1st Workshop on Personalization of Generative AI Systems (PERSONALIZE 2024)

St. Julian's, Malta
22 March 2024

ISBN: 978-1-7138-9458-2

Printed from e-media with permission by:

Curran Associates, Inc.
57 Morehouse Lane
Red Hook, NY 12571

Some format issues inherent in the e-media version may also appear in this print version.

Printed with permission by Curran Associates, Inc. (2025)

Association for Computational Linguistics
209 N. Eighth Street
Stroudsburg, Pennsylvania 18360

Phone: 1-570-476-8006
Fax: 1-570-476-0860

acl@aclweb.org

Additional copies of this publication are available from:

Curran Associates, Inc.
57 Morehouse Lane
Red Hook, NY 12571 USA
Phone: 845-758-0400
Fax: 845-758-2633
Email: curran@proceedings.com
Web: www.proceedings.com

PERSONALIZE 2024

The 1st Workshop on Personalization of Generative AI Systems

Proceedings of the Workshop

March 22, 2024

Association for Computational Linguistics (ACL)
209 N. Eighth Street
Stroudsburg, PA 18360
USA
Tel: +1-570-476-8006
Fax: +1-570-476-0860
acl@aclweb.org

Introduction

We are excited to welcome you to the first edition of PERSONALIZE: Personalization of Generative AI Systems.

Personalization of generative AI is a key step to make generic systems tangibly useful to a diverse demographic user group. Our workshop studies personalization from technical, legal, and philosophical angles.

The exponential growth of generative AI and foundation models has spurred significant development, adoption, and capital investment across various industries. However, an important challenge lies in the generic nature of these systems, lacking personalization, which hinders their effectiveness for diverse user demographics.

Addressing this issue has become a major focus for both model developers and firms, with billions of dollars and extensive research efforts dedicated to personalization initiatives, exemplified by projects like Snap's MyAI and Meta's Abraham Lincoln bot plans.

Despite this progress, there are three key challenges being overlooked: technical, legal, and philosophical. Technical challenges encompass issues with existing personalization methods, such as computational efficiency, quality, and safety concerns. Meanwhile, legal and philosophical considerations are vital due to the potential for misuse, harmful consequences, biased behavior, and privacy violations associated with personalized AI systems.

Our workshop will serve as a platform for diverse stakeholders to explore these multifaceted challenges and engage in discussions and guide the future of personalized generative AI.

Organizing Committee

General Chair

Ameet Deshpande, Princeton University, USA
EunJeong Hwang, University of British Columbia, Canada
Vishvak Murahari, Princeton University, USA
Joon Sung Park, Stanford University, USA
Diyi Yang, Stanford University, USA
Ashish Sabharwal, Allen Institute for Artificial Intelligence (AI2), USA
Karthik Narasimhan, Princeton University, USA
Ashwin Kalyan, Allen Institute for Artificial Intelligence (AI2), USA

Program Committee

Program Committee

Pranjal Aggarwal, Indian Institute of Technology Delhi, India
Atharvan Dogra, Indian Institute of Technology Madras, India
Creston Brooks, Princeton University, USA
Anika Maskara, Princeton University, USA
Anirudh Ajith, Princeton University, USA
Akshara Prabhakar, Princeton University, USA
Victoria Graf, Princeton University, USA
Adithya Bhaskar, Princeton University, USA
John Yang, Princeton University, USA
Howard Yen, Princeton University, USA
Sabhya Chabria, Princeton University, USA
Jens Tuyls, Princeton University, USA
Abhishek Panigrahi, Princeton University, USA
Carlos Jimenez, Princeton University, USA
Yash Kant, University of Toronto, Canada
Shunyu Yao, Princeton University, USA
Mehar Bhatia, UBC, Canada
Sahithya Ravi, UBC, Canada
Maksym Taranukhin, Dalhousie University, Canada
Soheil Alavi, UBC, Canada
Saiyue Lyu, UBC, Canada
Xincheng (Peter) Huang, UBC, Canada
Bu Li, UBC, Canada
Zhe Liu, UBC, Canada
Vasile Negrescu, Raytheon, USA
Michael F. Liu, UBC, Canada

Table of Contents

Program

Friday, March 22, 2024

09:00 - 09:15	*Opening Remarks*
09:15 - 09:45	*Invited Talk 1*
09:45 - 10:15	*Invited Talk 2*
10:15 - 11:00	*Coffee Break*
11:00 - 12:00	*Panel discussion*
12:00 - 14:00	*Lunch Break*
14:00 - 15:30	*In-Person Poster Session*
15:30 - 16:00	*Coffee Break*
16:00 - 16:30	*Invited Talk 3*
16:30 - 17:00	*Best Paper Talks (General & Theme)*
17:00 - 17:30	*Virtual poster session*

RoleCraft-GLM: Advancing Personalized Role-Playing in Large Language Models

Meiling Tao[1]*, **Xuechen Liang**[2]*, **Tianyu Shi**[3]†, **Lei Yu**[3], **Yiting Xie**[4]
[1]Guangdong University of Technology, Guangzhou, China
[2]East China Jiaotong University, Nanchang, China
[3] University of Toronto, Toronto, Canada
[4]Genfun.ai, Beijing, China

Abstract

This study presents RoleCraft-GLM, an innovative framework aimed at enhancing personalized role-playing with Large Language Models (LLMs). RoleCraft-GLM addresses the key issue of lacking personalized interactions in conversational AI, and offers a solution with detailed and emotionally nuanced character portrayals. We contribute a unique conversational dataset that shifts from conventional celebrity-centric characters to diverse, non-celebrity personas, thus enhancing the realism and complexity of language modeling interactions. Additionally, our approach includes meticulous character development, ensuring dialogues are both realistic and emotionally resonant. The effectiveness of RoleCraft-GLM is validated through various case studies, highlighting its versatility and skill in different scenarios. Our framework excels in generating dialogues that accurately reflect characters' personality traits and emotions, thereby boosting user engagement. In conclusion, RoleCraft-GLM marks a significant leap in personalized AI interactions, and paves the way for more authentic and immersive AI-assisted role-playing experiences by enabling more nuanced and emotionally rich dialogues[1].

1 Introduction

Large Language Models (LLMs) have become a cornerstone in understanding and generating natural language, showcasing remarkable capabilities that often surpass human proficiency in certain language reasoning tasks. Consequently, they have excelled notably excelled as conversational agents, offering high-level responses in various dialogues and significantly influencing human-AI interactions, thus hinting at their potential to reshape numerous aspects of daily life (Bender and Koller, 2020).

Despite these advancements in generative AI (Baidoo-Anu and Ansah, 2023),challenges persist, particularly in meeting the diverse requirements of different user groups.Presently, many AI systems rely on generic models, which may not adequately address the specific needs of varied users. This limitation can negatively influence user experiences and the applicability of AI in certain scenarios (Ackerman et al., 2022). Thus, there is a burgeoning recognition of the importance of personalization within AI, gradually influencing the direction of the field. There is a growing trend toward developing AI systems that are more attuned to individual preferences and needs (Brandtzæg and Følstad, 2018; Lee and Koubek, 2010), emphasizing the need for a deeper understanding of user behaviors and a more tailored approach to AI interactions. This evolving trend suggests a move toward more personalized, user-centric AI models, potentially transforming the generative AI sector to offer more individualized and effective solutions.

Existing open-source LLMs, while trained across broad domains, may not always offer the specialized optimization desired for nuanced role-playing tasks. This suggests that additional customization might be beneficial to more effectively meet the specific requirements of role-playing scenarios. On the other hand, advanced LLMs such as GPT-4 (OpenAI, 2023) showcase enhanced abilities in role-playing due to their extensive training and sophisticated algorithms. However, this closed-source model may introduce practical limitations. These include higher costs associated with API usage, limited scope for fine-tuning to tailor the models for specific role-playing contexts, and restrictions in context window sizes which can impact the fluidity and depth of generated dialogues in complex role-playing scenarios.

In this paper, as illustrated in the figure 1, we

* Equal contribution. This work is done during internship at Genfun.ai.

†Corresponding author: ty.shi@mail.utoronto.ca

[1]Access models, demos at https://github.com/tml2002/RoleCraft

Proceedings of the 1st Workshop on Personalization of Generative AI Systems (PERSONALIZE 2024), pages 1–9
March 22, 2024 ©2024 Association for Computational Linguistics

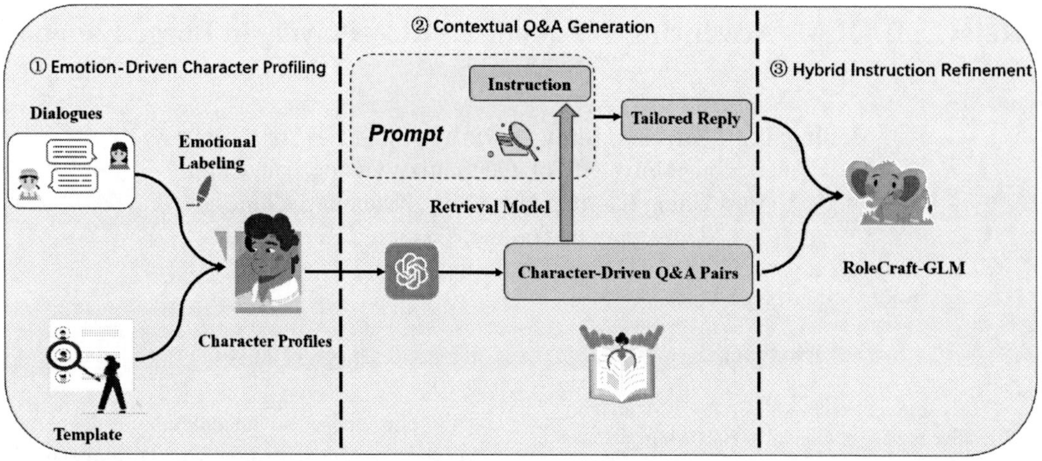

Figure 1: Overview of the RoleCraft-GLM framework: (1)Emotionally annotated dialog datasets play a key role in creating role profiles that reflect specific emotional traits. (2)The generation of Q&A pairs, based on context and known character traits, ensures that dialogues are consistent with the character profiles. (3) A hybrid approach of generic and character-specific instructions is used to train the GLM for various dialog scenarios.

introduce the RoleCraft-GLM framework designed to enhance personalized role-playing experiences with LLMs. Moving beyond traditional celebrity-focused characters, we focus on diverse, non-celebrity personas, each with unique emotional annotations. This approach aims to enrich realism and emotional depth in language interactions. We compiled a novel dataset encompassing a wide array of real-world dialogues, with careful consideration for personal privacy and copyright laws. Our data analysis highlights the potential benefits of integrating emotional labels in dialogue datasets for improved natural language processing. We conducted comparative experiments using models like ChatGLM3, fine-tuned with the Low-Rank Adaptation (LoRA) method, to assess RoleCraft-GLM's effectiveness in producing nuanced and character-consistent dialogues.

The main contributions of our work are as follows:

- We introduce a groundbreaking dataset that centers on non-celebrity characters, each characterized by unique emotional annotations. This innovative shift away from the traditional focus on celebrity-centric characters greatly enhances the realism and intricacy of everyday interactions within language modeling.

- We have developed a novel training strategy that considers more detailed personal role data. This strategy includes a fine-grained approach to character portrayal, emphasizing emotional depth, and fostering contextual awareness in dialogue generation.

- Our framework has shown promising performance, as evidenced by multi-dimensional evaluations, in comparison to current state-of-the-art models. These evaluations rigorously assess aspects such as dialogue authenticity, emotional accuracy, and contextual relevance, highlighting our framework's advanced capabilities in these critical areas.

2 Related Work

2.1 Personalization of LLMs

The recent strides in LLMs, particularly in understanding user context and preferences, have significantly propelled the personalization aspect of AI interactions.Consequently, technologies like effective prompt design and feedback mechanisms, including similarity-based retrievers, enhance AI's ability to learn from past interactions and adapt to user needs more precisely. These methods enable AI systems to proactively identify and rectify errors, thus enhancing their performance over time (Dalvi et al., 2022; Madaan et al., 2022).Furthermore,this evolution in LLMs lays the groundwork for AI applications that are not only more personalized and intuitive but also deeply aligned with user-centric principles.The evolution of personalization in AI interactions highlights a crucial shift towards understanding and catering to individual user preferences. Projects like Snap's MyAI[2] and Meta's Abraham Lincoln bot[3] serve as prime examples, demonstrating how AI can be customized for enhanced user engagement and specific functional needs., illustrating AI's potential for enhanced user engagement and functionality through customization (Bender et al., 2021). These initiatives emphasize the importance of tailoring AI systems to meet specific user needs. Against this backdrop, our work in RoleCraft-GLM aims to build upon these advancements to offer nuanced, emotionally rich AI interactions that align with individual user contexts and needs.

2.2 Role-Playing

The evolution of role-playing in AI, marked by the transition from basic text-based interactions to intricate character simulations (Park et al., 2023), reflects the strides made in natural language processing and AI technologies. Initially, AI role-playing systems offered only fundamental exchanges, limited in their ability to craft dialogues with emotional depth and contextual relevance. With the emergence of advanced models such as GPT-3 (Brown et al., 2020), LLaMA (Touvron et al., 2023), and ChatGLM, there was a notable enhancement in AI's capability for engaging in more sophisticated, context-aware conversations. Yet, these improvements also underscored a significant gap in personalization for role-playing applications. Predominantly, LLMs trained on wide-ranging, generic datasets fell short in handling scenarios that demanded a deeper understanding of nuanced emotional nuances (Radford et al., 2018) and specific character traits. To address these shortcomings, we have meticulously developed the RoleCraft-GLM framework. It stands out with its unique dataset, focusing on diverse, non-celebrity personas enriched with detailed emotional annotations (Bender and Koller, 2020). This dataset is key to overcoming previous limitations, facilitating a new level of personalization and emotional intricacy in AI role-playing interactions.

3 Methodology

As shown in Figure 1, the RoleCraft-GLM framework, rooted in 'Role' and 'Craft', represents our approach to enhancing AI role-playing. 'Role' emphasizes creating distinct, multi-dimensional characters, each with unique personality traits and emotional depths. 'Craft' involves the intricate process of constructing dialogues that genuinely reflect these character traits, thereby adding depth and realism to conversations.

Building on this foundation, the RoleCraft-GLM framework is underpinned by key principles to elevate the authenticity of role-playing (Wang et al., 2023). The first principle, 'Fine-Grained Character Portrayal', is pivotal in endowing each character with detailed and nuanced traits and backgrounds, integral to the 'Role' aspect of RoleCraft. This approach is focused on creating characters that are reflective of real-life individuals in their personality, and behaviors (Kim et al., 2023), setting the stage for realistic and compelling character portrayals. Progressing to the second principle, 'Mastery of Emotion and Style', we concentrate on the emotional expressions and speaking styles of characters (Li et al., 2023). This principle, key to the 'Craft' element of RoleCraft, enriches dialogues with diverse emotions and distinctive speech patterns, effectively capturing the unique emotional states and communication styles of each character. Furthermore, the 'Accurate Application of Character Knowledge' principle emphasizes incorporating each character's background and experiences into the dialogue generation process (Shao et al., 2023). This ensures that the dialogues are in harmony with the characters' personas, encompassing their unique experiences and insights. Concluding with the 'Context-Aware Dialogue Generation' principle, our system is designed to dynamically tailor dialogues based on the prevailing context (Zhanga et al., 2023). This is crucial for maintaining a seamless and logically consistent conversation flow, essential for immersive and credible role-playing experiences.

3.1 RoleCraft-GLM Framework

Our methodology, guided by key design principles, uniquely advances the capabilities of LLMs in role-playing. Setting ourselves apart from approaches such as RoleGLM (Wang et al., 2023), we focus on an innovative integration of fine-grained character portrayal, profound emotional depth, and heightened contextual awareness in dialogue generation. This approach differentiates our work from existing models and addresses challenges in a novel way, enhancing how LLMs can be utilized for creating

[2] https://www.personal.ai/

[3] https://ai.meta.com/

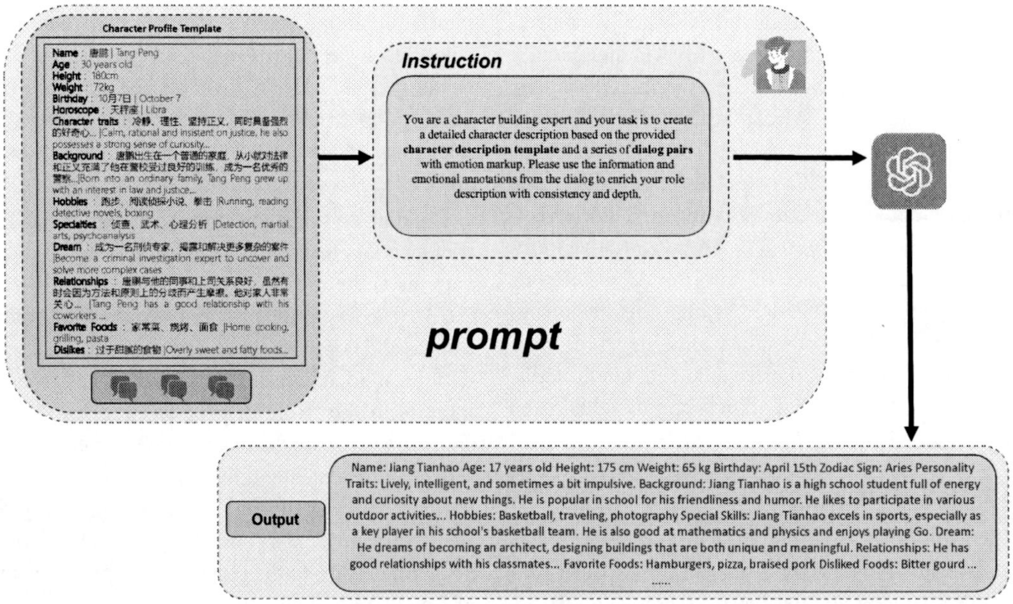

Figure 2: Here is an example of generating a detailed character description. Utilizing a character description template along with an emotionally annotated dialogue dataset facilitates the generation of detailed character descriptions based on prompts.(The instruction and output have been translated into English.)

more realistic and engaging role-playing scenario.

Emotion-Driven Character Profiling

To address the challenges of limited emotional diversity and unconvincing character portrayals in dialogues generated by LLMs, we've adopted a detailed emotion classification strategy. This approach involves meticulously annotating emotions within the dialogue dataset, thereby steering the GPT-4 to craft character profiles that mirror these identified emotions. Consider a character who displays a spectrum of emotions from joy to disappointment. Marking these diverse emotional states allows for a natural and fluid transition in their dialogues within a single scene, effectively capturing the complexity and dynamism of human emotions. This approach challenges the LLMs to accurately depict these emotional shifts, ensuring that the dialogues genuinely represent the intricate and ever-evolving nature of human emotions, thus enhancing the overall user interaction experience.

Contextual Q&A Generation

To address the challenge of context-irrelevant responses, which is a common issue in dialogue systems where interactions often lack relevance to the ongoing scenario or character specifics, we employ GPT-4 to generate contextually coherent Q&A pairs. For example, when a character faces a dilemma, the system is designed to produce queries and responses that align with the character's established traits, such as indecisiveness and anxiety, thereby maintaining the authenticity of the dialogue in relation to the character's profile.

Hybrid Instruction-Based GLM Refinement

Our methodology employs a hybrid training approach that seamlessly integrates general instructions with character-specific Q&A pairs. This strategy is carefully crafted to strike a balance between the flexibility required for dynamic dialogue generation and the need to uphold character integrity. In practical terms, this means equipping the LLMs to adeptly navigate a spectrum of conversational scenarios. These range from broad, general interactions to more intricate exchanges that demand responses finely tuned to the unique profiles of individual characters. By training the LLM with this diverse mix of inputs, the model becomes proficient in handling various situational dialogues, accurately reflecting each character's distinct attributes and the specific subtleties of the conversation. As a result, this hybrid training method fosters the creation of dialogues that are both contextually adaptive and consistent with the characters' distinct personalities.

3.2 Semantic-Enhanced Retrieval Optimization

Addressing the issue of inaccurate and semantically irrelevant information retrieval in dialogues, we have adopted the BGE[4] retrieval method. BGE is an efficient Chinese and English semantic vector model that ensures the accuracy of responses, especially when dealing with sensitive topics, and remains semantically sensitive to the context, significantly enhancing the quality of interaction. (Xiao et al., 2023). This familiarity allows models to generate dialogue based on a wealth of pre-existing knowledge. In contrast, modern datasets prioritize the nuanced portrayal of personal and everyday characters. These datasets are derived from diverse sources, including real chat logs, customer service interactions, and fictional narratives from less mainstream media. Such characters might include a typical office worker dealing with daily stressors or a mother showing love and responsibility in a family setting. The dialogues here involve specific, real-life scenarios, such as office interactions or typical family conversations, which lack the broad pre-existing knowledge base associated with public figures.

4 Experiments

4.1 Dataset

In the evaluation of machine learning models, the role of datasets is paramount, particularly in language processing and character portrayal. Traditional datasets predominantly highlight eminent figures, such as the legendary Sun Wukong, whose familiar attributes and stories are widely acknowledged, facilitating model development (Sabadoš, 2021). However, these datasets often neglect the finer details and emotional complexity of lesser-known or everyday characters, leading to a representation gap (Rolf et al., 2021). Our unique dataset bridges this gap by focusing on the rich, nuanced depiction of ordinary individuals. It involves an in-depth exploration and portrayal of each character's distinct personality traits and emotional depths, delving into aspects usually overshadowed in dominant narratives.

In constructing our dataset, we designed 20 unique and personalized Chinese characters to mirror a wide spectrum of real-world dialogues. These characters ranged from everyday individuals to fictional ones inspired by scripts. Our diverse data sources included social media interactions, film and television scripts, and customer service dialogues. We emphasized personal privacy and copyright law compliance, ensuring all data was cleansed and anonymized.

We filtered out redundant data and multi-party conversations to reshape the original data into contextually relevant dialogues. For example, script-based dialogues were restructured to better depict character interactions and emotional dynamics. Table 1 provides basic statistics for RoleCraft-GLM. Our final dataset comprises 27,259 multi-turn dialogues, distinctly different from datasets like Reddit comments (Al-Rfou et al., 2016), Sina Weibo (Shang et al., 2015), and Twitter datasets (Ritter et al., 2011), which mostly capture less structured, multi-participant interactions.

In addition, we annotated each dataset entry with emotion labels to capture characters' distinct emotional traits, adding an emotional layer to model training. We used Ekman's "Six Basic Emotions Theory" (Ekman, 1992) to label utterances and included additional emotions like neutral, excited, and depressed, totaling ten categories. The use of emotion labels in dialogue datasets has been proven to enhance natural language processing by improving response retrieval and emotional relevance (Zhou et al., 2017). These labels also enrich conversational analysis and aid in building natural dialogue systems (Bothe et al., 2019).

4.2 Experiment Settings

In our research, we anticipate that fine-tuning our model using a specifically designed dataset for role-playing will result in superior performance in character portrayal compared to baseline models. This expectation is based on the customized nature of the dataset, which includes detailed emotional annotations and context-specific scenarios that are essential for nuanced character interactions. Through this specialized training, we expect our model to accurately capture and express the intricacies of character-specific language styles and emotional responses, surpassing baseline models that may lack such targeted training. Our experiments aim to validate this hypothesis and showcase the advanced capabilities of our model in role-playing tasks.

[4]https://github.com/FlagOpen/FlagEmbedding

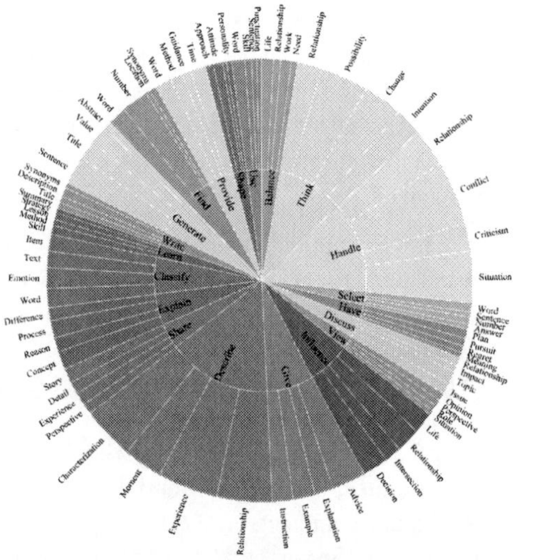

Figure 3: Verb-noun structure of Instructions. The inner circle representing the top 20 verbs and the outer circle listing the direct noun objects.

Category	Value
# Total Dialogues	2,7259
Avg.round of dialogues	14.64
# Characters	20
Character Personality Traits	45
Avg.length of profile	394.05
# Instructions	3,9422
Character-specific instructions	9842
General instructions	2,9580
Avg. instruction length	28.93
# Response	15,7742
Character-specific response	9842
General response	14,7900
Avg.response length	33.86

Table 1: Statistics of datasets

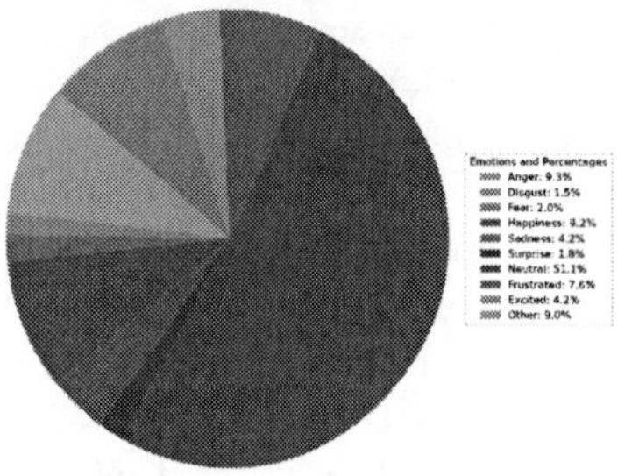

Figure 4: Emotion distributions in dialogues

Figure 5: The word cloud represents a visual distribution of personality traits for Chinese characters within the dataset, with larger words indicating a higher frequency of associated traits.

4.2.1 Baselines

We assessed the ChatGLM3 model[5], enhancing its performance on specific datasets using the Low-Rank Adaptation (LoRA) fine-tuning method (Hu et al., 2021). LoRA's precision in fine-tuning, essential for handling personalized and emotionally rich content, maintains the model's core capabilities while adapting to new data features. We benchmarked our RoleCraft-GLM's performance against industry standards such as GPT-3.5 and GPT-4, and leading Chinese dialogue generation technologies like ChatGLM2[6] and ChatGLM3, along with Baichuan2 (Yang et al., 2023) and Qwen (Bai et al., 2023). In our comparative experiments, we evaluated RoleGLM, which was fine-tuned using LoRA on specific datasets, as a benchmark. To match RoleGLM's setup, we also focused on a similar number of Chinese roles for consistency in our training approach. By selecting ChatGLM2 over ChatGLM3, we aimed to closely compare performances under equivalent conditions. This extensive evaluation underlined our model's distinctive advancements in dialogue generation.

4.2.2 Evaluation criteria

(1) Rouge-L Score: A commonly used metric (Lin, 2004) for evaluating natural language generation, measuring the overlap between model-generated text and real (ground truth) text. We focused on average score (Avg), general instruction response (RAW), role-playing speaking style (CUS), and specific role knowledge (SPE).

[5]https://github.com/THUDM/ChatGLM3

[6]https://github.com/THUDM/ChatGLM2-6B

Case	周小北，听说有两个泰国同学给你起了绰号，这让你感觉如何呢？ | Zhou Xiaobei, I heard that two of your Thai classmates gave you a nickname, how does that make you feel?
GPT-4	我对这个昵称其实感到既好笑又有点受宠若惊。虽然绰号听起来可能有点滑稽，但我知道我的泰国同学并没有恶意，他们只是在轻松地与我交流。 I actually felt both amused and a little flattered by the nickname. While the nickname may sound a bit funny, I know that my Thai classmates didn't mean any harm, they were just interacting with me in a relaxed manner.
Baichua2	听到有两个泰国同学给我起了绰号，我会感到好奇和高兴。这对我来说是一种友好的社交互动，我会以开放和幽默的态度来接受它。 I would be curious and happy to hear that two of my Thai classmates had given me a nickname. This is a friendly social interaction for me and I will accept it with openness and humor.
Qwen	我开始有点生气，因为他们是在取笑我，但后来我意识到或许我需要更了解文化差异，逐渐学习怎么应对。 I was a little angry at first because they were making fun of me, but then I realized that maybe I needed to be more aware of cultural differences and gradually learn how to deal with them.
Chatglm3	哦，那两个泰国同学给我起绰号吗？我觉得挺有趣的，我喜欢新奇和幽默，所以绰号对我来说是友情和创意的一部分，很开心！ Oh, those two Thai classmates gave me a nickname? I think it's funny, I like novelty and humor, so nicknames are part of friendship and creativity for me, it's fun!
Ours	哈哈，泰国同学给我起绰号？太有趣了！我好奇他们怎么想的，可能是因为我的奇思妙想吧！这个绰号我可得好好珍藏！ Haha, Thai classmates giving me nicknames? That's so funny! I wonder what they thought, probably because of my whimsy! That's a nickname I'm going to treasure!

Figure 6: A case of generated responses from our model and baseline models to a character-specific introduction.

Table 2: Rouge-L Evaluation

Model	Avg	RAW	CUS	SPE
GPT-3.5	0.4532	0.5569	0.5197	0.2831
GPT-4	0.4633	**0.5661**	**0.5264**	0.2973
ChatGLM2	0.4054	0.5104	0.4063	0.2996
ChatGLM3	0.4161	0.5218	0.4159	0.3108
Baichuan2	0.4273	0.5308	0.4576	0.2934
Qwen	0.4264	0.5297	0.4617	0.2879
Ours	**0.4704**	0.5385	0.5154	**0.3573**

Model	Avg. Ranking
ChatGLM3	1.86
Baichuan2	2.95
Qwen	3.38
Ours	**1.42**

Table 3: GPT-4 Evaluation

(2) **Average Ranking Using GPT Scoring:** In our work, we used the GPT-4 score (Fu et al., 2023) to evaluate the average rank of models on different dialogue-generating tasks, focusing on two main criteria for scoring: first, the distinctiveness and accuracy of the character's speaking style in matching their profile, and second, the richness of character-related knowledge and memory incorporated into the dialogues.

(3) **Comparison of Emotionally Annotated and Non-Annotated Models:** We compared models with and without emotional annotations in specific role knowledge memory (SPE) to evaluate the role of emotional annotation in enhancing model performance.

4.3 Performance Analysis

Results from Tables 2 and 3 clearly demonstrate our model's exceptional performance across multiple key performance indicators, particularly in specific role knowledge memory (SPE). Our model significantly outperformed GPT-4 and other models with a score of 0.3573 in this dimension, highlighting its superior ability in understanding and generating complex dialogues involving specific roles. However, GPT-4 leads in general instruction response accuracy (RAW) with a score of 0.5661, reflecting its strong capability in interpreting and responding to general instructions. Our model, while slightly less efficient in this dimension, still maintains a high score, proving its effectiveness in handling everyday dialogues. These findings underscore our method's significant effectiveness in deepening role understanding and enhancing dialogue generation quality. In particular, in emotion-driven role portrayal, our model demonstrated precise capture of each role's emotional traits and personality, surpassing traditional role-playing models in expressing role-specific knowledge. Moreover, our model not only excelled in generating role-specific dialogue content but also showed remarkable ability in maintaining natural flow and contextual consistency.

Table 4: Rouge-L Evaluation

model	Avg	RAW	CUS	SPE
RoleGLM	0.4570	0.5255	0.5049	0.3406
Ours	0.4641	0.5251	0.5128	0.3544

The Rouge-L assessment results from Table 4 indicate our model's performance improvement in three dimensions compared to RoleGLM. This suggests that our dataset enabled the model to more accurately capture and reflect the everyday characteristics and emotional states of roles, thereby enhancing the dialogue's realism and personalization. Additionally, the inclusion of emotional annotation

Method	SPE
RoleCraft-GLM(w/o emo)	0.3362
RoleCraft-GLM(w emo)	0.3573

Table 5: Comparing Emotion-Annotated and Non-Annotated Data

further enhanced the model's ability to understand and generate nuanced emotional dialogues, especially evident in the high SPE scores, indicating our method's outstanding performance in specific role knowledge and memory.

In our ablation experiments (see Table 5), we compared two versions of the RoleCraft-GLM model: one incorporating emotional annotations and the other without them. The primary objective was to assess the specific impact of emotional annotation on improving the model's scores in specific role knowledge memory (SPE). The results showed that the RoleCraft-GLM model with emotional annotation scored higher in SPE than the version without it. This difference emphasized the importance of emotional annotation in improving the model's understanding and generation of dialogues for non-celebrity roles that are closer to everyday life and lack extensive public knowledge or prior information. In these cases, emotional annotation not only provided the model with key information to deeply understand the roles' emotional states and personality traits but also ensured that the generated dialogues were closer to the roles' true feelings and personalized expressions.

5 Conclusions

In this paper, we present RoleCraft-GLM, our innovative framework aimed at enhancing personalized role-playing experiences. Central to this framework is a unique dataset featuring 20 diverse, non-celebrity Chinese characters, each with distinct emotional annotations. This shift from traditional celebrity-focused characters to more authentic, everyday personas marks a significant advancement in language modeling. RoleCraft-GLM's dataset emphasizes real-life scenarios and emotional depth, setting new standards in natural language processing. Our evaluations demonstrate that RoleCraft-GLM excels in creating dialogues that are not only contextually rich but also emotionally nuanced, outperforming conventional models. In the future, we hope to to develop behavioral agents that excel in personalization and interactivity, skillfully tailored to individual user preferences, thereby elevating the level of user engagement.

Acknowledgment

We would like to thank Genfun.ai for providing computation resources and APIs. We would also thank Minkun Yu and Zekun Wang for helpful suggestions.

References

Samuel Ackerman, Ateret Anaby-Tavor, E. Farchi, Esther Goldbraich, George Kour, Ella Ravinovich, O. Raz, Saritha Route, Marcel Zalmanovici, and Naama Zwerdling. 2022. High-quality conversational systems. *ArXiv*, abs/2204.13043.

Rami Al-Rfou, Marc Pickett, Javier Snaider, Yun-Hsuan Sung, Brian Strope, and Ray Kurzweil. 2016. Conversational contextual cues: The case of personalization and history for response ranking. *arXiv preprint arXiv:1606.00372*.

Jinze Bai, Shuai Bai, Yunfei Chu, Zeyu Cui, Kai Dang, Xiaodong Deng, Yang Fan, Wenbin Ge, Yu Han, Fei Huang, Binyuan Hui, Luo Ji, Mei Li, Junyang Lin, Runji Lin, Dayiheng Liu, Gao Liu, Chengqiang Lu, Keming Lu, Jianxin Ma, Rui Men, Xingzhang Ren, Xuancheng Ren, Chuanqi Tan, Sinan Tan, Jianhong Tu, Peng Wang, Shijie Wang, Wei Wang, Shengguang Wu, Benfeng Xu, Jin Xu, An Yang, Hao Yang, Jian Yang, Shusheng Yang, Yang Yao, Bowen Yu, Hongyi Yuan, Zheng Yuan, Jianwei Zhang, Xingxuan Zhang, Yichang Zhang, Zhenru Zhang, Chang Zhou, Jingren Zhou, Xiaohuan Zhou, and Tianhang Zhu. 2023. Qwen technical report. *arXiv preprint arXiv:2309.16609*.

David Baidoo-Anu and Leticia Owusu Ansah. 2023. Education in the era of generative artificial intelligence (ai): Understanding the potential benefits of chatgpt in promoting teaching and learning. *Journal of AI*, 7(1):52–62.

Emily M Bender, Timnit Gebru, Angelina McMillan-Major, and Shmargaret Shmitchell. 2021. On the dangers of stochastic parrots: Can language models be too big? In *Proceedings of the 2021 ACM conference on fairness, accountability, and transparency*, pages 610–623.

Emily M Bender and Alexander Koller. 2020. Climbing towards nlu: On meaning, form, and understanding in the age of data. In *Proceedings of the 58th annual meeting of the association for computational linguistics*, pages 5185–5198.

Chandrakant Bothe, C. Weber, S. Magg, and S. Wermter. 2019. Enriching existing conversational emotion datasets with dialogue acts using neural annotators. *ArXiv*, abs/1912.00819.

P. Brandtzæg and A. Følstad. 2018. Chatbots: changing user needs and motivations. *Interactions*, 25:38–43.

Tom Brown, Benjamin Mann, Nick Ryder, Melanie Subbiah, Jared D Kaplan, Prafulla Dhariwal, Arvind Neelakantan, Pranav Shyam, Girish Sastry, Amanda Askell, et al. 2020. Language models are few-shot learners. *Advances in neural information processing systems*, 33:1877–1901.

Bhavana Dalvi, Oyvind Tafjord, and Peter Clark. 2022. Towards teachable reasoning systems: Using a dynamic memory of user feedback for continual system improvement. In *Proceedings of the 2022 Conference on Empirical Methods in Natural Language Processing*, pages 9465–9480.

Paul Ekman. 1992. An argument for basic emotions. *Cognition & emotion*, 6(3-4):169–200.

Jinlan Fu, See-Kiong Ng, Zhengbao Jiang, and Pengfei Liu. 2023. Gptscore: Evaluate as you desire. *arXiv preprint arXiv:2302.04166*.

Edward J Hu, Yelong Shen, Phillip Wallis, Zeyuan Allen-Zhu, Yuanzhi Li, Shean Wang, Lu Wang, and Weizhu Chen. 2021. Lora: Low-rank adaptation of large language models. *arXiv preprint arXiv:2106.09685*.

Seungone Kim, Jamin Shin, Yejin Cho, Joel Jang, Shayne Longpre, Hwaran Lee, Sangdoo Yun, Seongjin Shin, Sungdong Kim, James Thorne, et al. 2023. Prometheus: Inducing fine-grained evaluation capability in language models. *arXiv preprint arXiv:2310.08491*.

Sangwon Lee and Richard J Koubek. 2010. Understanding user preferences based on usability and aesthetics before and after actual use. *Interacting with Computers*, 22(6):530–543.

Cheng Li, Jindong Wang, Kaijie Zhu, Yixuan Zhang, Wenxin Hou, Jianxun Lian, and Xing Xie. 2023. Emotionprompt: Leveraging psychology for large language models enhancement via emotional stimulus. *arXiv preprint arXiv:2307.11760*.

Chin-Yew Lin. 2004. Rouge: A package for automatic evaluation of summaries. In *Text summarization branches out*, pages 74–81.

Aman Madaan, Niket Tandon, Peter Clark, and Yiming Yang. 2022. Memory-assisted prompt editing to improve gpt-3 after deployment. *arXiv preprint arXiv:2201.06009*.

OpenAI. 2023. Gpt-4 technical report.

Joon Sung Park, Joseph O'Brien, Carrie Jun Cai, Meredith Ringel Morris, Percy Liang, and Michael S Bernstein. 2023. Generative agents: Interactive simulacra of human behavior. In *Proceedings of the 36th Annual ACM Symposium on User Interface Software and Technology*, pages 1–22.

Alec Radford, Karthik Narasimhan, Tim Salimans, Ilya Sutskever, et al. 2018. Improving language understanding by generative pre-training.

Alan Ritter, Colin Cherry, and Bill Dolan. 2011. Data-driven response generation in social media. In *Empirical Methods in Natural Language Processing (EMNLP)*.

Esther Rolf, Theodora Worledge, B. Recht, and M.I. Jordan. 2021. Representation matters: Assessing the importance of subgroup allocations in training data. *ArXiv*, abs/2103.03399.

Noemi Sabadoš. 2021. Automatsko generisanje skupa podataka za treniranje modela za automatsko prepoznavanje osobe na slici. 36:536–539.

Lifeng Shang, Zhengdong Lu, and Hang Li. 2015. Neural responding machine for short-text conversation. *arXiv preprint arXiv:1503.02364*.

Yunfan Shao, Linyang Li, Junqi Dai, and Xipeng Qiu. 2023. Character-llm: A trainable agent for role-playing. *arXiv preprint arXiv:2310.10158*.

Hugo Touvron, Thibaut Lavril, Gautier Izacard, Xavier Martinet, Marie-Anne Lachaux, Timothée Lacroix, Baptiste Rozière, Naman Goyal, Eric Hambro, Faisal Azhar, et al. 2023. Llama: Open and efficient foundation language models. *arXiv preprint arXiv:2302.13971*.

Zekun Moore Wang, Zhongyuan Peng, Haoran Que, Jiaheng Liu, Wangchunshu Zhou, Yuhan Wu, Hongcheng Guo, Ruitong Gan, Zehao Ni, Man Zhang, et al. 2023. Rolellm: Benchmarking, eliciting, and enhancing role-playing abilities of large language models. *arXiv preprint arXiv:2310.00746*.

Shitao Xiao, Zheng Liu, Peitian Zhang, and Niklas Muennighof. 2023. C-pack: Packaged resources to advance general chinese embedding. *arXiv preprint arXiv:2309.07597*.

Aiyuan Yang, Bin Xiao, Bingning Wang, Borong Zhang, Chao Yin, Chenxu Lv, Da Pan, Dian Wang, Dong Yan, Fan Yang, et al. 2023. Baichuan 2: Open large-scale language models. *arXiv preprint arXiv:2309.10305*.

Hongbo Zhanga, Chen Tang, Tyler Loakmana, Chenghua Lina, and Stefan Goetze. 2023. Cadge: Context-aware dialogue generation enhanced with graph-structured knowledge aggregation. *arXiv preprint arXiv:2305.06294*.

Zhi-Min Zhou, Man Lan, Yuanbin Wu, and Jun Lang. 2017. Single turn chinese emotional conversation generation based on information retrieval and question answering. *2017 International Conference on Asian Language Processing (IALP)*, pages 103–106.

How to use Language Models for Synthetic Text Generation in Cerebrovascular Disease-specific Medical Reports

Byoung-Doo Oh[1], Gi-Youn Kim[2], Chulho Kim[3] and Yu-Seop Kim[2]
[1]Cerebrovascular Disease Research Center, Hallym University, Republic of Korea
[2]Department of Convergence Software, Hallym University, Republic of Korea
[3]Department of Neurology, Chuncheon Sacred Heart Hospital, Republic of Korea
{iambd822, dekmj001}@gmail.com, gumdol52@hallym.or.kr, yskim01@hallym.ac.kr

Abstract

The quantity and quality of data have a significant impact on the performance of artificial intelligence (AI). Consequently, there is a growing interest in synthetic data generation for medical AI. However, research has primarily focused on medical images, with little given to text-based data such as medical records. This is because in the biomedical field, text data often contains sensitive information such as personal information, making it difficult to access a sufficient amount of data required for medical AI. Therefore, this study explores the application of language models (LMs) for synthetic text generation in low-resource domains like medical records. It compares the results of synthetic text generation based on different LMs. To achieve this, we focused on two criteria for LM-based synthetic text generation of medical records using two keywords entered by the user: 1) the impact of the LM's knowledge, 2) the impact of the LM's size. Additionally, we objectively evaluated the generated synthetic text, including quantitative metrics such as BLUE and ROUGE, along with clinician's evaluations.

1 Introduction

The performance of artificial intelligence (AI) is greatly influenced by the quantity and quality of data, including computational resources (Whang et al., 2023). For example, massive language model (LM) services like ChatGPT (OpenAI, 2023), with 20 billion parameters, require large-scale datasets and high-performance computing resources. However, building extensive datasets in the biomedical domain is challenging for the following reasons (Kalkman et al., 2022): 1) Inclusion of sensitive information such as personal details require ensuring privacy protection, information security, transparency, and related considerations. 2) Caution must be exercised due to concerns such as the potential failure to maintain anonymity and the possibility of data misuse. Consequently, despite the existing demand, accessing the necessary data in the biomedical domain can be difficult, with only a limited subset being publicly available.

Nevertheless, medical AI has consistently advanced, primarily in fields with less sensitive information, such as medical image analysis. However, text data containing extensive information, like Electronic Medical Records (EMR), is organized in different formats depending on regions or institutions and poses a challenge for effective utilization due to the inclusion of a considerable amount of sensitive information (Lee and Kim, 2021). Therefore, there is a need for a technique of synthetic text generation, one of the text augmentation methods, to enable the effective utilization of medical records in medical AI.

In this study, we explored methods to synthetic text generation using LMs for text augmentation in low-resource medical records. We compared the following aspects: 1) the impact of the LM's knowledge, and 2) the impact of the LM's size. To do so, we compared ChatGPT, BioGPT (Luo et al., 2023), distilGPT2 (Sanh et al., 2019), and our own GPT2 (we called CerebroGPT). At this time, we conducted experiments using low-resource medical records related to cerebrovascular diseases. Finally, for objective evaluation, we performed clinician's evaluations along with four quantitative metrics (BLUE, ROUGE, Cosine similarity with sentence embeddings and TF-IDF).

This paper is structured as follows: In Chapter 2, we provide a review of prior research on text augmentation methods. Chapter 3 describes the medical records we utilized in this study. Chapter 4 details the methodology, while Chapter 5 details

Proceedings of the 1st Workshop on Personalization of Generative AI Systems (PERSONALIZE 2024), pages 10–17
March 22, 2024 ©2024 Association for Computational Linguistics

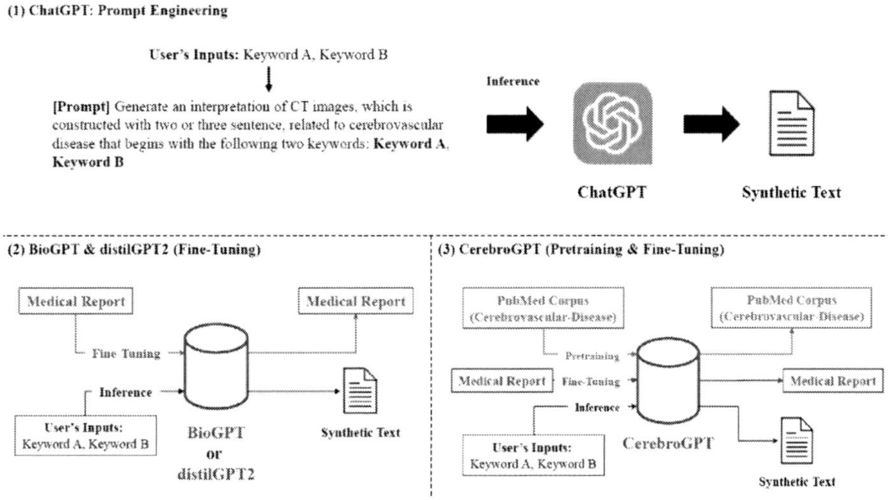

Figure 1. Overviews of the proposed methods for synthetic text generation by LMs.

the experimental setup and results. In Chapter 6, we summarize our observations and present the conclusion.

2 Related Work

Rule-based methods involve traditional techniques such as synonym replacement, random word insertion and deletion, collectively known as Easy Data Augmentation (Wei and Zou, 2019). Due to their simple principles, they have addressed good performance when applied to small-scale datasets. However, it may not be suitable for the medical domain when applied to text, as they could incorrectly represent the location of abnormalities or describe diseases inaccurately in medical records.

Model-based methods augment text based on the language understanding derived from the knowledge of LMs. Rakshit et al. (2022) enhanced text generation by fine-tuning GPT2 using the generative abilities of the LM. It involved adding new special tokens ("<|startoftext|>") to the model during fine-tuning, enabling it to generate text learned based on knowledge of LMs.

After the release of ChatGPT, prompt engineering based on ChatGPT has also been attempted (Ubani et al., 2023; Dai et al., 2023; Møller et al., 2023). In these efforts, suitable prompts for specific tasks were explored when using ChatGPT for generating synthetic training data in low-resource tasks. They focused on the fact that ChatGPT, pretrained on a large corpus, has a broad semantic space, allowing it to generate various expressions for the same meaning.

3 Medical Reports in Cerebrovascular Disease

The dataset consists of radiologist's reports on CT images collected from Hallym University Sacred Heart Hospital [1] and Chuncheon Sacred Heart Hospital [2] from 2012 to 2020, involving a total of 35,511 individuals which is intracerebral hemorrhage (ICH), non-ICH, and normal patients. While it includes a total of 90,489 reports, but there are many duplicate reports with the same content. Therefore, we utilized 47,675 reports after removing duplicates. Additionally, to standardize different report formats by radiologists and to address sensitive information such as personal details, we conducted preprocessing using regular expressions. All procedures in this study were performed in accordance with the Decla-ration of Helsinki, and it was approved by the Institutional Review Board at Chuncheon Sacred Heart Hospital (IRB No. 2021-10-012). The examples of medical reports are shown in Appendix A.

4 Language Models for Synthetic Text Generation

As shown in Figure 1, we compared the following LMs for LM-based synthetic text generation of medical records:

[1] https://hallym.hallym.or.kr/

[2] https://chuncheon.hallym.or.kr/

- **ChatGPT (20B)**: ChatGPT utilizes the GPT3.5-Turbo version, a LM that has been pretrained on diverse datasets for various domains and fine-tuned using methods like RLHF (Reinforcement Learning of Human Feedback) in InstructGPT (Ouyang et al., 2022). Therefore, we explored suitable prompts through prompt engineering and generated synthetic text using this prompt.
- **BioGPT (355M)**: BioGPT is structured with the same architecture as GPT2-medium: vocabulary size is 42,384, number of layers is 24, hidden size is 1024 dimensions, and number of heads is 16. It is a domain-specific LM fine-tuned for the biomedical domain, trained on a comprehensive biomedical dataset of 15 million papers (title and abstract) from PubMed. Therefore, we fine-tuned a BioGPT using medical record corpus.
- **distilGPT2 (82M)**: The architecture of distilGPT2 is as follows: vocabulary size is 50,260, number of layers is 6, hidden size is 768 dimensions, and number of heads is 12. It is a LM that underwent knowledge distillation from GPT2 (124M) trained on the OpenWebText Corpus (Gokaslan and Cohen, 2019), a corpus from a general domain, to achieve a smaller size and faster inference speed. Therefore, we fine-tuned a distilGPT2 using medical record corpus.
- **CerebroGPT (10M)**: CerebroGPT is a cerebrovascular disease-specific LM which is developed in-house and small-sized, with the following architecture: vocabulary size is 42,384, number of layers is 3, hidden size is 128 dimensions, and number of heads is 4. It was pretrained on a corpus of 396,826 papers (title and abstract) from the cerebrovascular disease, obtained by filtering out duplicate papers and items with only titles and no abstracts from PubMed. And Therefore, we fine-tuned a CerebroGPT using medical record corpus.

Synthetic text generation requires producing diverse expressions or sentence structures for the same content. Therefore, we compared four generation strategies (grid search, beam search, top-k sampling, top-p sampling) and employed the most suitable strategy for each LM. And all LMs are designed to generate synthetic text based on two keywords inputted by the user.

5 Experiments

5.1 Experimental Setup

The experiments were conducted on a server equipped with two Nvidia A100 GPUs. All LMs except ChatGPT used the Adam optimizer with a learning rate set to 1e-4. BioGPT and distilGPT2 had a batch size of 8, while CerebroGPT had a batch size of 64. Early stopping was set to 10. For actual clinician's evaluations, we selected 100 samples as the evaluation sets and split the remaining data into training and validation sets with a ratio of 9:1.

5.2 Results and Discussion

We employed quantitative metrics for the generated text: BLEU, ROUGE, cosine similarity with sentence embedding and TF-IDF. The detailed descriptions of these metrics are as follows: 1) **BLEU**: We use BLEU to evaluate how well the synthetic text well represents the cerebrovascular disease-specific vocabularies. 2) **ROUGE**: We use ROUGE-N and ROUGE-L for evaluation. It evaluates to the same goal as BLEU. 3) **Cosine similarity with sentence embedding**: We use BioGPT to represent the embeddings of the text. Subsequently, we calculated the cosine similarity between the two embeddings, evaluating the semantic similarity between medical records and synthetic text. 4) **Cosine similarity with TF-IDF**: We represented vectors of TF-IDF on a sentence-by-sentence basis after filtering out stop words and evaluated the cosine similarity for these vectors. At this time, we used the original report from which two keywords were extracted from the test data as a reference sentence. Additionally, we evaluated the quality of the synthetic text directly by clinicians to ensure an objective evaluation.

The results of the synthetic texts generated by each model are presented in Appendix B. And the results for the four quantitative metrics are shown in Table 1. In overall aspects such as semantics and representation ability of cerebrovascular disease-related vocabulary, distilGPT2 demonstrated the most superior performance. ChatGPT, considered as one of the most advanced LMs, effectively expressed grammatically complete sentences and medical knowledge. However, we consider that it received a lower score due to the inclusion of many general expressions and the format different to

	Sentence Embeddings	**TF-IDF**	**ROUGE-1**	**ROUGE-2**	**ROUGE-L**
ChatGPT	0.6692	0.1612	0.1154	0.0293	0.1131
BioGPT (top-p)	0.5711	0.2168	0.1045	0.0141	0.1011
distilGPT2 (top-k)	**0.8514**	**0.4549**	**0.4217**	**0.2618**	**0.4146**
CerebroGPT (top-k)	0.7997	0.3828	0.3223	0.1703	0.3179
	BLEU-1	**BLEU-2**	**BLEU-3**	**BLEU-4**	**BLEU**
ChatGPT	0.0689	0.1873	0.0021	0.0001	0.0004
BioGPT (top-p)	0.0452	0.0078	0.0001	2.16e-308	1.12e-80
distilGPT2 (top-k)	**0.2945**	**0.1916**	**0.1189**	**0.0734**	**0.1165**
CerebroGPT (top-k)	0.2057	0.1126	0.0516	0.0271	0.0503

Table 1: Evaluation results for synthetic text using evaluation metric.

<table>
<tr><th colspan="4">Best performance ranking</th></tr>
<tr><th>3</th><th>4</th><th>1</th><th>2</th></tr>
<tr><th>ChatGPT</th><th>BioGPT</th><th>distilGPT2</th><th>CerebroGPT</th></tr>
<tr><td>Excellent ability to express various sentences with the general fact.</td><td rowspan="4">Difficult to evaluate synthetic text because it is not created with a complete sentence structure.</td><td>Excellent ability to express various sentences with the medical fact.</td><td>The ability to represent sentences based on medical facts is excellent, but the ability to generate sentences with various expressions is slightly poor.</td></tr>
<tr><td>Excellent ability to express grammatically complete sentences.</td><td>Some ungrammatical sentence expressions.</td><td>Some ungrammatical sentence expressions.</td></tr>
<tr><td>Many additional general expressions appear in the synthetic text.</td><td rowspan="2">Represented in a format similar to actual medical reports.</td><td rowspan="2">Represented in a format most similar to actual medical reports.</td></tr>
<tr><td>Represented in a different format from actual medical reports.</td></tr>
</table>

Table 2: Human evaluation results (with clinician).

medical records. BioGPT, pretrained on a PubMed corpus of 15 million papers, effectively expresses medical knowledge. However, fine-tuned on low-resource medical records compared to large model sizes, it was judged to be unable to accurately represent incomplete sentence structures and the format of medical records. Furthermore, CerebroGPT, the model with the smallest size, demonstrated performance just below distilGPT2. Despite its compact size, it exhibited excellent capabilities in expressing cerebrovascular disease-related vocabulary and effectively represented the format of medical records. However, we consider that it tended to express less grammatical constructs compared to distilGPT2, contributing to these observed results. Lastly, In the case of BLEU and ROUGE, the overall scores are distributed low, because the goal is to generate synthetic text with diverse expressions rather than generating the same text as the reference sentence.

Next, we received evaluations from clinician, and detailed reviews are available in Table 2. The clinician evaluated 100 synthetic texts generated by each LM by directly reviewing them. As a result, distilGPT2 and CerebroGPT were evaluated to produce synthetic text that contained medical facts at the similar as a radiologist or other clinician. In addition, when checking the overall aspect, including grammatical sentence structure expressions, etc., the clinician's evaluation evaluated the quality of synthetic text in the same as the quantitative evaluation, in the order of distilGPT2, CerebroGPT, ChatGPT, and BioGPT.

6 Conclusion

In this study, we explored the use of LMs for synthetic text generation based on two keywords provided by the user to augment low-resource medical records. We compared ChatGPT, BioGPT, distilGPT2, and CerebroGPT (in-house). The experimental results indicated that, overall, distilGPT2 exhibited superior performance in semantic aspects and the expression of cerebrovascular disease-related vocabulary. Moreover, distilGPT2 demonstrated the most suitable quality of synthetic text in the evaluation by clinicians. Therefore, we conclude that selecting a LM tailored to the dataset size of the specific domain, rather than relying on large-scale LMs (LLMs), is crucial for augmenting low-resource domain text. Additionally, it is considered that generating high-quality synthetic text is possible by preprocessing the text into the desired format.

However, as data augmentation ultimately involves generating synthetic dataset, annotating for the synthetic data must also be conducted. Therefore, we will develop an annotation model for cerebrovascular disease-related synthetic text. In addition, we plan to obtain additional permission to build a database of not only radiologist's reports on CT images but also EMRs from a wide range of medical fields with sensitive information removed. Through this, we plan to use Retrieval-Augmented Generation (Lewis et al., 2020) to conduct research on an advanced text augmentation algorithm based on medical facts in EMR. These results are expected to play an important role in further improving synthetic text generation in the medical domain and utilizing the rich information contained in EMR in the future medical AI field.

Limitations

This work has several limitations. First, the cerebrovascular disease-related medical records used contain sensitive information and cannot be disclosed publicly. Second, the format of the preprocessed medical records may differ from those used in other countries or institutions. Third, the proposed method is limited to cerebrovascular diseases and does not cover the entire biomedical domain. The synthetic text generation in the broader medical domain, including the format and vocabulary expressions familiar to most clinicians (e.g., abbreviations), remains a future task.

Acknowledgements

This work was supported by the National Research Foundation of Korea (NRF) grant funded by the K orea government (MSIT) (No. 2022R1A5A80193 03) and Institute of Information & communication s Technology Planning & Evaluation (IITP) grant f unded by the Korea government (MSIT) [NO.202 1-0-02068, Artificial Intelligence Innovation Hub (Artificial Intelligence Institute, Seoul National Un iversity)].

References

Aaron Gokaslan and Vanya Cohen. 2019. OpenWebText corpus.

Anders Giovanni Møller, Jacob Aarup Dalsgaard, Arianna Pera, and Luca Maria Aiello. 2023. Is a prompt and a few samples all you need? Using GPT-4 for data augmentation in low-resource classification tasks. *arXiv preprint arXiv:2304.13861*.

Haixing Dai, Zhengliang Liu, Wenxiong Liao, Xiaoke Huang, Yihan Cao, Zihao Wu, Lin Zhao, Shaochen Xu, Wei Liu, Ninghao Liu, Sheng Li, Dajiang Zhu, Hongmin Cai, Lichao Sun, Quanzheng Li, Dinggang Shen, Tianming Liu, and Xiang Li. 2023. AugGPT: Leveraging ChatGPT for Text Data Augmentation. *arXiv preprint arXiv:2302.13007*.

Jason Wei and Kai Zou. 2019. EDA: Easy Data Augmentation Techniques for Boosting Performance on Text Classification Tasks. In *Proceedings of the 2019 Conference on Empirical Methods in Natural Language Processing*, pages 6382–6388, Hong Kong, China. Association for Computational Linguistics.

Long Ouyang, Jeff Wu, Xu Jiang, Diogo Almeida, Carroll L. Wainwright, Pamela Mishkin, Chong Zhang, Sandhini Agarwal, Katarina Slama, Alex Ray, John Schulman, Jacob Hilton, Fraser Kelton, Luke Miller, Maddie Simens, Amanda Askell, Peter Welinder, Paul Christiano, Jan Leike, and Ryan Lowe. 2022. Training language models to follow instructions with human feedback. *Advances in Neural Information Processing Systems*, pages 27730-27744.

OpenAI. 2023. Gpt-4 technical report.

Patrick Lewis, Ethan Perez, Aleksandra Piktus, Fabio Petroni, Vladimir Karpukhin, Naman Goyal,

Heinrich Küttler, Mike Lewis, Wen-tau Yih, Tim Rocktäschel, Sebastian Riedel, and Douwe Kiela. 2020. Retrieval-Augmented Generation for Knowledge-Intensive NLP Tasks. *Advances in Neural Information Processing Systems*, pages 9459-9474.

Pranati Rakshit, Anuj Kumar and Amlan Chakraborty. 2022. A Survey on Video Description and Summarization Using Deep Learning-Based Methods. *Machine Learning in Information and Communication Technology: Lecture Notes in Networks and Systems*, 498:213–223.

Renqian Luo, Liai Sun, Yingce Xia, Tao Qin, Sheng Zhang, Hoifung Poon, and Tie-Yan Lin. 2022. BioGPT: generative pre-trained transformer for biomedical text generation and mining. *Briefings in Bioinformatics*, 23(6): bbac409.

Shona Kalkman, Johannes van Delden, Amitava Banerjee, Benoît Tyl, Menno Mostert, and Ghislaine van Thiel. 2022. Patients' and public views and attitudes towards the sharing of health data for research: a narrative review of the empirical evidence. *Journal of medical ethics*, 48(1): 3-13.

Solomon Ubani, Suleyman Olcay Polat, Rodney Nielsen. 2023. ZeroShotDataAug: Generating and Augmenting Training Data with ChatGPT. *arXiv preprint arXiv:2304.14334*.

Steven Euijong Whang, Yuji Roh, Hwanjun Song, and Jae-Gil Lee. 2023. Data collection and quality challenges in deep learning: A data-centric ai perspective. *The VLDB Journal*, 32(4): 791-813.

Suehyun Lee and Hun-Sung Kim. 2021. Prospect of Artificial Intelligence Based on Electronic Medical Record. *Journal of Lipid and Atherosclerosis*, 10(3): 282-290.

Victor Sanh, Lysandre Debut, Julien Chaumond, and Thomas Wolf. 2019. DistilBERT, a Distilled Version of BERT: Smaller, Faster, Cheaper and Lighter. In *Proceeding of the NeurIPS EMC^2 Workshop*.

A Medical Report Corpus

Medical records were collected for a total of 35,511 people, and details are as follows: 1) Patients with intracranial hemorrhage: 10,249, 2) Patients with other cerebrovascular diseases or normal individuals: 25,262. Table 3 shows the original text and preprocessed results of the medical records.

B Generated Synthetic Texts

Each of the generated synthetic texts is a result created based on the same two keywords: "Multiple, both", "History, trauma", "Non-specific, small", "1, Diffuse". This has been put together for each LM, as shown in the following Table 4-7.

Intracerebral Hemorrhage Patient	
Original text	Preprocessed text
Diffuse cerebral subdural hemorrhage: decreased	Diffuse cerebral subdural hemorrhage. - decreased.
Diffuse cerebral subdural hygroma, subdural hemorrhage - No signficant interval change since the last examination.	Diffuse cerebral subdural hygroma, subdural hemorrhage. - No signficant interval change since the last examination. Both parietal craniostomy.
Non-ICH and Normal Patient	
Original text	Preprocessed text
Unremarkable finding of brain parenchyma and cerebrospinal fluid space	Unremarkable finding of brain parenchyma and cerebrospinal fluid space.
equivocal focal low density in both globus pallidus R/O) Acute carbon monoxide intoxication	equivocal focal low density in both globus pallidus. R/O: Acute carbon monoxide intoxication.

Table 3: Example of medical report (intracerebral hemorrhage patient, non-ich and normal patient).

distilGPT2
Mulitple both frontal contusional hematomas -resolving. Midline frontal epidural hemorrhage -No signficant interval change since the last examination. Diffuse both cerebral subdural hygromas. -decreased. Left frontal subcortical hemaL subarachnoid hemorrhages -mild decreased.
History -trauma, S/P coil embolization at ruptured aneurysm at left P-om. SAH, IVH and hydrocephalus. Otherwise, no demonstrable abnormal finding.
Non-specific small nodular calcification or post infectious calcified granuloma. -Meningioma or parasite infestation. Chronic right otomastoiditis.
1. Diffuse subarachnoid hemorrhage. 2. intraventricular hemorrhages in lateral, fourth and third ventricles. 3. intracerebral hemorrhlacranial arteries. -No signficant interval change since the last examination.

Table 4: Examples of synthetic text generated by distilGPT2.

CerebroGPT
Mulitple both frontal subcortical intracerebral hemorrhage. Small vessel disease of both frontal lobes. -remnant intraventricular hemorrhages in left basal ganglia.
History -trauma, both frontal deep white matters. Multifocal low density in both frontal lobes.
Non-specific small infarctions in left basal ganglia and left frontal lobe. No signficant interval change since the last examination. Otherwise no demonstrable abnormal finding. Left corona radiata and temporal cortical Intracerebral hemorrhage in both fronto-parietal lobe.
1. Diffuse subarachnoid hemorrhage in left fronto-parietal cortical subarachnoid hemorrhage -decreased.

Table 5: Examples of synthetic text generated by CerebroGPT.

ChatGPT
Multiple both large and small infarcts are present, indicative of a cerebrovascular disease affecting various regions of the brain. These findings suggest a significant compromise in blood flow leading to ischemic strokes. Prompt medical intervention should be considered to prevent further damage and assess the underlying cause.
History - trauma: The CT images reveal a vascular abnormality in the brain, suggesting a possible cerebrovascular disease. This may be indicative of a previous traumatic event, such as a head injury or blood vessel rupture, leading to impaired blood flow in the affected area. Further medical evaluation and treatment should be considered.
Non-specific small hypodensities are observed in the subcortical region of the brain, suggesting possible lacunar infarcts or chronic microvascular ischemic changes in a patient with cerebrovascular disease. Further clinical correlation and follow-up imaging may be necessary to ascertain the underlying cause and guide management decisions.
1. Diffuse subarachnoid hemorrhage is a condition characterized by bleeding throughout the spaces between the brain and the thin membranes covering it, suggesting a ruptured blood vessel. Immediate medical attention is vital as it can lead to significant brain damage or even life-threatening complications. 2. Diffuse subarachnoid hyperdensity is indicative of widespread blood extravasation within the subarachnoid spaces, typically caused by an aneurysm rupture. Timely intervention and interventions such as coiling or clipping are crucial to prevent further bleeding and minimize long-term neurological deficits.

Table 6: Examples of synthetic text generated by ChatGPT. Highlights are the results of generating sentences with general content, such as advice to consult a doctor or get tested at a hospital.

BioGPT
Mulitple both contuhematoma left-cortex subcortical. frontal hemorrhage counter ou. hemorrhage right ie@-@ cortical subcortical -interval. parietal hemorrhage Multiright-subdural ag. hemorrhages ght temporal. st/ of, to,.. of. / 1 Chronic. Chronic otomo., maxillary sphenoid. osclerotic calcification both vertebral. no abnormal. significant change last. C F U MRI. urther of age refer. to.-. c F Uporboth bone with cortex. dural. - 2 c f u, ension multistage. stified 3 considering. old and with as to 3 Mild in. not. 5 evidence subarachnoid,,-R O 1 Old. unal 2 No. 1 Multiple sional. lacunar. No change within. (), c no change 2 Multiple fracture right bone skull able 3 4 use. 3 Traumatic and, and contuhemorrhages mega significantly usp1 including elresolving reversible. both cortical and ernal. Non pecsubarachnoid. in frontal sul. suggvely 1--developed unres. right cerebral hyroma (5 4 5 Lt. brain. reversible edema urther. 4 Re). olstate 2 Suspously ventricular. ereus. R S O. Resving 2 Nontraumatic, with edema both ventricle post. 2 RE-brain and brain not how ressive - (2 4,) 4 4> than 4.44. hydrocephalus slightly C D. s 5 Mild. evidence diffuse swelling M1 other idum since. 4. able. considering significant MU4 4 2 2 8uschange. ending. nreversible of hydrocephalus 4 mild. with. lgprogressive involving a the. on aggrav. developed. post2 ...
History -trauma, /. x Trauma hemorrhagic.,. infarction hemorrhagic sions both and frontal. SDH right lobe left lobe Otherwise demonstrable finding or orwith ficlevel. urther, lutide of ost- discrete. C view within. stable how by than res.. / subarachnoid. of temporal. not. to. with arterial. aneor ymaneurysm and as more rather. ension use fic. developed el. able. 1 along dural. - 1 Chronic cerebral. dural with. c. Chronic. No chang. ogenic. R O metastasis 2 Old infarction left ganglia 3 Fungal. no change left otitis 4 Chronic otomo. in right sto. usion right jugular. 3 Chronic lesions both astand ara. within mastoid cells to developed. opp usein watershed a-. evidence 1- 1 Old. ward. lacunar. 4 Soft density left udspace. ified. -, t ...

Table 7: Examples of generated synthetic texts (BioGPT). BioGPT's synthetic text is very long and unstructured sentences.

Assessing Generalization for Subpopulation Representative Modeling via In-Context Learning

Gabriel Simmons
University of California, Davis
gsimmons@ucdavis.edu

Vladislav Savinov
Independent Researcher
vlad.al.savinov@gmail.com

Abstract

This study evaluates the ability of Large Language Model (LLM)-based Subpopulation Representative Models (SRMs) to generalize from empirical data, utilizing in-context learning with data from the 2016 and 2020 American National Election Studies. We explore generalization across response variables and demographic subgroups. While conditioning with empirical data improves performance on the whole, the benefit of in-context learning varies considerably across demographics, sometimes hurting performance for one demographic while helping performance for others. The inequitable benefits of in-context learning for SRM present a challenge for practitioners implementing SRMs, and for decision-makers who might come to rely on them. Our work highlights a need for fine-grained benchmarks captured from diverse subpopulations that test not only fidelity but generalization.

1 Introduction

Natural language processing research has plunged headlong into the new alchemical science of *prompt engineering* (Liu et al., 2023). Ask OpenAI's ChatGPT to "think step-by-step" and behold its improved reasoning performance (Wei et al., 2023). Tell it to behave as an expert and witness its expertise increasing (Salewski et al.).

The responsiveness of foundation models to prompt engineering has led researchers from diverse disciplines to explore their applications. This is certainly true in political science, where several recent studies investigate whether the malleability of LLMs would allow them to simulate the attitudes and behaviors of human subpopulations (Chu et al., 2023; Jiang et al., 2022; Kim and Lee, 2023; Simmons and Hare, 2023; Linegar et al., 2023).

Polling plays an important role in opinion aggregation, acting as a cornerstone of governance (Shapiro, 2011). The use of LLMs as subgroup

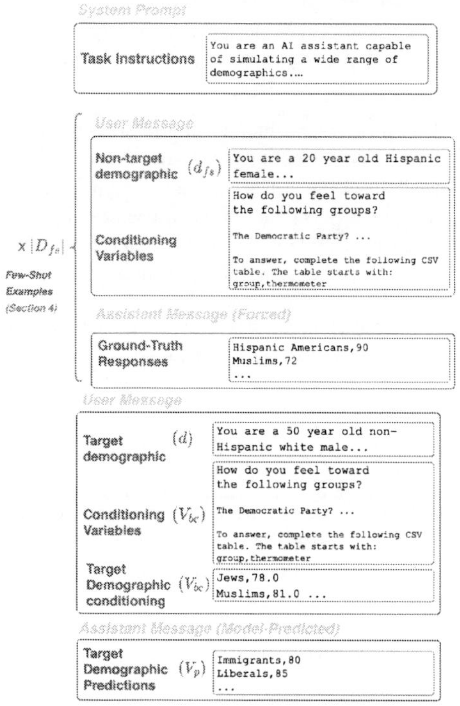

Figure 1: Description of a prompting strategy used for both RQ 1 and RQ 2. For Study 1, $|D_{fs}| = 0$.

simulators has hypothesized benefits including decreased cost and increased sample sizes (Argyle et al.). As response rates to traditional survey methods decline, social scientists are encouraged to explore new methods (Ziems et al.). More than a dozen examples of the subpopulation representative modeling approach are found in academic research (Simmons and Hare, 2023), and the approach has already garnered attention at local (Tal) and national levels (ION).

1.1 Limitations of LLMs as Subpopulation Representative Models

While the potential benefits are considerable, applying LLMs as a substitute or complement for polling

Proceedings of the 1st Workshop on Personalization of Generative AI Systems (PERSONALIZE 2024), pages 18–35
March 22, 2024 ©2024 Association for Computational Linguistics

should be taken with caution. Recent work shows that prompting LLMs with demographic information leaves much to be desired. Bisbee et al. show that when ChatGPT (gpt-3.5-turbo)[1] is prompted with demographic information from the ANES Survey[2] and asked to complete a Feeling Thermometer[3], its responses are more extreme and less variable than the responses collected from human participants (Bisbee et al.). Santurkar et al. show that overall fidelity[4] to human response distributions is low for OpenAI's ChatGPT when the model is not prompted with a demographic descriptor, that prompting is more effective for some population subgroups than others, and that the fidelity obtained using demographic prompting, while higher than without, is still far from perfect. These studies express a pessimistic stance about the potential of LLMs for subpopulation representative modeling, one that is rightly held based on the experimental evidence to date.

1.2 In-Context Learning for Better Fidelity

We contend here that we should not be prematurely pessimistic. As with chain-of-thought (Wei et al., 2023) and expert prompting, perhaps a straightforward technique to improve the performance of LLMs as subpopulation representative models has been overlooked. A hallmark of LLMs is their capability for in-context learning (ICL; Brown et al.; Dong et al. 2023). One popular mode of in-context learning is *few-shot learning*, where task examples are provided in the context window to condition generation (Song et al., 2023). Few-shot learning improves performance relative to prompting without examples, on tasks including translation and question answering (Brown et al.), clinical information extraction (Agrawal et al., 2022), reading comprehension and natural language inference (Chowdhery et al., 2022), and improves factual accuracy of model responses (Semnani et al., 2023).

The subpopulation representative modeling (SRM) task involves predicting the distribution of some response variables, such as candidate preference (Palakodety et al., 2020), feeling thermometer (Argyle et al.) or stance on divisive issues (Kim and Lee, 2023) for a population subgroup (target demographic) identified by a combination of demographic variables. Applying LLMs to this task typically involves prompting the language model with a natural language description of the demographic and adding instructions to encourage the model to predict the response distribution. Importantly, this zero-shot approach does not leverage observed data from the subpopulation other than its demographic descriptors.

The most straightforward way to apply ICL to the SRM task would be to condition the model with data from the target subpopulation and demographic variables. With sufficient grounding in the target task, we expect that models could become representative. However, in this setup the practitioner has gained little, since they have to provide data from the target subpopulation and response variables to elicit desirable performance.[5] For this reason, we expect that SRM practitioners would be enthusiastic to use available data to improve performance on unrelated subpopulations or unrelated response variables. In other words, *generalization* beyond the data presented in the few-shot examples would allow practitioners to apply SRMs with improved performance even if data was not abundant for the subpopulation of interest.

1.3 The Importance of Generalization

For the subpopulation representative modeling task, generalization can occur along two axes: (1) generalization across response variables and (2) generalization across demographics. If a model can generalize across response variables, this means that conditioning on observed response variables improves fidelity for unobserved response variables. If a model can generalize across demographics, this means that conditioning on observed demographics improves fidelity for unobserved demographics. If these capabilities are demonstrated, the outlook for subpopulation representative modeling via LLMs may not be as dire as it seems. In-context learning could mitigate known issues such as extremism (Bisbee et al.) or lack of representativeness (Santurkar et al.).

Successful generalization alone does not imply that LLMs are suitable for use as SRMs. However, we argue that if generalization were possible, it would encourage further development of LLM-

[1] https://openai.com/blog/chatgpt

[2] The American National Election Studies (ANES) are national surveys of voters in the United States, conducted before and after presidential elections, with data since 1948 (ANES)

[3] The ANES Feeling Thermometer measures respondent affinity to various political groups in the United States.

[4] Santurkar et al. refer to this as alignment. We use "fidelity" since alignment take several meanings.

[5] This setup could still be used for synthetic data generation for the subpopulation and response variables, similar to missing data imputation in Kim and Lee (2023)

Demographic Variables	Response Variables
age	The Democratic Party
race	The Republican Party
gender	Black Americans
income	White Americans
education	Hispanic Americans
political party	Asian Americans
	Muslims
	Christians
	Jews
	Liberals
	Conservatives

Table 1: Demographic and response variables used in this study.

based SRM technology. Integrating LLMs into the political infrastructure could have serious social consequences. For that reason, we believe that machine learning practitioners, social scientists, and policymakers should understand the viability of the technology, as greater viability may translate to an increased chance of real-world use. This motivates our study of the generalization capabilities of LLMs for the subpopulation representative modeling task.

Research Questions

We address the following research questions:

- **RQ 1 (Generalization across Response Variables)**: How does the fidelity of LLMs to some target **demographic** vary with the number of **response** variables from the target demographic used for conditioning? We address this in Section 3.

- **RQ 2 (Generalization across Demographics)**: How does the fidelity of LLMs to some target **demographic** vary with the number of **examples from other demographics** used for conditioning? We investigate this in Section 4.

2 Methods

This section documents methods shared across both studies. Specific methods for each study are documented in Section 3 and Section 4.

2.1 Data

We use data from the American National Election Studies (ANES). We used the time series cumulative data file for the ANES Survey[6], which contains six demographic variables (age, race, gender, income, education, and political party), and 11 Feeling Thermometer variables shown in Table 1. The ANES Feeling Thermometer is a series of ratings questions where survey participants rate their affinity towards various political groups on a continuous scale from 0-100. Across all years, the ANES data contains 68,224 observations. We selected observations from the years 2016 and 2020, yielding 12,550 observations. After removing observations with missing values, the dataset used for experiments contained 4,397 observations. See Appendix B for additional details on data processing steps applied before prompting.

2.2 The Subpopulation Representative Modeling Task

Subpopulation data consists of a number of observations of some set of variables V, with each observation corresponding to a single individual. Often, this set of variables contains some subset $V_d \subset V$ that describe the demographic characteristics of each individual, and some other subset $V_b \subset V$ capturing individual behaviors or attitudes. At a high level, the goal for the SRM task might be to approximate the distribution of V_b conditioned on V_d. However, it is equally likely that practitioners are interested in predicting a specific behavior and have some other behavioral data available for conditioning, requiring generalization across response variables. We investigate this setting in Section 3. Additionally, practitioners may have some paired (demographic, behavior) data available for certain demographic cells and want to predict the behavior for other demographic cells. We investigate generalization across demographics in Section 4.

2.3 Measuring Fidelity Error

We are interested in assessing how LLM fidelity to some target demographic varies with the amount of empirical data used to condition the model. We use the term *fidelity error* (E) to refer to the gap between the LLM response and ground truth data observed from humans in the demographic of interest. In our setting, the behavioral variables V_b are Feeling Thermometer ratings across 11 political groups. To explore generalization across response variables, we select some $V_{bc} \subset V_b$ to be used for

[6]available at https://electionstudies.org/data-center/anes-time-series-cumulative-data-file/

$$E(d, V_c, D_{fs}) = \frac{1}{|V_p|} \sum_{v_p \in V_p} |\hat{y}(d, V_c, v_p, D_{fs}) - y(d, v_p)|. \quad (1)$$

$$E(d, n_c, n_{fs}) = \frac{1}{n_r} \sum_{D_{fs} \sim \mathcal{D}(n_{fs}, d)} \frac{1}{|\mathcal{V}_c(n_c, d)|} \sum_{V_c \in \mathcal{V}_c(n_c, d)} E(d, V_c, D_{fs}). \quad (2)$$

conditioning. The LLM is tasked to predict the remaining variables $V_p = V_b \setminus V_{bc}$.

To obtain ground truth for V_b at the demographic level, we obtain an average respondent profile for each demographic cell by calculating the mean responses for each of the 220 demographic cells in the ANES data.

We define fidelity error for some target demographic d as the difference between the empirical mean and the LLM-predicted response, averaged over the Feeling Thermometer variables included in V_p. In general this error varies by the conditioning variables (V_c), see Equation (1). The term $y(d, v_p)$ is the empirical mean Feeling Thermometer for demographic d towards group v_p. The term $\hat{y}(d, V_c, v_p, D_{fs})$ is the LLM-predicted Feeling Thermometer data for demographic d towards group v_p, conditioned on variables V_c and few-shot data D_{fs}. In other words, Equation (1) describes the fidelity error of the model conditioned on a specific set of few-shot examples.

Equation (2) estimates the overall fidelity error of the model by sampling n_r sets of few-shot examples from the observed data. In our experiments we used $n_r = 5$. The term $\mathcal{V}_c(n_c, d)$ is the set of sets of conditioning variables having $|V_c| = n_c$ elements that are available for demographic d. The term $\mathcal{D}_{fs}(n_{fs}, d)$ is the set of sets of few-shot examples having $|D_{fs}| = n_{fs}$ elements that are available for demographic d.

2.4 Generating LLM Responses

Our prompting strategy is briefly outlined here and in Figure 1. In this study, we utilize OpenAI's `gpt-3.5-turbo`, accessed via the API. We adapt a similar prompting strategy to Bisbee et al., altering prompts to accommodate Research Questions 1 and 2. This approach comprises a consistent system prompt for directing the model's behavior and a variable user prompt, tailored for each research question. For RQ 1, each query features a *single* user prompt with an incomplete Feeling Thermometer table. For RQ 2, we supply the model with multiple user prompts, each paired with an example model response which contains a Feeling Thermometer table with ground truth data.

For a detailed view of our prompting setup, refer to the Appendix A.

3 Generalization of In-Context Learning Across Response Variables

This study investigates the generalization of in-context learning across response variables (Research Question 1). We are interested in finding out to what extent increasing the number of conditioning variables improves fidelity to unobserved response variables.

3.1 Methods

Each prompt includes all demographic variables, plus a subset of the behavioral variables $V_{bc} \subset V_b$. We are interested in relating the number of behavioral variables used for conditioning ($|V_{bc}|$) to the fidelity error. For each demographic cell, we compute the mean empirical response data. Then for each possible value of $|V_{bc}| \in [0, 10]$, we randomly sample n_r sets of conditioning variables. The empirical mean response data for these variables are presented in each prompt as a partially-completed Feeling Thermometer table in CSV format, as shown in Figure 8. The model then completes the remaining rows of the table. For each prompt, we parse the model-completed portion of the Feeling Thermometer table into CSV format. We then calculate the fidelity error for each prompt by comparing these responses to the empirical mean response data for variables V_p.

3.2 Fidelity Error Decreases with Increasing Conditioning Variables

Figure 2 shows the relationship between number of conditioning variables $|V_{bc}|$ and the fidelity error for varying number of few-shot examples. In general, in-context conditioning on observed behavioral variables improves fidelity to unobserved behavioral variables, with error decreasing as the number of conditioning variables increases.

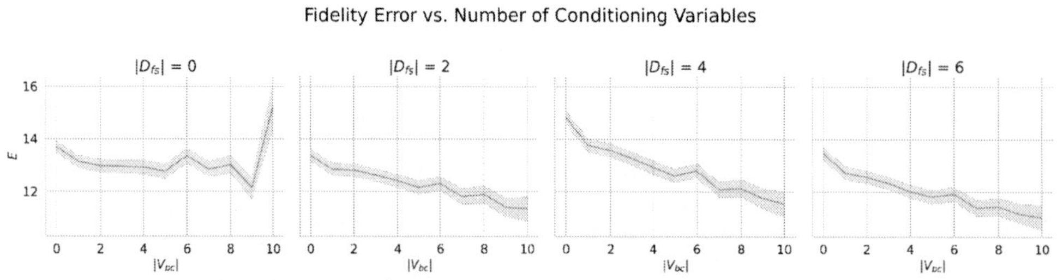

Figure 2: Changes in the fidelity error depending on the $|V_{bc}|$ averaged across all demographics. The fidelity decreases as the number of conditioning variables increases. This pattern holds for every number of few-shot examples checked.

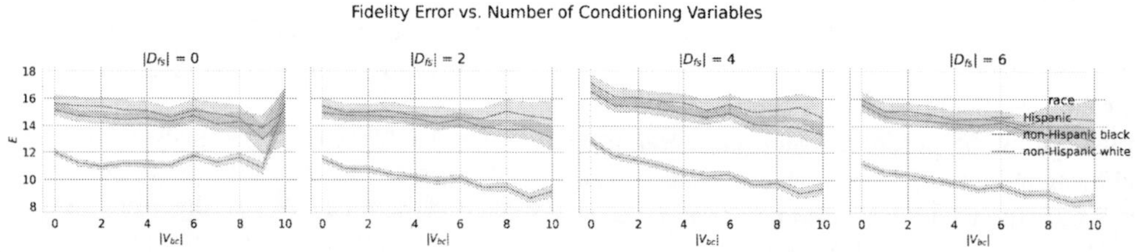

Figure 3: Changes in the fidelity error (E) depending on the number of conditioning variables ($|V_{bc}|$) for different racial groups. Error rates are lower in general for non-Hispanic Whites than for other racial groups.

3.3 Effectiveness of Response Variable Conditioning Varies by Demographic

We can observe discrepancies in error rates between demographics. For example, error rates are lower in general for non-Hispanic Whites than for other racial groups (Figure 3), and for Democratic party in comparison to the Republican one (Figure 4).

Reduction in error as a result of increased conditioning varies by demographic. For instance, error rates are roughly constant for $|V_{bc}| < 6$, then increase for the non-Hispanic black demographic, while continuing to decrease for the non-Hispanic white demographic (Figure 3). This suggests that conditioning on behavioral variables may be more effective for some demographics than for others.

Refer to Appendix C for figures showing relationships between the fidelity error and number of conditioning variables for other demographics.

4 Generalization of In-Context Learning Across Demographics

4.1 Methods

In this study, we investigate the generalization of in-context learning across demographics.

In this case, we select some empirical data $D_{fs} \subset D, \{d_{fs} \neq d \ \ \forall \ \ d_{fs} \in D_{fs}\}$ to be used as few-shot examples. Each prompt was constructed by selecting a target demographic, as in the previous study. Then $|D_{fs}| \in \{0, 2, 4, 6\}$ few-shot examples of complete demographic and Feeling Thermometer information for non-target demographics were randomly selected.

Selecting few-shot examples naturally raises the question of which examples to select. Few-shot example selection can be viewed as an information retrieval task, and many of the well-known methods from IR are applicable here. These include semantic similarity methods (Nan et al., 2023) as well as classic information retrieval algorithms such as max marginal relevance (MMR) (Carbonell and Goldstein, 1998). Few-shot example selection is also related to the problem of representative sampling in the social sciences (Manheim et al., 1981); stratified sampling by demographic could be applied (Barreto et al., 2018). Additionally, the recent trend towards larger models and LLM-as-a-service APIs has encouraged methods that maximize the number of few-shot examples to be included when the model input is restricted by total length (Sel).

However, the most straightforward approach is to sample uniformly at random from the observed data, and in this work we opt for this setup. Since the use of LLMs for SRM is relatively new and may be applied by practitioners who are not familiar with the aforementioned methods, we think it

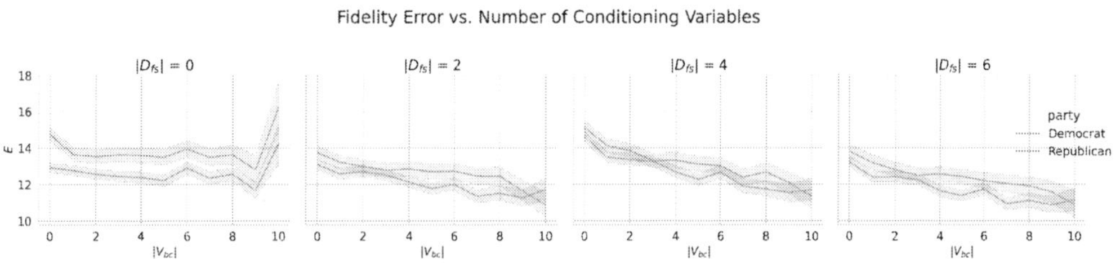

Figure 4: Changes in the fidelity error (E) depending on the number of conditioning variables ($|V_{bc}|$) for different political parties. Error rates are lower in general for Democrats than for Republicans.

is important to consider the performance of naive methods. We are aware that the choice of sampling method could influence the results of this study; see the Discussion for commentary on the effects of sampling strategy and our suggestions for additional experiments.

4.2 Fidelity Error Decreases with Increasing Few-Shot Examples

Figure 6 shows fidelity error as it relates to the number of few-shot examples. In general, fidelity error decreases with increasing number of few-shot examples.

4.3 Effectiveness of Few-Shot Learning Varies by Demographic

We can again observe discrepancies in error rates between various demographics, including race, age income, and party. For instance, from Figure 5 it can be seen that not only the fidelity error for non-Hispanic whites is smaller in general, but also that in-context learning is more efficient for this ethnicity.

We draw heavily on the prompting methods used in Bisbee et al. - this was done intentionally, for the sake of comparison. The key difference is the use of conditioning based on ground-truth data. Bisbee et al.'s study is one of the sharpest criticisms of LLM-based SRMs to date and raises important questions about the viability of LLM-based SRMs. If the deficiencies highlighted in this work are ameliorated by in-context learning, this would be an important consideration. We use similar methods so that results are attributable to the use of in-context learning, rather than differences in prompting strategy.

5 Discussion: Subpopulation Representative Modeling via In-Context Learning

Recent criticisms have argued that Large Language Models do not sufficiently represent the opinions or behaviors of human subpopulations when these subpopulations are specified in the context (Santurkar et al.; Bisbee et al.). However, extant work neglects the capability for models to learn via in-context learning.

Our experiments demonstrate that LLMs *can* learn the subpopulation representative modeling task in-context. The experiments in Section 3 show that providing the model with partial information about subpopulation behavior improves model fidelity on unobserved response variables. Section 4 shows that providing the model with information about other subpopulations can improve model fidelity to an unrelated subpopulation of interest.

In this experiment, we selected few-shot examples uniformly at random. This is only one of several few-shot example selection strategies available to the practitioner (see Section 4, Methods). We believe it is likely that the example selection strategy has some influence over the performance disparities between majority and minority groups. Appendix Figure 13 shows that the ANES data is imbalanced with repsect to the demographic variables – for example, approximately three fourths of respondents were non-Hispanic white, as opposed to Hispanic or non-Hispanic black. The minority categories account for approximately 1/8th of the observations each. For a given target example, the likelihood to select a few-shot example with the same race is proportional to the distribution of the data over the race variable. In general, it is more likely that a randomly-selected few-shot example will share demographic values with the target example when the target example belongs to the majority demographic. Assuming that the

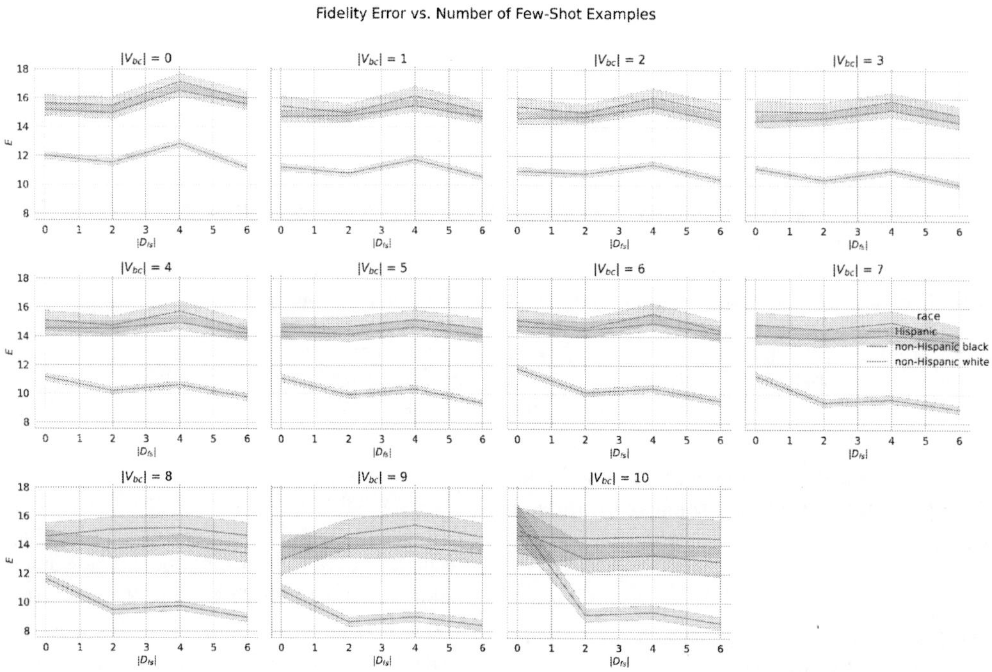

Figure 5: Changes in the fidelity error (E) depending on the number of few-shot examples ($|D_{fs}|$) for different racial groups. Error rates are lower for non-Hispanic Whites. While with increased number of few-shot examples the fidelity error for other race groups remain nearly constant, the fidelity rate for non-Hispanic white racial group decreases.

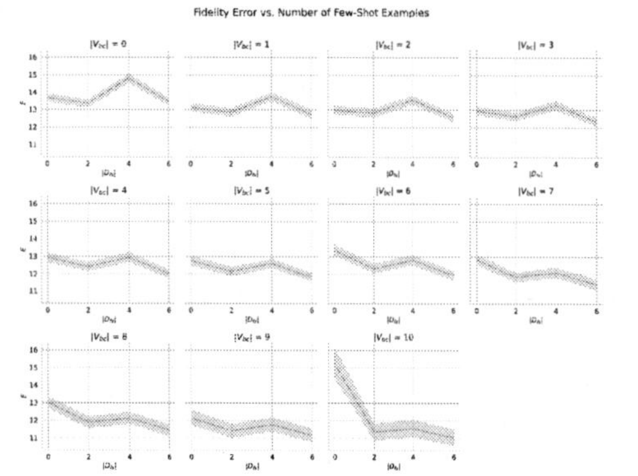

Figure 6: Changes in the fidelity error depending on the $|D_{fs}|$ averaged across all demographics. The fidelity decreases as the number of few-shot examples increases. This pattern holds for every number of conditioning variables checked.

similarity between few-shot examples correlates to their utility for the predictive task, this dataset bias could result in few-shot prompting being more effective for majority groups. This applies both in absolute terms, and in terms of the marginal benefit of additional few-shot examples. We encourage further investigation of the relationship between demographic representation in the few-shot data, performance discrepancies across demographics, and few-shot example selection strategies, and plan to explore this theme in future work.

These aggregate results seem promising for the potential of LLMs to perform the subpopulation modeling task. However, upon closer analysis, we find that the effectiveness of in-context learning is variable across demographics. While additional conditioning data boosts performance for some demographics, it has negligible or even deleterious effects for others. This result extends prior work showing variation across demographics in the exaggeration of stereotypical response patterns (Bisbee et al.) and the fidelity of LLMs to human responses without conditioning (Santurkar et al.). The subgroup-specific effectiveness of in-context learning for SRM presents challenges for SRM practitioners, as well as decision-makers using the results of SRMs. We suggest three directions for future work. The inequitable performance of LLMs on subpopulation simulation calls the ethicality of the endeavor into question. In tasks like recidivism prediction, theoretical results indicate mutual unsatisfiability of model bias criteria (Kleinberg et al., 2016; Chouldechova, 2017). These impossibility results influence why the field views machine learning models as appropriate for certain use cases and possibly unfit for others. We encourage similar investigation into the ethical nature of the subpopulation representative modeling task. This should take into consideration the dual-use nature of subpopulation representative models – that they could be leveraged for positive use cases (improving existing political representation processes) as well as negative (used to steer misinformation campaigns). Secondly, our results highlight the need for fine-grained benchmarking for subpopulation representative models, in terms of generalization performance in few-shot settings as studied here, as well as absolute performance in zero-shot settings. Finally, we note that several approaches have been proposed to ameliorate issues with existing subpopulation representation techniques (Santurkar et al.; Lahoti et al., 2023). We see potential for further research in this area of improving subpopulation representative model performance.

References

ION - Primul Consilier cu Inteligență Artificială al Guvernului. https://ion.gov.ro/.

Select by length - langchain.

Talk to the City. https://ai.objectives.institute/talk-to-the-city.

Monica Agrawal, Stefan Hegselmann, Hunter Lang, Yoon Kim, and David Sontag. 2022. Large language models are few-shot clinical information extractors. In *Proceedings of the 2022 Conference on Empirical Methods in Natural Language Processing*, pages 1998–2022, Abu Dhabi, United Arab Emirates. Association for Computational Linguistics.

ANES. History.

Lisa P. Argyle, Ethan C. Busby, Nancy Fulda, Joshua R. Gubler, Christopher Rytting, and David Wingate. Out of One, Many: Using Language Models to Simulate Human Samples. pages 1–15.

Matt A. Barreto, Lorrie Frasure-Yokley, Edward D. Vargas, and Janelle Wong. 2018. Best practices in collecting online data with Asian, Black, Latino, and White respondents: Evidence from the 2016 Collaborative Multiracial Post-election Survey. *Politics, Groups, and Identities*, 6(1):171–180.

James Bisbee, Joshua Clinton, Cassy Dorff, Brenton Kenkel, and Jennifer Larson. Artificially Precise Extremism: How Internet-Trained LLMs Exaggerate Our Differences.

Tom Brown, Benjamin Mann, Nick Ryder, Melanie Subbiah, Jared D Kaplan, Prafulla Dhariwal, Arvind Neelakantan, Pranav Shyam, Girish Sastry, Amanda Askell, Sandhini Agarwal, Ariel Herbert-Voss, Gretchen Krueger, Tom Henighan, Rewon Child, Aditya Ramesh, Daniel Ziegler, Jeffrey Wu, Clemens Winter, Chris Hesse, Mark Chen, Eric Sigler, Mateusz Litwin, Scott Gray, Benjamin Chess, Jack Clark, Christopher Berner, Sam McCandlish, Alec Radford, Ilya Sutskever, and Dario Amodei. Language Models are Few-Shot Learners. In *Advances in Neural Information Processing Systems*, volume 33, pages 1877–1901. Curran Associates, Inc.

Jaime Carbonell and Jade Goldstein. 1998. The use of MMR, diversity-based reranking for reordering documents and producing summaries. In *Proceedings of the 21st Annual International ACM SIGIR Conference on Research and Development in Information Retrieval*, pages 335–336, Melbourne Australia. ACM.

Alexandra Chouldechova. 2017. Fair Prediction with Disparate Impact: A Study of Bias in Recidivism Prediction Instruments. *Big Data*, 5(2):153–163.

Aakanksha Chowdhery, Sharan Narang, Jacob Devlin, Maarten Bosma, Gaurav Mishra, Adam Roberts, Paul Barham, Hyung Won Chung, Charles Sutton, Sebastian Gehrmann, Parker Schuh, Kensen Shi, Sasha Tsvyashchenko, Joshua Maynez, Abhishek Rao, Parker Barnes, Yi Tay, Noam Shazeer, Vinodkumar Prabhakaran, Emily Reif, Nan Du, Ben Hutchinson, Reiner Pope, James Bradbury, Jacob Austin, Michael Isard, Guy Gur-Ari, Pengcheng Yin, Toju Duke, Anselm Levskaya, Sanjay Ghemawat, Sunipa Dev, Henryk Michalewski, Xavier Garcia, Vedant Misra, Kevin Robinson, Liam Fedus, Denny Zhou, Daphne Ippolito, David Luan, Hyeontaek Lim, Barret Zoph, Alexander Spiridonov, Ryan Sepassi, David Dohan, Shivani Agrawal, Mark Omernick, Andrew M. Dai, Thanumalayan Sankaranarayana Pillai, Marie Pellat, Aitor Lewkowycz, Erica Moreira, Rewon Child, Oleksandr Polozov, Katherine Lee, Zongwei Zhou, Xuezhi Wang, Brennan Saeta, Mark Diaz, Orhan Firat, Michele Catasta, Jason Wei, Kathy Meier-Hellstern, Douglas Eck, Jeff Dean, Slav Petrov, and Noah Fiedel. 2022. PaLM: Scaling Language Modeling with Pathways.

Eric Chu, Jacob Andreas, Stephen Ansolabehere, and Deb Roy. 2023. Language Models Trained on Media Diets Can Predict Public Opinion.

Qingxiu Dong, Lei Li, Damai Dai, Ce Zheng, Zhiyong Wu, Baobao Chang, Xu Sun, Jingjing Xu, Lei Li, and Zhifang Sui. 2023. A Survey on In-context Learning.

Hang Jiang, Doug Beeferman, Brandon Roy, and Deb Roy. 2022. CommunityLM: Probing Partisan Worldviews from Language Models. In *Proceedings of the 29th International Conference on Computational Linguistics*, pages 6818–6826, Gyeongju, Republic of Korea. International Committee on Computational Linguistics.

Junsol Kim and Byungkyu Lee. 2023. AI-Augmented Surveys: Leveraging Large Language Models for Opinion Prediction in Nationally Representative Surveys. ArXiv:2305.09620 [cs].

Jon Kleinberg, Sendhil Mullainathan, and Manish Raghavan. 2016. Inherent Trade-Offs in the Fair Determination of Risk Scores.

Preethi Lahoti, Nicholas Blumm, Xiao Ma, Raghavendra Kotikalapudi, Sahitya Potluri, Qijun Tan, Hansa Srinivasan, Ben Packer, Ahmad Beirami, Alex Beutel, and Jilin Chen. 2023. Improving Diversity of Demographic Representation in Large Language Models via Collective-Critiques and Self-Voting. ArXiv:2310.16523 [cs].

Mitchell Linegar, Rafal Kocielnik, and R. Alvarez. 2023. Large language models and political science. *Frontiers in Political Science*, 5.

Pengfei Liu, Weizhe Yuan, Jinlan Fu, Zhengbao Jiang, Hiroaki Hayashi, and Graham Neubig. 2023. Pre-train, Prompt, and Predict: A Systematic Survey of Prompting Methods in Natural Language Processing. *ACM Computing Surveys*, 55(9):195:1–195:35.

Jarol B. Manheim, R. Rich, Lars Willnat, Donna Bahry, and Philip A. Schrodt. 1981. Empirical Political Analysis: Research Methods in Political Science.

Linyong Nan, Yilun Zhao, Weijin Zou, Narutatsu Ri, Jaesung Tae, Ellen Zhang, Arman Cohan, and Dragomir Radev. 2023. Enhancing Few-shot Text-to-SQL Capabilities of Large Language Models: A Study on Prompt Design Strategies.

Shriphani Palakodety, Ashiqur R. KhudaBukhsh, and J. Carbonell. 2020. Mining Insights from Large-Scale Corpora Using Fine-Tuned Language Models. https://www.cs.cmu.edu/ akhudabu/ECAI-2019-BERTElection.pdf.

Leonard Salewski, Stephan Alaniz, Isabel Rio-Torto, Eric Schulz, and Zeynep Akata. In-Context Impersonation Reveals Large Language Models' Strengths and Biases.

Shibani Santurkar, Esin Durmus, Faisal Ladhak, Cinoo Lee, Percy Liang, and Tatsunori Hashimoto. Whose Opinions Do Language Models Reflect?

Sina Semnani, Violet Yao, Heidi Zhang, and Monica Lam. 2023. WikiChat: Stopping the Hallucination of Large Language Model Chatbots by Few-Shot Grounding on Wikipedia. In *Findings of the Association for Computational Linguistics: EMNLP 2023*, pages 2387–2413, Singapore. Association for Computational Linguistics.

R. Y. Shapiro. 2011. Public Opinion and American Democracy. *Public Opinion Quarterly*, 75(5):982–1017.

Gabriel Simmons and Christopher Hare. 2023. Large Language Models as Subpopulation Representative Models: A Review.

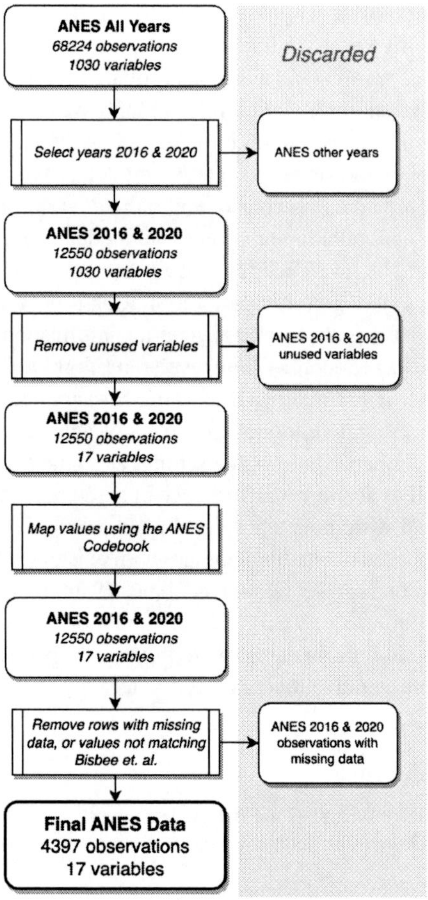

Figure 7: Data processing pipeline.

Yisheng Song, Ting Wang, Puyu Cai, Subrota K. Mondal, and Jyoti Prakash Sahoo. 2023. A Comprehensive Survey of Few-shot Learning: Evolution, Applications, Challenges, and Opportunities. *ACM Computing Surveys*, 55(13s):1–40.

Jason Wei, Xuezhi Wang, Dale Schuurmans, Maarten Bosma, Brian Ichter, Fei Xia, Ed Chi, Quoc Le, and Denny Zhou. 2023. Chain-of-Thought Prompting Elicits Reasoning in Large Language Models.

Caleb Ziems, William Held, Omar Shaikh, Zhehao Zhang, Diyi Yang, and Jiaao Chen. Can Large Language Models Transform Computational Social Science?

A Prompting Setup

This section provides specific prompts used for our study, further explaining Figure 1. Our strategy is adapted from the methodology used in Bisbee et al., with several modifications to better suit our research objectives.

```
The table starts with:
group,thermometer
Muslims,30.0
Jews,72.0
```

Figure 8: Possible end of the table to condition on two response variables for the target demographic (ground-truth responses).

The prompting setup consists of task instructions (the system prompt) and the user prompt. The system prompt is a constant element in all the requests, designed to guide the AI model towards displaying a subpopulation representative behavior (see Figure 9 for the exact structure of the system prompt). User prompts vary based on the research question. For research question 1, a single user prompt is used. This prompt consists of three parts:

1. Target demographic description (d), which provides demographic data to the model (see Figure 10);
2. A number of conditioning variables, constant across all requests, posing a concrete question with respect to the current study (see Figure 11);
3. Target demographic conditioning, providing a partial Feeling Thermometer table of $V_{bc} \subset V_b$ variables into the model (see Figure 8).

For research question 2, multiple user prompts are employed, each paired with an example model response. The structure of additional user prompts remains consistent with that of the RQ 1, but instead of the target demographic data, a non-target demographic conditioning is used. All but one of these prompts serve as few-shot examples. In RQ 2, a single few-shot example consists of:

1. **Non**-target demographic data (d_{fs}), fed into the model in the same format as in the Figure 10;
2. A number of conditioning variables, similarly to RQ 1 (refer to Figure 11);
3. Ground-truth responses from the cleaned ANES data – a Feeling Thermometer table for the same non-target demographic. The format is the same as in Figure 8.

Few-shot examples are followed by the final user prompt (same as in the RQ 1), soliciting a model prediction for the feeling thermometer table for the target demographic.

B Notes on Data Processing

Many observations in the ANES data were incomplete. Missing value rates for the data are shown in Figure 12. Counts of observations for each demographic variable are shown in Figure 13. Removing rows containing missing demographic and response variables, and observations with variable values other than those in Table 1 resulted in 4,397 observations, with 570 unique demographic cells. The end-to-end data processing pipeline is shown in Figure 7.

C Figures

Figures 14, 15, 16, 17, 18, 19, 20, 21, 22, 23, 24 and 25 show our findings for different demographic variables.

```
You are an AI assistant capable of simulating a wide range of demographics.

You receive demographic data describing a single person as an input.
Provide responses from this person's perspective.
Use only knowledge about politics that they would have.

The user asks about individuals' feelings toward different groups.
Responses should be given on a scale from 0 (meaning cold feelings) to 100 (
    meaning warm feelings).
Ratings between 50 degrees and 100 degrees mean that you feel favorable and warm
     toward the group.
Ratings between 0 degrees and 50 degrees mean that you don't feel favorable
    toward the group and that you don't care too much for that group.
You would rate the group at the 50 degree mark if you don't feel particularly
    warm or cold toward the group.
```

Figure 9: System prompt used for all studies (task instructions).

```
You are a {age} year old {race} {gender} with a {education}, earning ${income}
    per year.
You are a registered {party} living in the USA in 2019.
```

Figure 10: User message, used either for non-target (d_{fs}) or target demographic d.

```
How do you feel toward the following groups?
The Democratic Party?
The Republican Party?
Black Americans?
White Americans?
Hispanic Americans?
Asian Americans?
Muslims?
Christians?
Jews?
Liberals?
Conservatives?

To answer, complete the following CSV table.

The table starts with:
group,thermometer
```

Figure 11: Conditioning variables (V_{bc}).

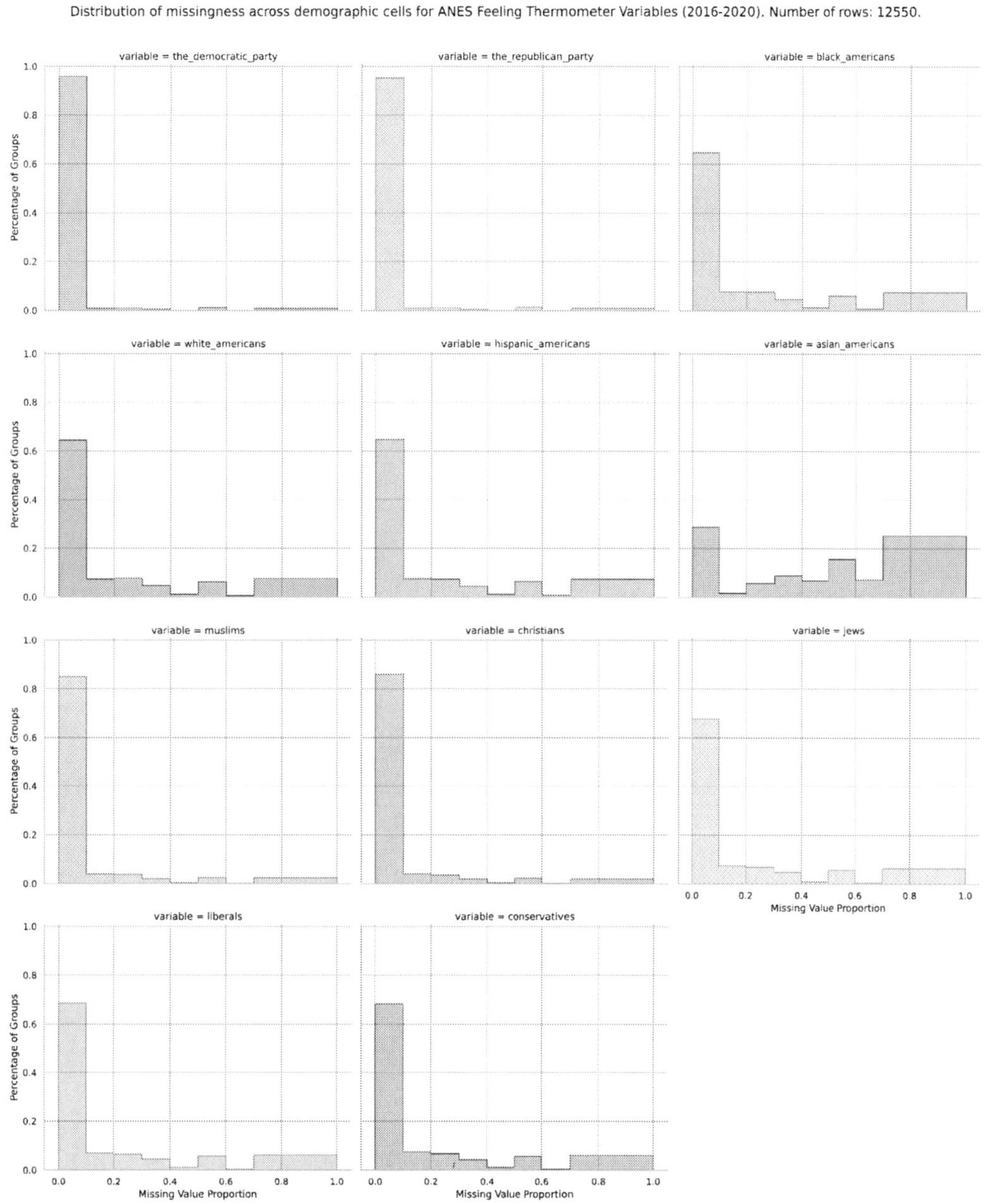

Figure 12: Distribution of missingness across demographic cells for ANES feeling thermometer Variables (2016-2020).

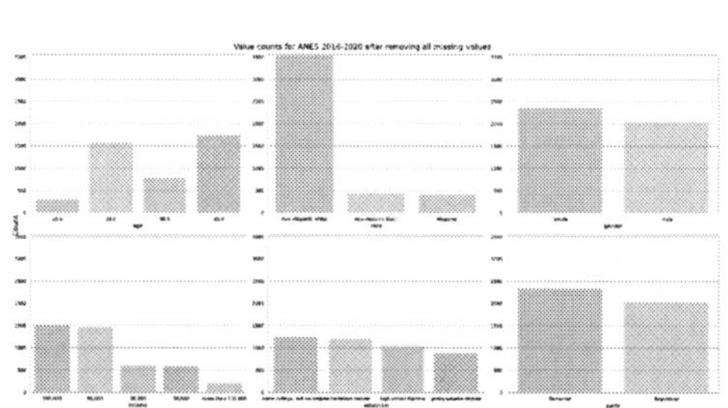

Figure 13: Value counts for ANES 2016-2020 after removing all missing values.

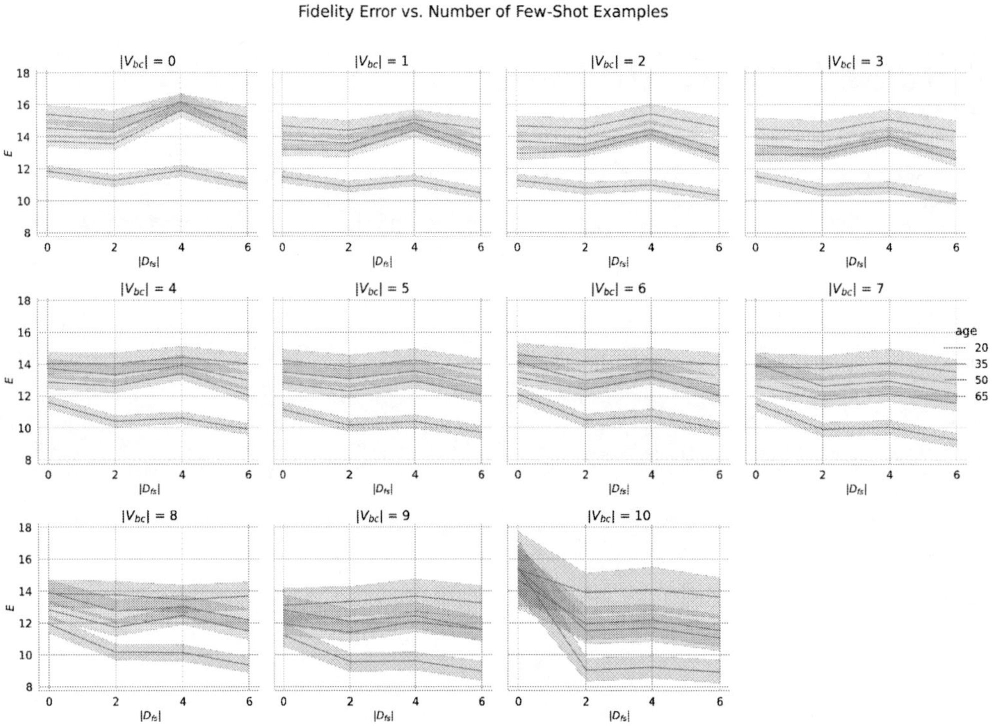

Figure 14: Fidelity error vs. $|D_{fs}|$ for age.

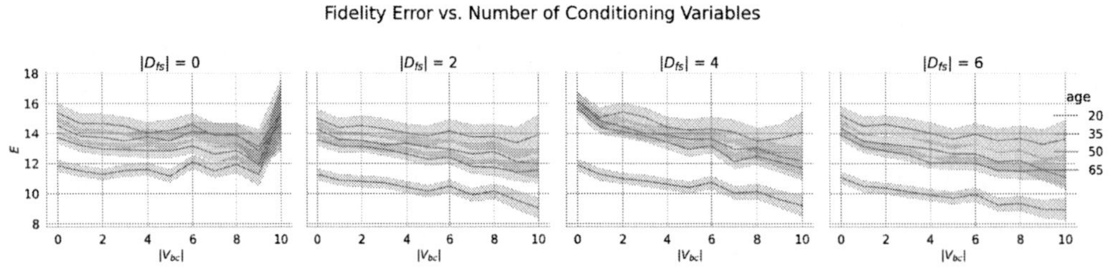

Figure 15: Fidelity error vs. $|V_{bc}|$ for age.

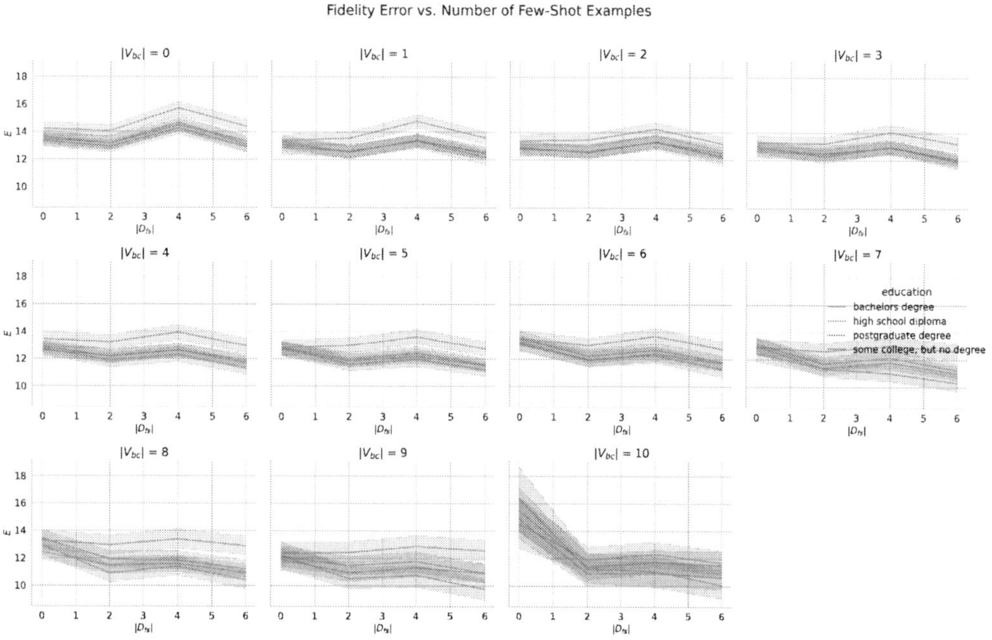

Figure 16: Fidelity error vs. $|D_{fs}|$ for education.

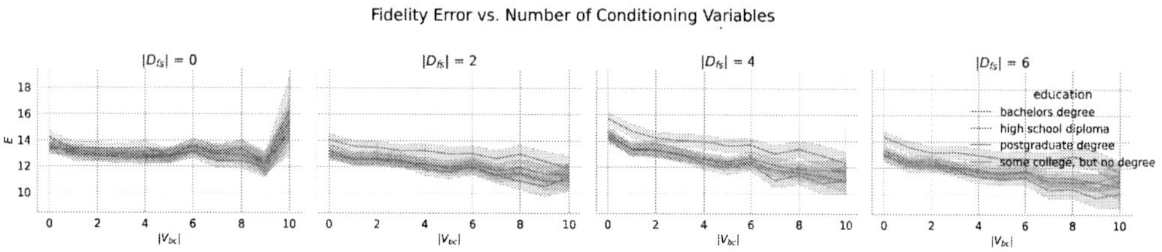

Figure 17: Fidelity error vs. $|V_{bc}|$ for education.

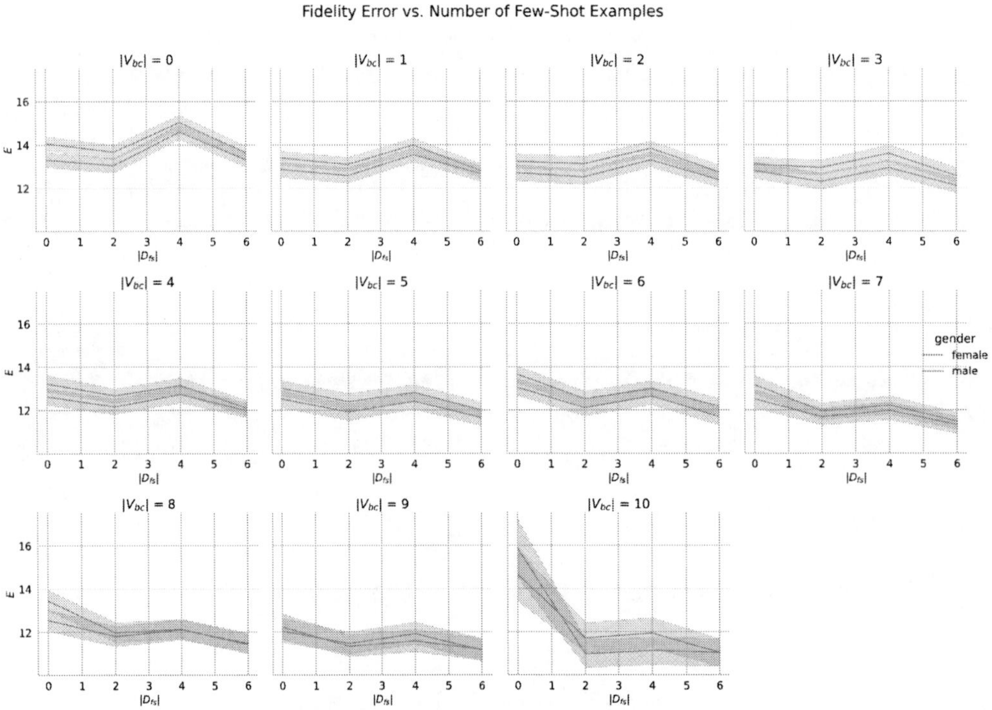

Figure 18: Fidelity error vs. $|D_{fs}|$ for gender.

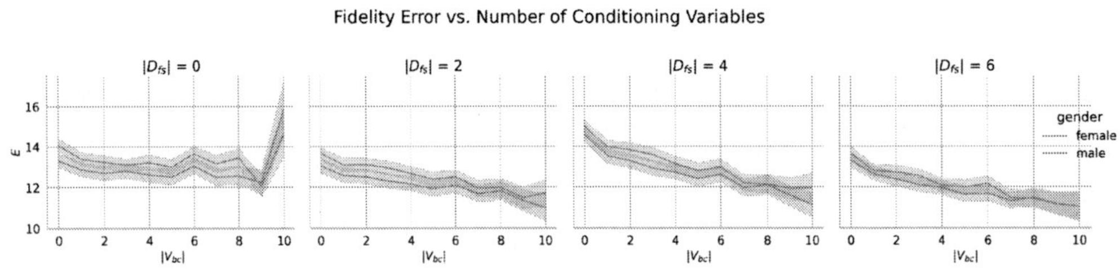

Figure 19: Fidelity error vs. $|V_{bc}|$ for gender.

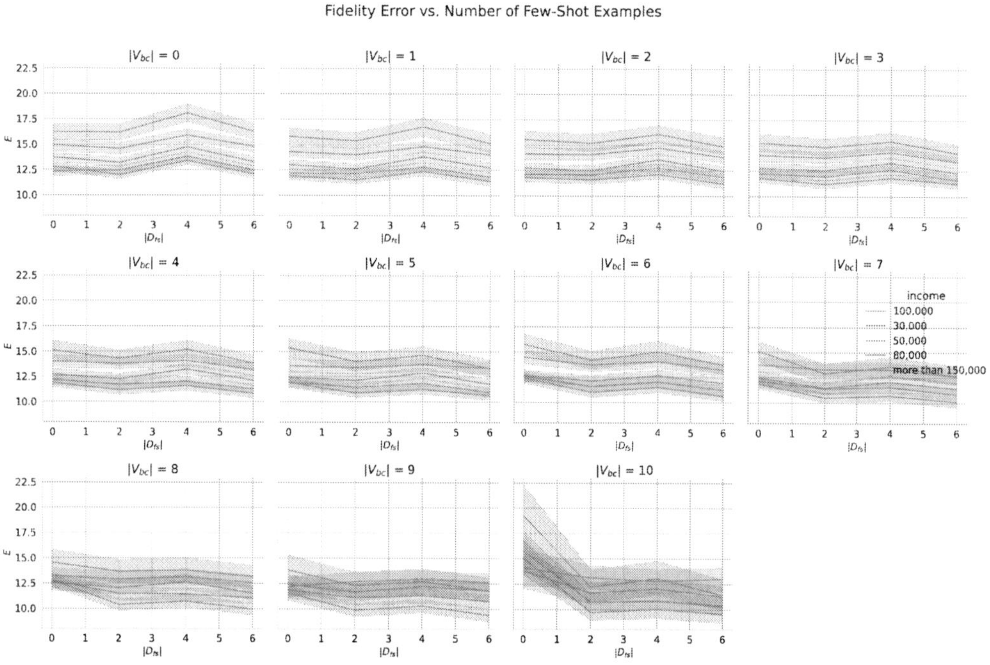

Figure 20: Fidelity error vs. $|D_{fs}|$ for income.

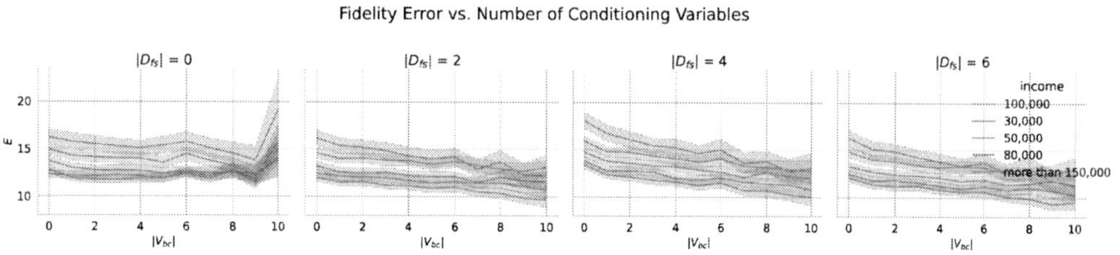

Figure 21: Fidelity error vs. $|V_{bc}|$ for income.

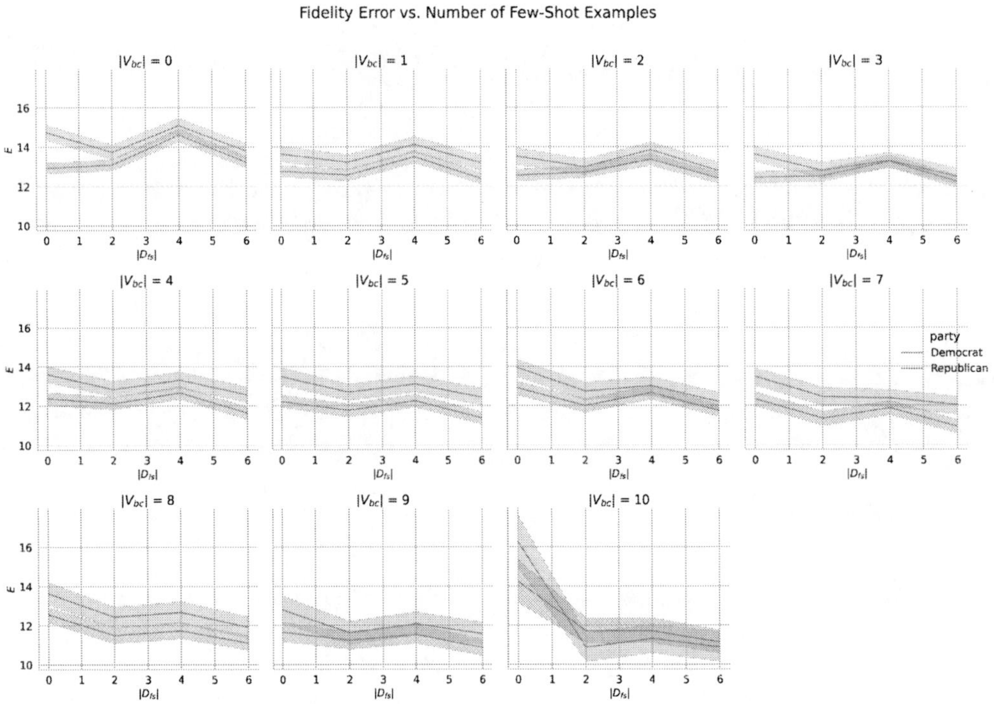

Figure 22: Fidelity error vs. $|D_{fs}|$ for party.

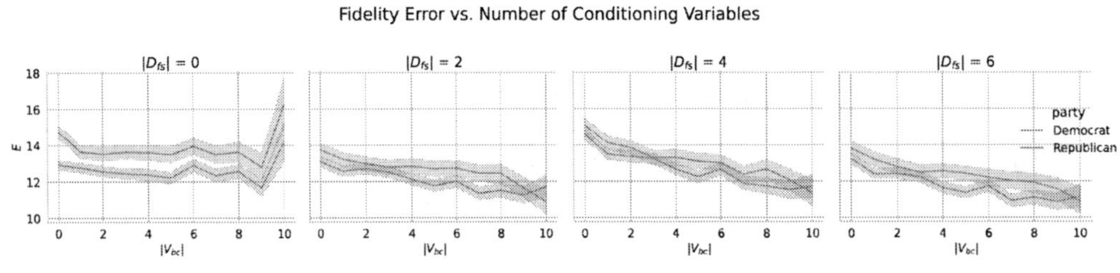

Figure 23: Fidelity error vs. $|V_{bc}|$ for party.

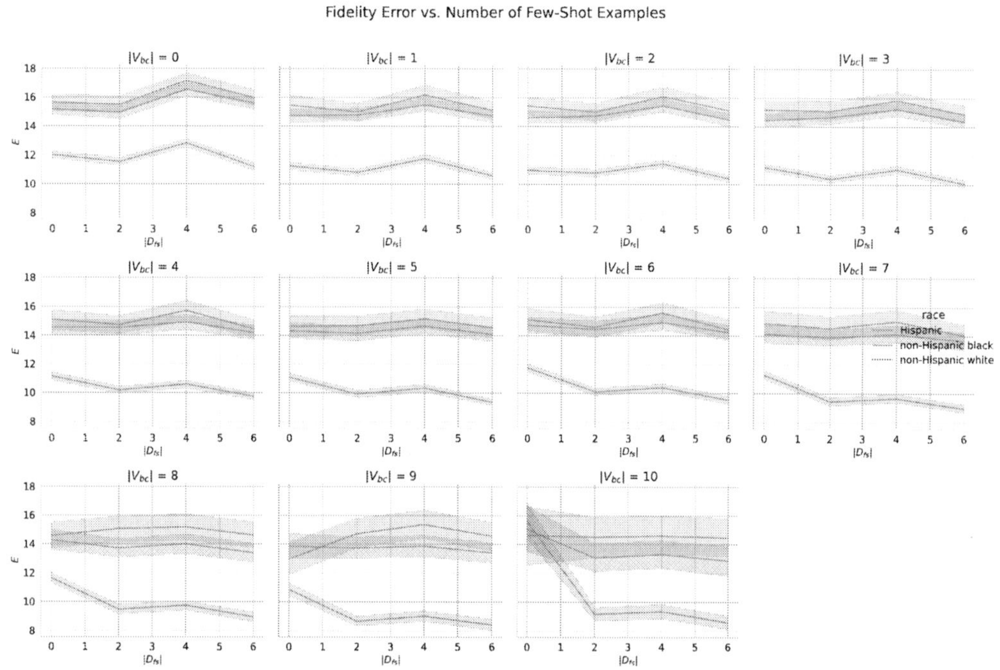

Figure 24: Fidelity error vs. $|D_{fs}|$ for race.

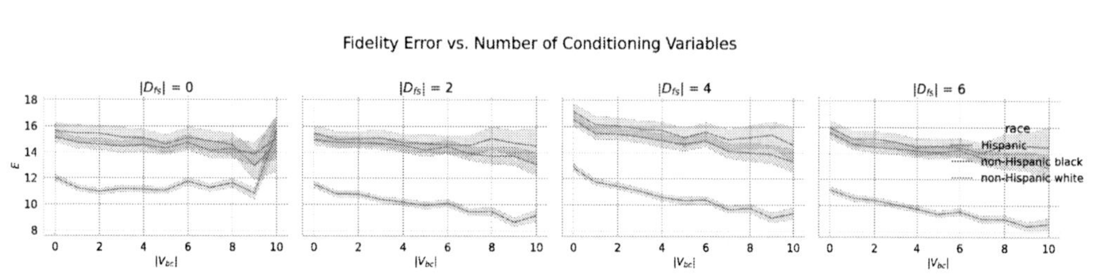

Figure 25: Fidelity error vs. $|V_{bc}|$ for race.

HumSum: A Personalized Lecture Summarization Tool for Humanities Students Using LLMs

Zahra Kolagar
Fraunhofer IIS
Erlangen, Germany
zahra.kolagar@iis.fraunhofer.de

Alessandra Zarcone
Fraunhofer IIS, Erlangen, Germany
Technische Hochschule Augsburg, Germany
alessandra.zarcone@tha.de

Abstract

Generative AI systems aim to create customizable content for their users, with a subsequent surge in demand for adaptable tools that can create personalized experiences.

This paper presents HumSum, a web-based tool tailored for humanities students to effectively summarize their lecture transcripts and to personalize the summaries to their specific needs. We first conducted a survey driven by different potential scenarios to collect user preferences to guide the implementation of this tool.

Utilizing Streamlit, we crafted the user interface, while Langchain's Map Reduce function facilitated the summarization process for extensive lectures using OpenAI's GPT-4 model. HumSum is an intuitive tool serving various summarization needs, infusing personalization into the tool's functionality without requiring personal user data collection.

1 Introduction and Motivation

The educational landscape underwent a significant shift with the advent of e-learning platforms and educational applications, particularly during the global pandemic. The increased reliance on remote learning highlighted the necessity of digital tools to support students' educational needs (Maatuk et al., 2022; Fauzi, 2022; Lynch, 2020; Radha et al., 2020). The surge in online learning applications underscores the critical need for personalized tools capable of meeting diverse student requirements. One-size-fits-all approaches often struggle to accommodate the varied learning paces, preferences, and strengths of individual students (Tetzlaff et al., 2021; Reber et al., 2018). An essential aspect lies in creating educational applications and tools that go beyond generic content delivery, ensuring tailored experiences that resonate with each student's unique learning trajectory. Personalization not only enhances academic outcomes but can also serve as a motivational factor, fostering student enthusiasm and persistence in learning endeavors (Maghsudi et al., 2021a; Sadovaya et al., 2016).

The evolution of Large Language Models (LLMs) represents a recent advancement in artificial intelligence, with the possibility of significantly influencing various facets of education. Models such as pre-trained GPT-3/4 (Koubaa, 2023; OpenAI, 2023), Llama models (Touvron et al., 2023), or dialogue-optimized models like InstructGPT (Ouyang et al., 2022), ChatGPT (OpenAI, 2022), characterized by their extensive knowledge and language proficiency, have gained attention in many natural language processing (NLP) and natural language generation (NLG) tasks (Xi et al., 2023; Liu et al., 2023). LLMs possess the capability to process vast volumes of text, allowing for nuanced and context-aware understanding — a feature fundamental to aligning their output to match the user requests (Wang et al., 2023). The adaptability and versatility inherent in these models enable the development of tailored educational tools and applications, empowering students by providing personalized content that aligns with their learning styles and preferences (Cen et al., 2023; Qu et al., 2022; Embarak, 2022; Maghsudi et al., 2021b). By harnessing the capabilities of LLMs, educational platforms can offer interactive and adaptive content, contributing to enhanced engagement, deeper comprehension, and a more impactful learning experience for students across diverse disciplines.

We present a personalized summarization tool catered explicitly to the needs of humanities students, harnessing the capabilities of LLMs to provide tailored lecture summaries. LLM-based ap-

Proceedings of the 1st Workshop on Personalization of Generative AI Systems (PERSONALIZE 2024), pages 36–70
March 22, 2024 ©2024 Association for Computational Linguistics

proaches to automatic summarization have shown promising results in capturing long-range dependencies, handling complex sentence structures, and producing coherent and contextually appropriate summaries (Bražinskas et al., 2020; Fabbri et al., 2020; Adams et al., 2022).

Our work addresses the following questions:

- RQ 1: How can we assess the diverse learning preferences of students for the development of a personalized summarization tool?
- RQ 2: How will users perceive and interact with this personalized summarization tool?
- RQ 3: How can we create a personalized tool without necessitating the acquisition of user data?

Section 3 presents the collection and preprocessing of transcribed university lectures on humanities studies, which were used as material for the summarizations. Section 4 presents the design of a survey, centered on scenarios and multiple options, followed by an analysis of survey results highlighting user trends and preferences. These insights have provided the requirements for the development of the summarization tool. Section 5 reports on the development of the tool, which was based on OpenAI's GPT-4 model (OpenAI, 2023), illustrating the integration of user preferences derived from the survey into the tool's framework. Finally, Section 6 presents an in-depth analysis of user engagement and perceptions regarding the tool, evaluating user feedback and satisfaction to assess the effectiveness and quality of personalized summaries.

2 Background and Related Work

2.1 Personalization and Education

In the field of education, personalization operates as a method rooted in evidence, centering on individualized learning abilities and study goals to tailor educational content to individual needs. This strategy entails adjusting, realigning, or reshaping components of the curriculum to harmonize with distinct individual requirements. As a result, it has the potential to tackle learning challenges faced by marginalized learners as well as to boost the overall efficacy of teaching and learning methodologies (Bhutoria, 2022; Yonezawa et al., 2012). Personalization stands as a fundamental principle in education, involving customized educational materials and accurate interventions to address distinct learning requirements. This approach, rooted in problem analysis and precise identification of student needs, constitutes the fundamental essence of personalized education (Cook et al., 2018; Fryer et al., 2017).

The emergence of Artificial Intelligence (AI) in education has broadened the scope for personalization, as AI-powered systems, such as Interactive Personalized Learning Spaces (PLS) and Intelligent Tutoring Systems (ITS), actively recommend tailored learning paths, customize educational content, and enrich learning experiences. These AI-driven platforms can effectively support pedagogical planning and language studies, as validated by empirical studies conducted across diverse educational environments (Qu et al., 2022; Zhang and Aslan, 2021; Hwang et al., 2020; Liu et al., 2017).

2.2 Personalizing Summaries for Educational Purposes

Summarization is an important NLP task aimed at condensing extensive amounts of information into cohesive and concise summaries. Its application spans diverse domains, from news articles to scientific papers, or legal documents (Altmami and Menai, 2022; El-Kassas et al., 2021; Kanapala et al., 2019). The surge in digital content since the 1950s has brought attention to automated summarization techniques, owing to the escalating need for efficient information retrieval and assimilation (Luhn, 1958; Allahyari et al., 2017).

The summarization of educational content has gained some attention even before the pandemic, due to the increasing popularity of E-learning. Yang et al. (2013) highlighted the shift toward mobile-based learning and the challenges posed by lengthy texts on such devices. Their research emphasized that well-crafted summaries could enhance learning experiences, particularly when aligning content with the device's constraints. Miller (2019) employed a BERT model to create a lecture summarization service for student use, indicating the move from traditional approaches to more AI-driven approaches.

On the other hand, personalization in summarization can be viewed as stylization, the ability to generate summaries that exhibit specific writing styles, tones, or levels of formality. By incorporating stylization techniques into the summarization

Department	Courses per Department	Transcripts per Department	Avg. Tokens per Transcript	Tot. Tokens	RTTR	MTLD
English	5	152	30843.8	819678.0	24.0	59.2
History	7	149	37662.3	604999.0	28.9	67.2
Philosophy	2	52	35588.4	498541.0	16.2	52.0
Psychology	2	43	51075.8	565734.0	21.7	63.2

Table 1: Descriptive statistics of the Yale Open Course lectures containing a total of 396 transcripts (RTTR = root type-token ratio; MTLD = measure of textual lexical diversity - both are average per transcript).

process, it becomes possible to align the summary's linguistic characteristics with the target audience (Díaz and Gervás, 2007; Yan et al., 2011; Móro et al., 2012). For example, in an educational setting, summaries can be stylized to match the level of understanding and familiarity of the students or their learning styles. This personalization allows students to engage with the summary in a manner that is comfortable and conducive to their learning style, enhancing their comprehension and retention of the lecture content.

While LLMs' capabilities have been investigated for providing personalized recommendations (Sidahmed et al., 2022; Chen, 2023; Lyu et al., 2023) and language learning interfaces (Kwon, 2023), they have not been studied for the specific task of lecture summarization. However, LLMs can generate summaries that are tailored to individual preferences and needs, and aligning the generated text to the user preference has been shown to improve usability by conditioning the model on specific prompts or incorporating external knowledge sources (Bai et al., 2022). LLMs can thus significantly contribute to the customization of lecture summaries.

3 Lecture Transcripts Acquisition and Preprocessing

We created a dataset comprising lecture transcripts suitable for students in the humanities, collecting data from Open Yale Courses (OYC)[1] (Kleiner, 2023). This platform hosts numerous courses across various disciplines, including subjects pertinent to humanities students such as English studies, history, psychology, and philosophy. Each course includes video content along with supplementary materials like syllabi, suggested readings, and searchable transcripts for every lecture, available in HTML format. Table 1 summarizes the dataset's descriptive statistics, including the average length of the transcripts. For tokenization, we utilized the English SpaCy model en_core_web_sm version 3.6.0 (Honnibal et al., 2020).[2]. We also assess lexical richness across topics by utilizing two metrics: the root type-token ratio (RTTR; Guiraud, 1958) and the textual lexical diversity measure (MTLD; McCarthy and Jarvis, 2010). These metrics were computed using the Lexical-Richness library (Shen, 2022), with MTLD employing a threshold of 0.72 to mitigate the influence of text length (Shen, 2022)[3]. The lectures demonstrate notably high scores for both RTTR and MTLD, highlighting a significant level of lexical diversity.

In the preprocessing phase, minimal adjustments were made to the data. Verbatim descriptions of non-verbal cues or actions, denoted as '[Crosstalk]', '[Laughter]', and '[Points at Student]', among others, which originated from the transcription of video elements, were removed. Additionally, indicators of pauses within the transcripts, delimited by timestamps such as [00:08:47], were also eliminated. These modifications were implemented to streamline the content for subsequent processing and analysis. Finally, incorporating the lecture transcripts into our summarization tool development involved storing essential details, including departmental information, course titles, professor names, and lecture session numbers, alongside the respective lecture transcripts.

4 Survey Design and Personalization Analysis

4.1 Scenario-Based Survey Development

To collect requirements for personalization options in lecture summarization, we conducted a scenario-based survey, designed to explore user preferences for a summarization tool. To replicate various decision-making scenarios for creating summaries, we crafted 36 scenarios.

For each survey question, we collected responses from 10 participants from the Amazon Mechanical Turk (AMT) platform, accumulating a total

[1]https://oyc.yale.edu/courses

[2]https://github.com/explosion/spacy-models/releases/tag/en_core_web_sm-3.3.0

[3]https://github.com/LSYS/LexicalRichness

of 360 responses for the entire survey. To ensure that our survey focused on a demographic close to university students, we restricted participants' age range to 20-25 and required a Turker approval rate exceeding 98%. To craft authentic and engaging scenarios, we asked the participants to adopt the persona of a humanities student, embedding academic requirements specific to this field within the instructions, for instance, that humanities students often engage in extensive reading, utilize critical and analytical thinking, and compose diverse types of essays (cf. Fig. 15).

Participants were presented with one scenario at a time, for example, *"You took a lot of courses this semester and you have a busy schedule balancing multiple courses and extracurricular activities. How would you prefer the summaries for your courses this semester?"*, and were then asked what type of summary would they need in this scenario, as multiple-choice questions. Scenarios provide realistic contexts for participants to envision practical usage and inform their preferences accordingly. The varied scenarios allow for a comprehensive exploration of diverse needs, aiding in tailoring the tool.

We identified different aspects of summary personalization and asked the participants to express their preference for each aspect by choosing one out of three given options. For each aspect, several scenarios were crafted to collect the requirements.

Length & Depth (8 scenarios): choice between

- Concise Summaries
- Moderately Detailed Summaries
- In-depth Summaries Summaries

here the participants could express their preference for brief, essential summaries to a more comprehensive coverage

Tone & Style (8 scenarios): choice between

- Formal and Academic Summaries
- Neutral and Objective Summaries
- Conversational and Informal Summaries

here the participants could request academic language or a casual, easy-to-understand conversational style

Complexity (7 scenarios): choice between

- Simplified Summaries
- Balanced or Neutral Summaries
- Detailed or Complex Summaries

here we catered to varying levels of complexity from straightforward to elaborate information

Summary Format (7 scenarios): choice between

- Bullet Point Summaries
- Paragraph-based Summaries
- Keyword Summaries

presenting information through bulleted lists, narrative-style elaboration, or structured keywords

Extra Features (6 scenarios): choice between

- Reflection Questions
- Entity Extraction
- Debate Focus

to enhance understanding by posing reflective queries, extracting essential entities, and highlighting debates or perspectives discussed in the lectures.

We also included a fourth option, "other", allowing participants to articulate any additional preferences for the summarization tool, in case the first three options did not match their preferences (cf. Figures (5-13) depict the scenarios presented to the participants and the responses, while Figures (14-15) showcase the assigned task in AMT platform).

4.2 Interpreting User Preferences and Identified Patterns

The analysis of the survey responses provides insights into the diverse preferences of students regarding the summarization of lecture content across various scenarios. For instance, in scenarios focusing on extracting specific information like names or crucial details from summaries, participants predominantly leaned towards the "Entity Extraction" option. This indicates a preference for tools that can efficiently identify and extract essential elements, aiding in information retrieval for specific queries. Similarly, scenarios involving the preparation of academic or formal materials, such as thesis content or consultation with professors, exhibited a strong inclination towards "Formal and Academic" style summaries, aligning with the need for structured and scholarly formats in such contexts.

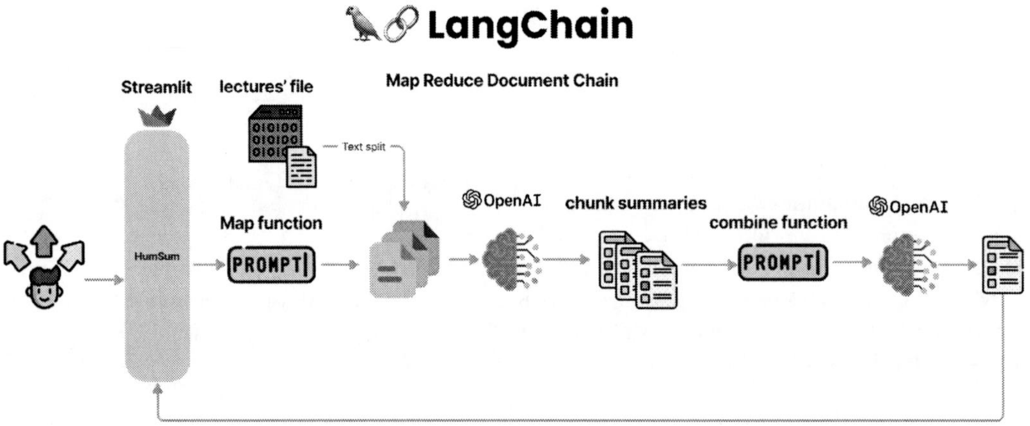

Figure 1: Summarization process using Streamlit, Langchain, and OpenAI's GPT4-8K model.

Furthermore, scenarios emphasizing comprehension and preparation for discussions or examinations revealed interesting trends. Participants favored different styles depending on their intended use. For instance, those preparing for discussions or debates leaned towards "Debate Focus" or "Reflection Question" options, indicating a preference for content stimulating critical thinking and discourse. In contrast, respondents preparing for exams or dealing with a busy schedule sought either "Concise Summaries" or "Moderately Detailed Summaries" that encapsulate essential concepts without excessive detail. Ultimately, regarding queries about the summary output style, participants tended to favor "Bullet point" or "Keyword" summaries when time constraints were a factor.

5 Summarization Tool Development

To craft the summarization tool, we leverage the insights collected from the analysis of scenario-driven survey outcomes. The tool aims at a straightforward design, enabling users to easily engage with the content, and personalizing the summaries to their needs.

5.1 User Interface

We created a user-friendly web-based tool named 'HumSum' designed specifically for the summarization process utilizing streamlit library[4]. HumSum features a convenient sidebar interface on the left-hand side, enabling users to input their preferences for the department, course, and session for which they seek a summary. Additionally, users can customize various aspects of the summary to suit their preferences as shown in figure 2. They can adjust the summary length, choosing from concise, moderate, or detailed options. Similarly, they can tailor the tone of the summary, opting for conversational, neutral, or formal language. Users can also select the complexity level — ranging from simplified to balanced to sophisticated — based on their comprehension needs. Moreover, the tool allows users to choose the format of the summary, whether it be in bullet-point, paragraph, or keyword style. Furthermore, users can opt for additional features such as extracting extra information like questions, entities, or debates from the lecture contents to enhance their summaries.

5.2 Langchain and LLM Chaining for Summarization

To generate lecture content summaries, we utilized Langchain[5], an open-source library compatible with Streamlit, offering access to various LLMs including those provided by OpenAI. Langchain encompasses diverse components such as Prompts, Memory, Chains, and Agents, which facilitate handling data stored in CSV files and support multiple NLP tasks involving information extraction and text generation. Specifically, we leveraged its 'Map Reduce Document Chain'[6] summarization chain feature, which allows for the summarization of long documents. As lecture contents are usually long and might exceed the input token limit of the LLM

[4]https://streamlit.io/

[5]https://www.langchain.com/

[6]https://js.langchain.com/docs/modules/chains/-popular/summarize

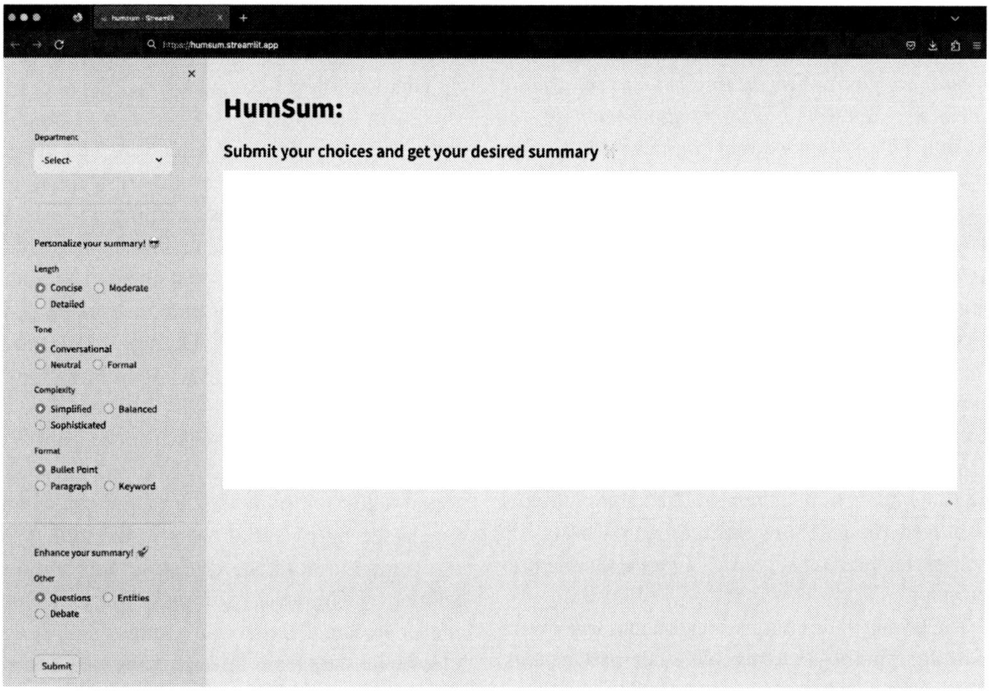

Figure 2: HumSum Interface - The slider on the left contains the customization options for the user.

models, we used this setup that enables the summarization of extensive document collections within a map-reduce style architecture. Langchain's Map Reduce involves dividing documents into smaller chunks that fit within the token limit of the model. For our lectures, we've specifically set this limit to 2000 tokens per chunk using Langchain's "Recursive Character Text Splitter"[7]. Each chunk is then summarized giving the user-selected preferences submitted via HumSum as instruction to the model (the map function), followed by the consolidation of these summaries into a final summary (combine or reduce function). To create the summaries, we made use of OpenAI's GPT-4-8k model (cf. Fig. 3 for the custom map prompt and Fig. 1 for the summarization process).

Summarise the lecture content from the course titled "{course_title}" for session {session_num} in the {department_name} department. The summary should meet the specified criteria:

- Length: {length_type}
- Tone: {tone_type}
- Complexity level: {complexity_type}
- Format: {format_type}
- Additional features: {other_features}

If the additional feature is "questions," generate five questions based on the lecture content. If it is "entities," extract names, dates, and locations from the lecture content. If the additional feature is "debate," extract opposing viewpoints or presented ideas from the lecture content.

Figure 3: Custom prompt to replace the default map prompt.

6 Assessing Preferences and Effectiveness through User Evaluation

6.1 Assessing User Preferences based on the Given Options

To evaluate the effectiveness of the HumSum summarization tool and the user-customizable options, we carried out a follow-up survey by recruiting three participants per scenario, all of whom were humanities students. This second survey utilized the same scenarios as the initial one, albeit with slight modifications, including additional information prompting participants to select their department, course title, and session. For instance the first survey's question such as *You took a lot of courses this semester and you have a busy schedule balancing multiple courses and extracurricular*

[7]https://python.langchain.com/docs/-modules/data_connection/document_transformers-/text_splitters/recursive_text_splitter

activities. how would you prefer the summaries for your courses this semester? has been modified to *Imagine yourself as an English student at Yale University. You would like to create a summary for Session Three of the course "Introduction to Theory of Literature", keeping in mind that you took a lot of courses this semester and you have a busy schedule balancing multiple courses and extracurricular activities.*. The students were asked to explore the tool and select their preferred options for personalizing the summaries of lecture transcripts. Throughout this process, no additional instructions were provided, and the students navigated the tool seamlessly without asking any questions or encountering difficulties. Once they finalized their choices, the students submitted them, and the HumSum tool displayed the resulting summarization based on their preferences (cf. Fig. 16 - 20 for a sample user journey).

The primary aims of this subsequent survey were twofold: firstly, to assess whether participants' choices remained consistent now that they had complete access to the application interface, and secondly, to discern the most prevalent user choices overall. This analysis aims to identify recurring preferences among participants, to inform future further development of the tool. Figure 4 shows the personalization options that received the highest number of selections per aspect (cf. Fig. 21 to 23 to see the frequency of all the provided options per aspect).

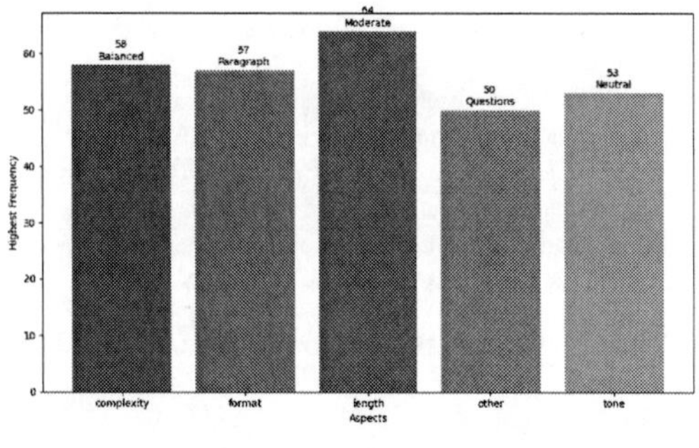

Figure 4: The options that received the highest number of selections within each aspect.

As depicted in Figure 4, users predominantly favored middle-ground choices as their primary selection, opting for moderate length, neutral tone, or balanced complexity. This tendency might be attributed to users' cautious approach, potentially stemming from their lack of prior experience with the tool and limited exposure to the generated summaries or real-world scenario analysis of the tool's efficacy.

This assertion finds additional support in Figure 24 in the appendix, displaying a comparison between our anticipated selections and the actual number of user preferences aligned with our expectations. Notably, options entailing more complex summaries, tailored to specific scenario requirements, were consistently not chosen. When questioned about this, users unanimously expressed concerns about handling such complexity, especially when required to memorize summaries for classroom discussions or exams.

While the infrequent selection of non-middle-ground options suggests a cautious approach by users, it doesn't imply that these options will never be chosen by potential users of the tool. We recognize the importance of further exploration and subsequent iterations to assess the tool's performance in actual classroom settings. Collecting real classroom data from multiple usage cycles by students in subsequent iterations will provide valuable insights into the tool's practical utility and user preferences.

6.2 Assessing the Tool Efficacy and the Personalization of the Summaries

To collect feedback regarding the effectiveness of the summarization tool and the resultant summaries based on users' selections, we administered a concise questionnaire featuring six rating-scale questions ranging from 1 to 5, as shown below. Overall, the average rating across all questions was 4 out of 5, indicating a favorable reception of this tool for summarizing humanities-related content, with users showing a high level of satisfaction when navigating the tool. The outcome of this questionnaire is displayed in Figure 25.

1. How satisfied are you with the summarization tool's user interface and ease of navigation?

2. Rate the accuracy of the summaries generated based on your selected preferences.

3. How well did the summaries reflect your specified preferences for length, tone, complexity, and format?

4. Rate the relevance and usefulness of the additional features (e.g., questions, entity extraction, debates) provided with the summaries.

5. How would you rate the personalization options provided in this summarization tool?

6. How likely are you to recommend this summarization tool to other students?

7 Conclusion and Future Work

In this study, we developed a personalized summarization tool, "HumSum," tailored for humanities students to efficiently condense lecture transcripts. We carried out a scenario-driven survey to identify and integrate personalization features within the tool, accommodating users' preferences for summary types. Utilizing the Streamlit library, Langchain, and OpenAI's GPT-4-8k model facilitated the tool's development and the summarization process. Subsequently, we evaluated the tool's effectiveness through a user journey based on the pre-defined scenarios and a straightforward rating questionnaire, to evaluate the tool's performance along with the users' anticipated outcomes.

This tool offers some advantages: it offers personalized summarization without relying on users' private information, in addition to being an easy-to-use tool. However, for future improvements, we aim to implement a feedback integration mechanism, enabling users to provide real-time insights to refine the summary output iteratively. Addressing the issue of hallucination, a critical concern in utilizing language models remains a future task (Huang et al., 2023). Additionally, integrating external knowledge sources, such as highlighting key information or providing links to supplementary materials like Wikipedia, could significantly enrich the tool's usability and enhance the learning experience for students.

Limitations

While our research yielded valuable insights, addressing its limitations is crucial. One such constraint, as identified in Section 6.1, pertains to users' predominant inclination towards moderate options within the summarization tool. This predilection could be attributed to users' unfamiliarity with the tool, limiting their perception of how specific options might shape a customized summary. Additionally, the scenarios employed might not have effectively elicited all feasible options, suggesting that continuous iterations over time could offer a more comprehensive understanding of the tool's efficacy and available options.

Regarding the Map Reduce method employed, its merits lie in scalability for larger documents and the independent nature of LLM calls on individual document segments, enabling concurrent processing. Nonetheless, several drawbacks should be considered. Primarily, this approach requires higher LLM calls to create a summary for one large document. Furthermore, there is a risk of information loss during the final reduction or combination phase. These limitations underscore areas for potential refinement and call for cautious consideration when employing the method in practical applications.

Ethics Statement

The turkers we recruited on the AMT platform as well as the students maintain their anonymity, a practice aligned with ethical norms within the community. They were recruited voluntarily and provided a written consent form to participate in the study and were allowed to opt out at any point in time. Moreover, the AMT workers were compensated following the norms and regulations of the AMT platform for their time and effort spent on our tasks. We encouraged feedback and offered to promptly address any concerns or issues that might arise during the research process. However, we did not record any issues and we received positive feedback regarding the experiments.

The icons showcased in Figure 1 have been sourced from the freely available collection at https://www.flaticon.com/.

Acknowledgements

We extend our sincere thanks to the AMT participants and the students whose invaluable contributions were essential in completing this research.

References

David Adams, Gandharv Suri, and Yllias Chali. 2022. Combining state-of-the-art models with maximal marginal relevance for few-shot and zero-shot multi-document summarization. *arXiv preprint arXiv:2211.10808*.

Mehdi Allahyari, Seyedamin Pouriyeh, Mehdi Assefi, Saeid Safaei, Elizabeth D Trippe, Juan B Gutierrez, and Krys Kochut. 2017. Text summarization techniques: a brief survey. *arXiv preprint arXiv:1707.02268*.

Nouf Ibrahim Altmami and Mohamed El Bachir Menai. 2022. Automatic summarization of scientific articles:

A survey. *Journal of King Saud University-Computer and Information Sciences*, 34(4):1011–1028.

Yuntao Bai, Andy Jones, Kamal Ndousse, Amanda Askell, Anna Chen, Nova DasSarma, Dawn Drain, Stanislav Fort, Deep Ganguli, Tom Henighan, et al. 2022. Training a helpful and harmless assistant with reinforcement learning from human feedback. *arXiv preprint arXiv:2204.05862*.

Aditi Bhutoria. 2022. Personalized education and artificial intelligence in the united states, china, and india: A systematic review using a human-in-the-loop model. *Computers and Education: Artificial Intelligence*, 3:100068.

Arthur Bražinskas, Mirella Lapata, and Ivan Titov. 2020. Few-shot learning for opinion summarization. *arXiv preprint arXiv:2004.14884*.

Chenghong Cen, Guang Luo, Lujia Li, Yilin Liang, Kang Li, Tan Jiang, and Qiang Xiong. 2023. User-centered software design: User interface redesign for blockly–electron, artificial intelligence educational software for primary and secondary schools. *Sustainability*, 15(6):5232.

Zheng Chen. 2023. Palr: Personalization aware llms for recommendation. *arXiv preprint arXiv:2305.07622*.

Clayton R. Cook, Stephen P. Kilgus, and Matthew K. Burns. 2018. Advancing the science and practice of precision education to enhance student outcomes. *Journal of School Psychology*, 66:4–10. Advancing the Science and Practice of Precision Education.

Alberto Díaz and Pablo Gervás. 2007. User-model based personalized summarization. *Information Processing & Management*, 43(6):1715–1734.

Wafaa S El-Kassas, Cherif R Salama, Ahmed A Rafea, and Hoda K Mohamed. 2021. Automatic text summarization: A comprehensive survey. *Expert systems with applications*, 165:113679.

Ossama H Embarak. 2022. Internet of behaviour (iob)-based ai models for personalized smart education systems. *Procedia Computer Science*, 203:103–110.

Alexander R Fabbri, Simeng Han, Haoyuan Li, Haoran Li, Marjan Ghazvininejad, Shafiq Joty, Dragomir Radev, and Yashar Mehdad. 2020. Improving zero and few-shot abstractive summarization with intermediate fine-tuning and data augmentation. *arXiv preprint arXiv:2010.12836*.

Muhammad Ashraf Fauzi. 2022. E-learning in higher education institutions during covid-19 pandemic: current and future trends through bibliometric analysis. *Heliyon*.

Luke K. Fryer, Mary Ainley, Andrew Thompson, Aaron Gibson, and Zelinda Sherlock. 2017. Stimulating and sustaining interest in a language course: An experimental comparison of chatbot and human task partners. *Computers in Human Behavior*, 75:461–468.

P. Guiraud. 1958. *Problèmes et Méthodes de La Statistique Linguistique*. Dodrecht: D. Reidel.

Matthew Honnibal, Ines Montani, Sofie Van Landeghem, and Adriane Boyd. 2020. spaCy: Industrial-strength Natural Language Processing in Python.

Lei Huang, Weijiang Yu, Weitao Ma, Weihong Zhong, Zhangyin Feng, Haotian Wang, Qianglong Chen, Weihua Peng, Xiaocheng Feng, Bing Qin, and Ting Liu. 2023. A survey on hallucination in large language models: Principles, taxonomy, challenges, and open questions.

Gwo-Jen Hwang, Han-Yu Sung, Shao-Chen Chang, and Xing-Ci Huang. 2020. A fuzzy expert system-based adaptive learning approach to improving students' learning performances by considering affective and cognitive factors. *Computers and Education: Artificial Intelligence*, 1:100003.

Ambedkar Kanapala, Sukomal Pal, and Rajendra Pamula. 2019. Text summarization from legal documents: a survey. *Artificial Intelligence Review*, 51:371–402.

Diana E. E. Kleiner. 2023. Open yale courses (oyc).

Anis Koubaa. 2023. Gpt-4 vs. gpt-3.5: A concise showdown.

Taeahn Kwon. 2023. *Interfaces for Personalized Language Learning with Generative Language Models*. Ph.D. thesis, Columbia University.

Danny Yen-Ting Liu, Kathryn Bartimote-Aufflick, Abelardo Pardo, and Adam J. Bridgeman. 2017. Data-driven personalization of student learning support in higher education. In Alejandro Peña-Ayala, editor, *Learning Analytics: Fundaments, Applications, and Trends: A View of the Current State of the Art to Enhance e-Learning*, pages 143–169. Springer International Publishing, Cham.

Yiheng Liu, Tianle Han, Siyuan Ma, Jiayue Zhang, Yuanyuan Yang, Jiaming Tian, Hao He, Antong Li, Mengshen He, Zhengliang Liu, et al. 2023. Summary of chatgpt-related research and perspective towards the future of large language models. *Meta-Radiology*, page 100017.

Hans Peter Luhn. 1958. The automatic creation of literature abstracts. *IBM Journal of research and development*, 2(2):159–165.

Maggie Lynch. 2020. E-learning during a global pandemic. *Asian Journal of Distance Education*, 15(1):189–195.

Hanjia Lyu, Song Jiang, Hanqing Zeng, Qifan Wang, Si Zhang, Ren Chen, Chris Leung, Jiajie Tang, Yinglong Xia, and Jiebo Luo. 2023. Llm-rec: Personalized recommendation via prompting large language models.

Abdelsalam M Maatuk, Ebitisam K Elberkawi, Shadi Aljawarneh, Hasan Rashaideh, and Hadeel Alharbi. 2022. The covid-19 pandemic and e-learning: challenges and opportunities from the perspective of students and instructors. *Journal of computing in higher education*, 34(1):21–38.

Setareh Maghsudi, Andrew Lan, Jie Xu, and Mihaela van Der Schaar. 2021a. Personalized education in the artificial intelligence era: what to expect next. *IEEE Signal Processing Magazine*, 38(3):37–50.

Setareh Maghsudi, Andrew Lan, Jie Xu, and Mihaela van der Schaar. 2021b. Personalized education in the artificial intelligence era: What to expect next. *IEEE Signal Processing Magazine*, 38(3):37–50.

Philip M McCarthy and Scott Jarvis. 2010. Mtld, vocd-d, and hd-d: A validation study of sophisticated approaches to lexical diversity assessment. *Behavior research methods*, 42(2):381–392.

Derek Miller. 2019. Leveraging bert for extractive text summarization on lectures. *arXiv preprint arXiv:1906.04165*.

Róbert Móro et al. 2012. Personalized text summarization based on important terms identification. In *2012 23rd International Workshop on Database and Expert Systems Applications*, pages 131–135. IEEE.

OpenAI. 2022. OpenAI: Introducing ChatGPT. [Online; posted 30-November-2022].

OpenAI. 2023. Gpt-4 technical report.

Long Ouyang, Jeff Wu, Xu Jiang, Diogo Almeida, Carroll L. Wainwright, Pamela Mishkin, Chong Zhang, Sandhini Agarwal, Katarina Slama, Alex Ray, John Schulman, Jacob Hilton, Fraser Kelton, Luke Miller, Maddie Simens, Amanda Askell, Peter Welinder, Paul Christiano, Jan Leike, and Ryan Lowe. 2022. Training language models to follow instructions with human feedback.

Jianjing Qu, Yanan Zhao, and Yongping Xie. 2022. Artificial intelligence leads the reform of education models. *Systems Research and Behavioral Science*, 39(3):581–588.

Rajapandian Radha, K Mahalakshmi, V Sathish Kumar, and AR Saravanakumar. 2020. E-learning during lockdown of covid-19 pandemic: A global perspective. *International journal of control and automation*, 13(4):1088–1099.

Rolf Reber, Elizabeth A Canning, and Judith M Harackiewicz. 2018. Personalized education to increase interest. *Current directions in psychological science*, 27(6):449–454.

Victoriya V Sadovaya, Olga V Korshunova, and Zhumagali Zh Nauruzbay. 2016. Personalized education strategies. *International Electronic Journal of Mathematics Education*, 11(1):199–209.

Lucas Shen. 2022. LexicalRichness: A small module to compute textual lexical richness.

Hakim Sidahmed, Sameer Ahuja, and Manoj Kumar Tiwari. 2022. Generating personalized recommendations via large language models (llms).

Leonard Tetzlaff, Florian Schmiedek, and Garvin Brod. 2021. Developing personalized education: A dynamic framework. *Educational Psychology Review*, 33:863–882.

Hugo Touvron, Thibaut Lavril, Gautier Izacard, Xavier Martinet, Marie-Anne Lachaux, Timothée Lacroix, Baptiste Rozière, Naman Goyal, Eric Hambro, Faisal Azhar, Aurelien Rodriguez, Armand Joulin, Edouard Grave, and Guillaume Lample. 2023. Llama: Open and efficient foundation language models.

Yufei Wang, Wanjun Zhong, Liangyou Li, Fei Mi, Xingshan Zeng, Wenyong Huang, Lifeng Shang, Xin Jiang, and Qun Liu. 2023. Aligning large language models with human: A survey. *arXiv preprint arXiv:2307.12966*.

Zhiheng Xi, Wenxiang Chen, Xin Guo, Wei He, Yiwen Ding, Boyang Hong, Ming Zhang, Junzhe Wang, Senjie Jin, Enyu Zhou, et al. 2023. The rise and potential of large language model based agents: A survey. *arXiv preprint arXiv:2309.07864*.

Rui Yan, Jian-Yun Nie, and Xiaoming Li. 2011. Summarize what you are interested in: An optimization framework for interactive personalized summarization. In *Proceedings of the 2011 conference on empirical methods in natural language processing*, pages 1342–1351.

Guangbing Yang, Nian-Shing Chen, Kinshuk, Erkki Sutinen, Terry Anderson, and Dunwei Wen. 2013. The effectiveness of automatic text summarization in mobile learning contexts. *Computers & Education*, 68:233–243.

Susan Yonezawa, Larry McClure, and Makeba Jones. 2012. Personalization in schools. *Education Digest*, 78(2):41–47.

Ke Zhang and Ayse Begum Aslan. 2021. Ai technologies for education: Recent research & future directions. *Computers and Education: Artificial Intelligence*, 2:100025.

A Appendix

A.1 Comparison of Expected and Actual Responses: Analysis of AMT Participants' Survey Data

The displayed bar plots represent the responses obtained from AMT participants for each scenario. The orange color indicates the anticipated or expected responses from participants. In the majority of cases, the participants' responses aligned with our anticipated patterns.

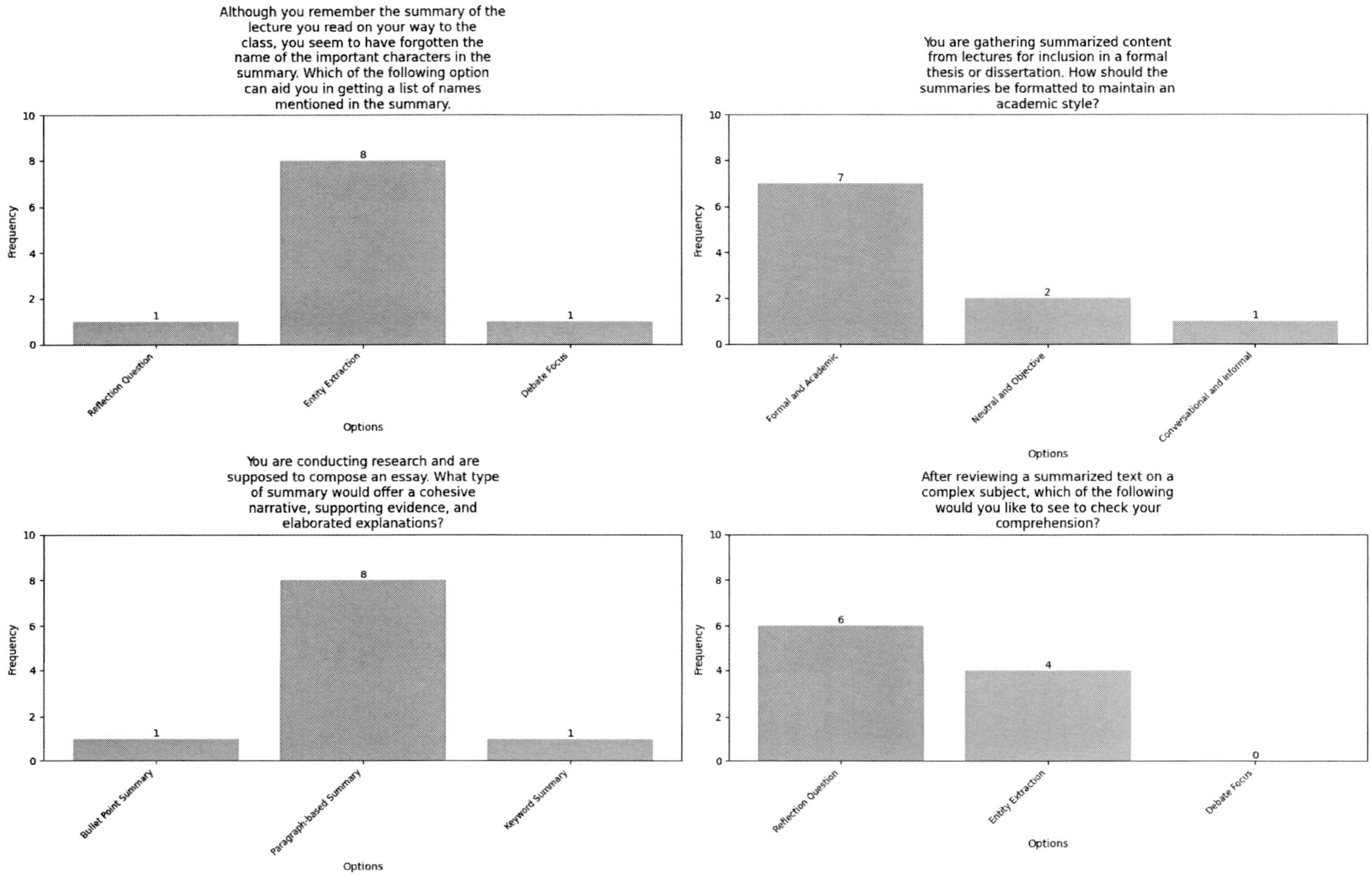

Figure 5: Results from scenarios 1-4

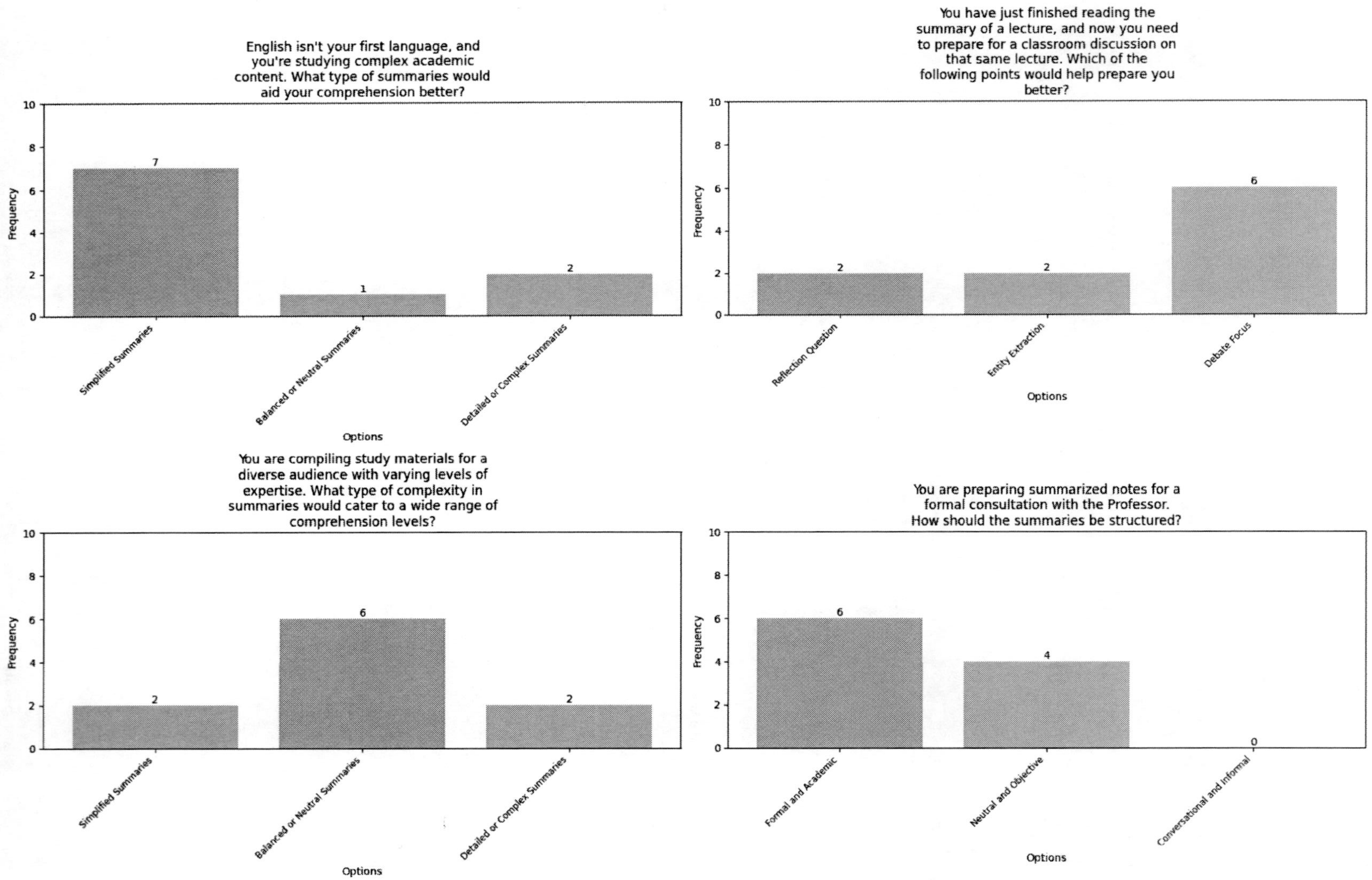

Figure 6: Results from scenarios 5-8

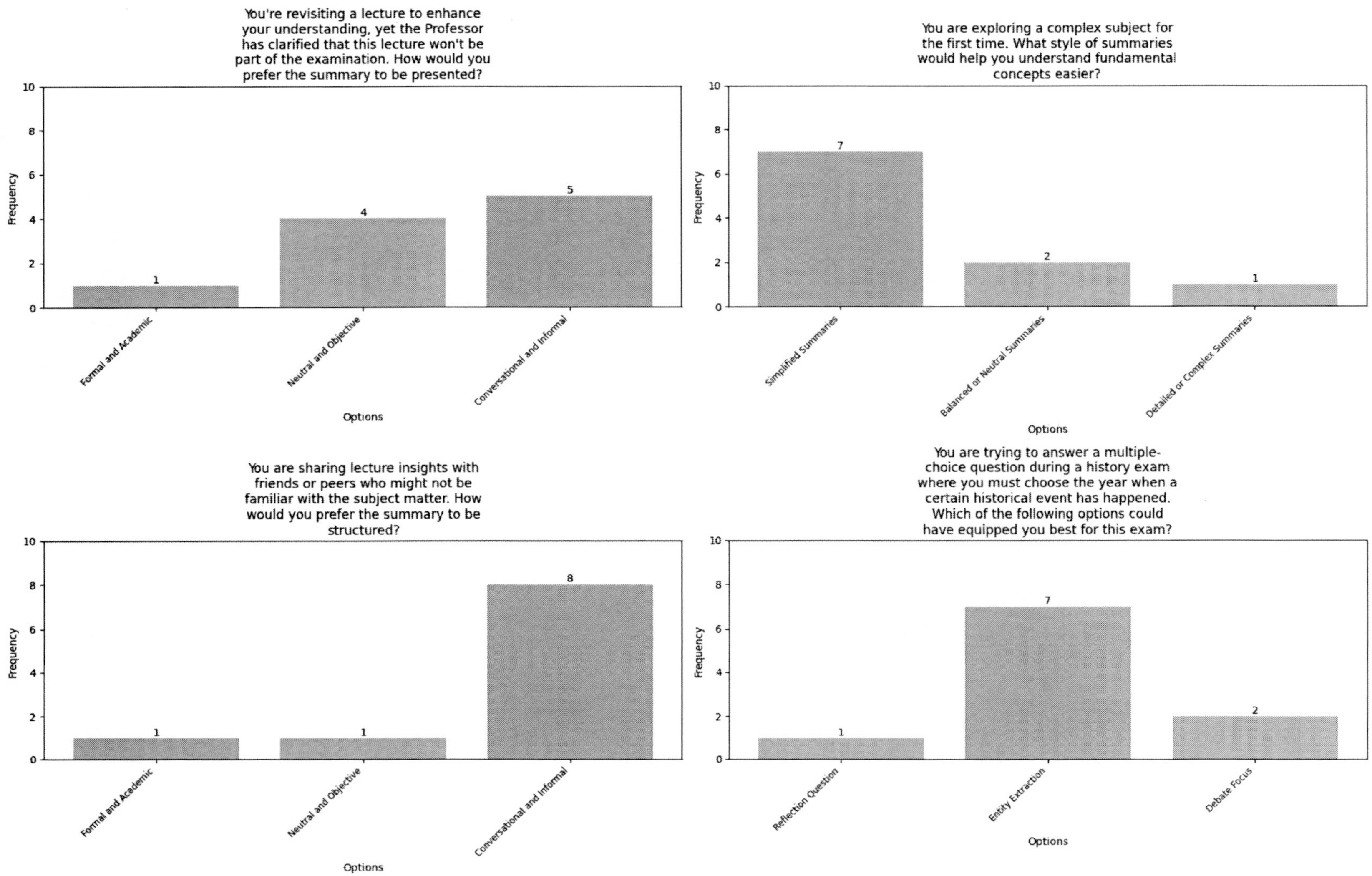

Figure 7: Results from scenarios 9-12

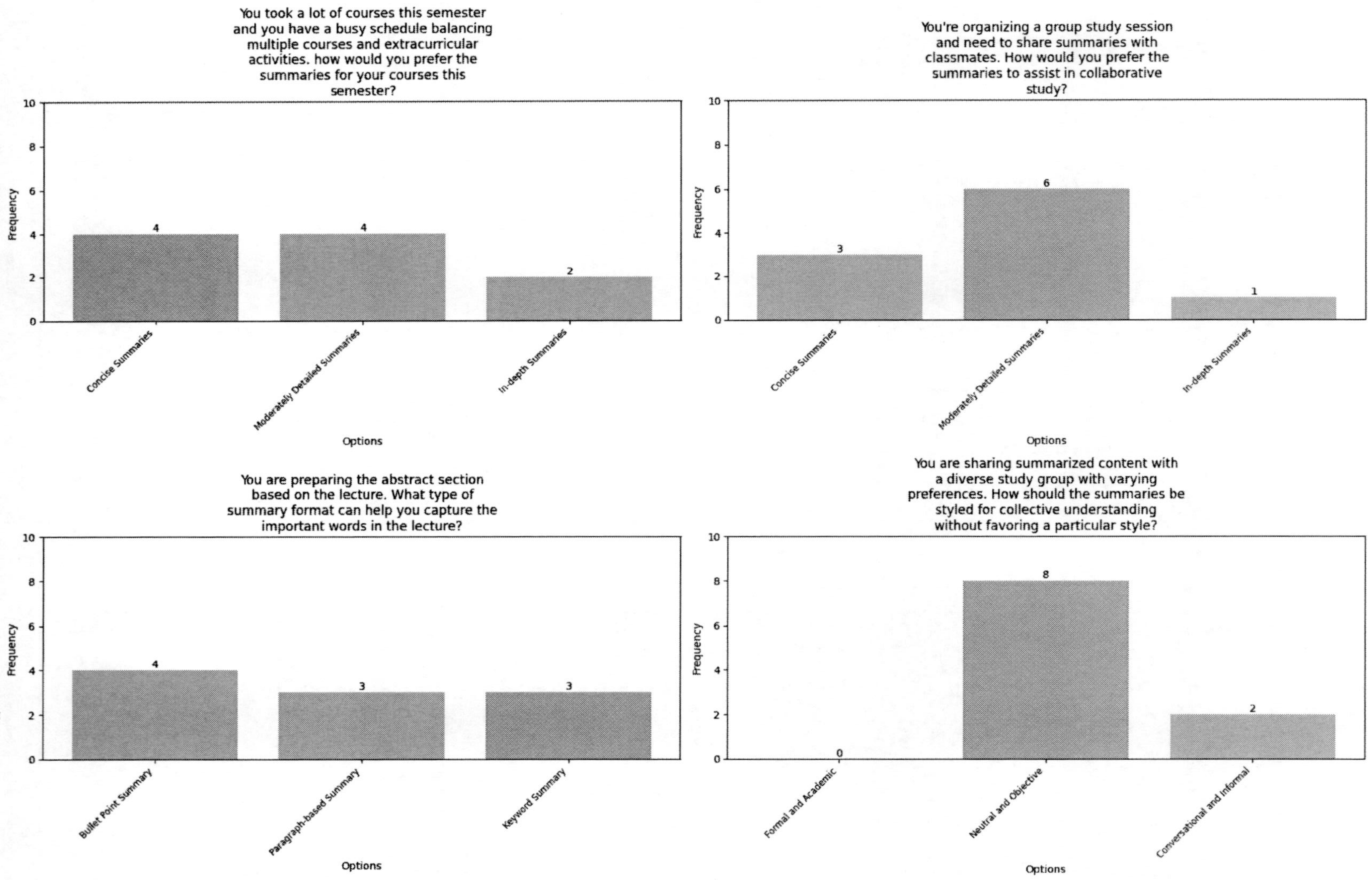

Figure 8: Results from scenarios 13-16

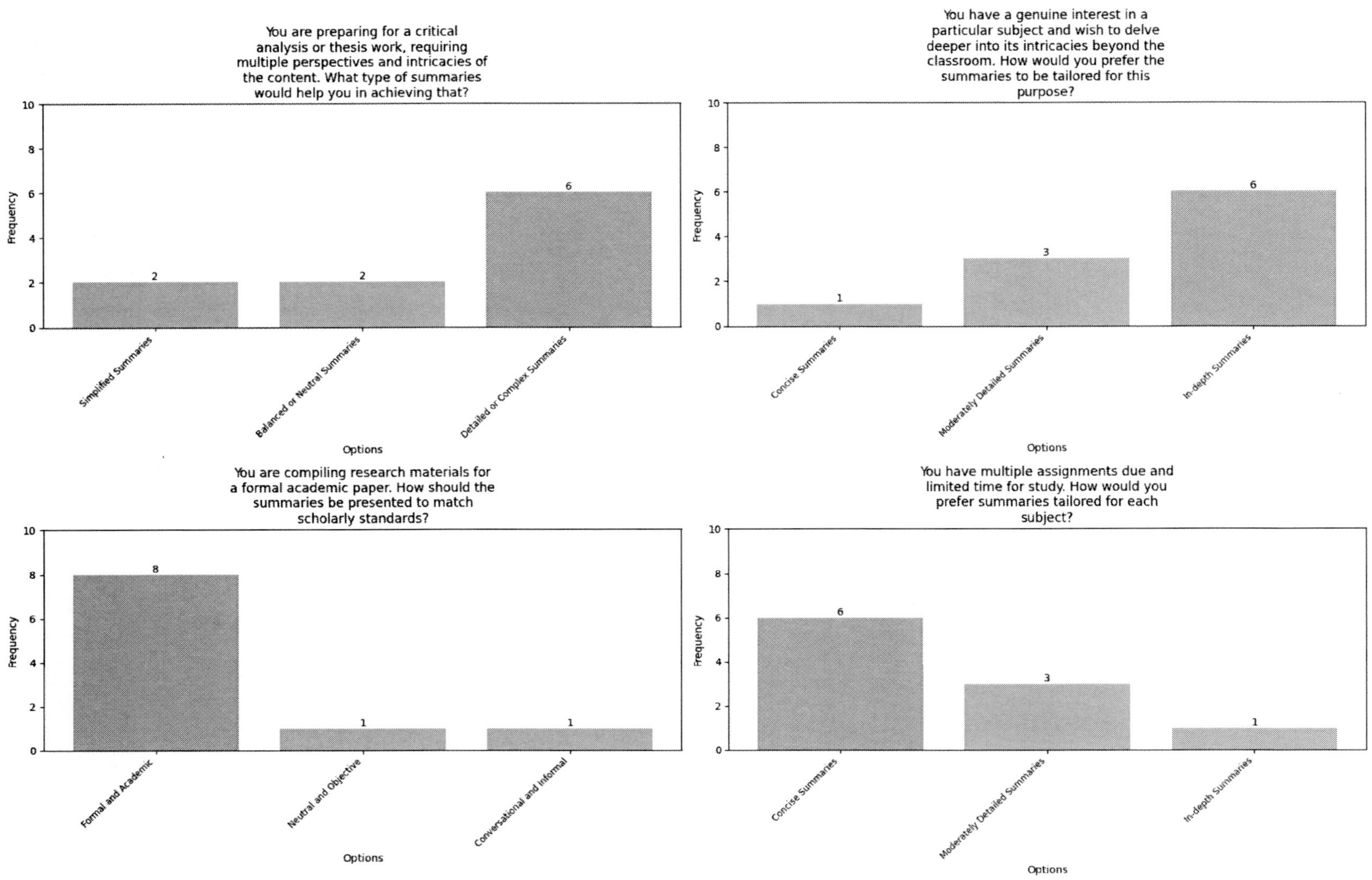

Figure 9: Results from scenarios 17-20

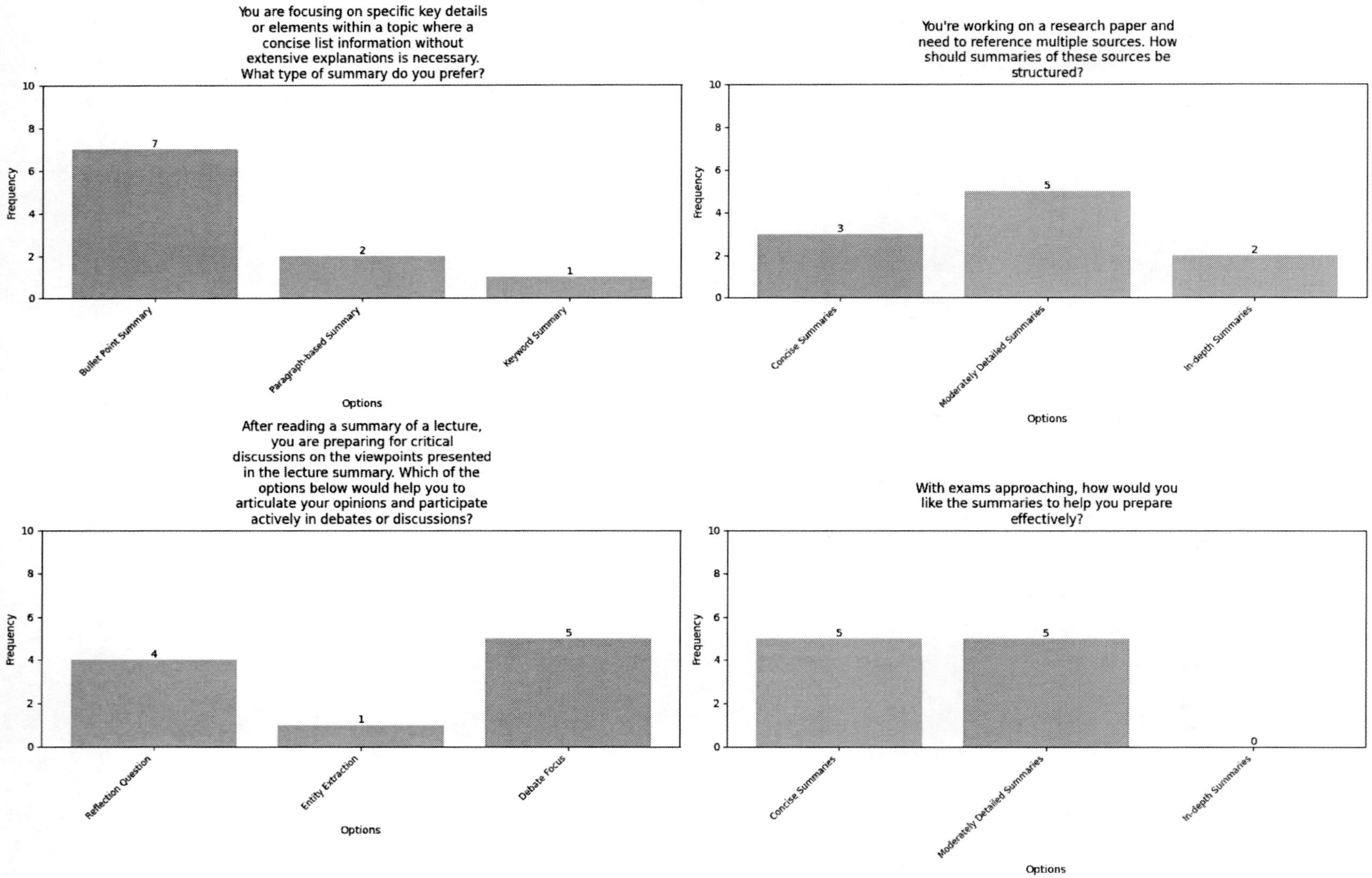

Figure 10: Results from scenarios 21-24

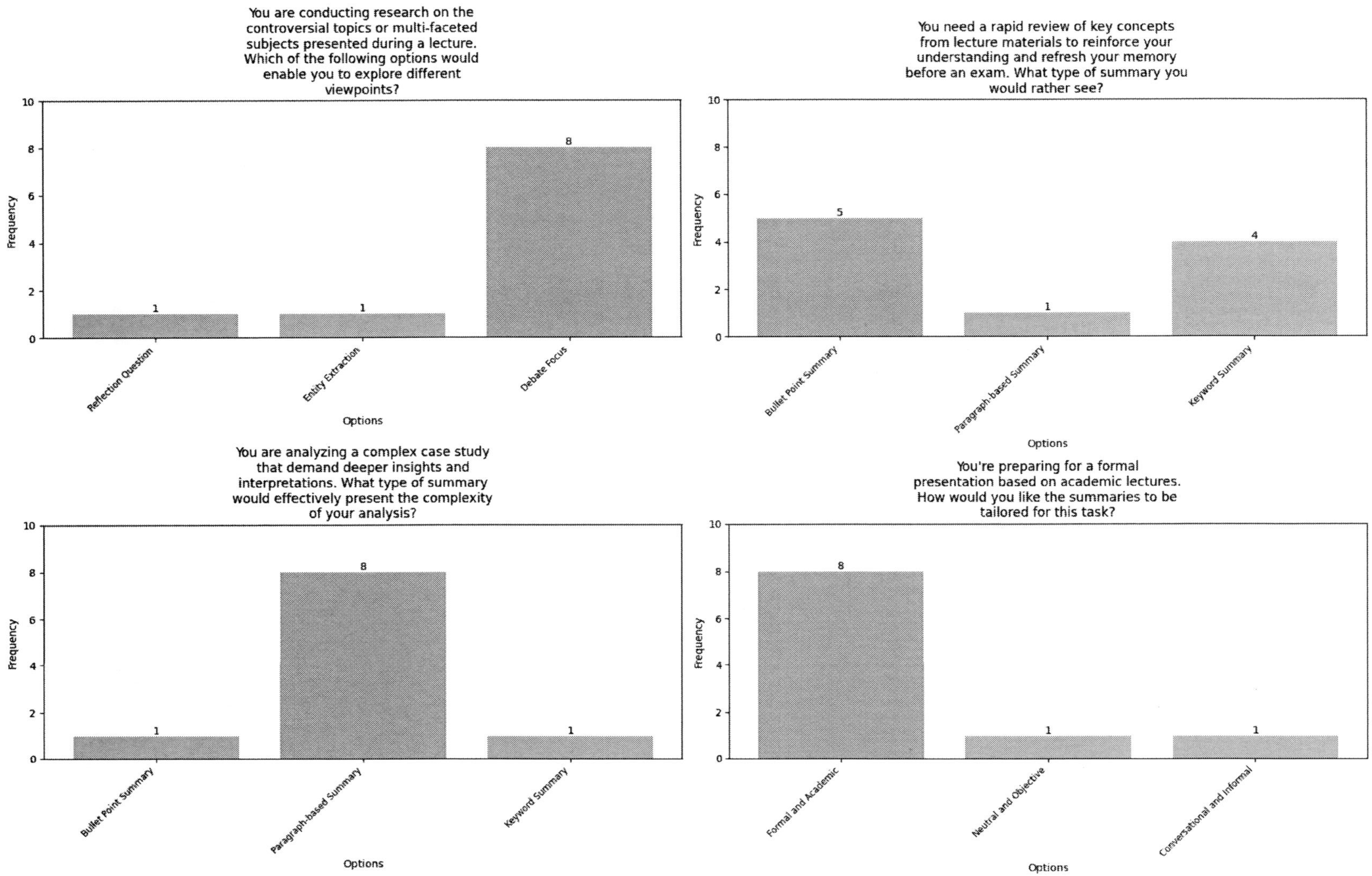

Figure 11: Results from scenarios 25-28

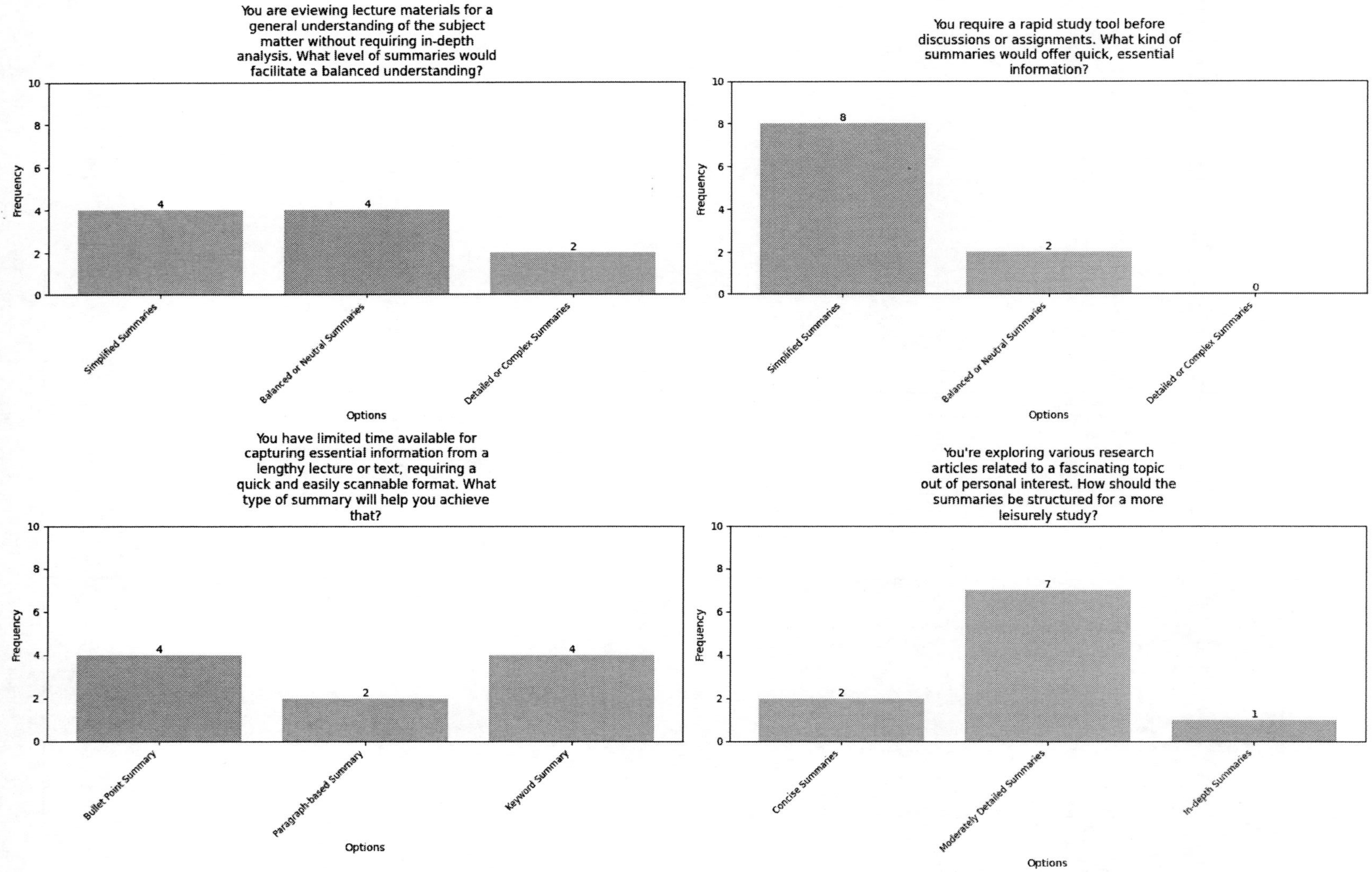

Figure 12: Results from scenarios 29-32

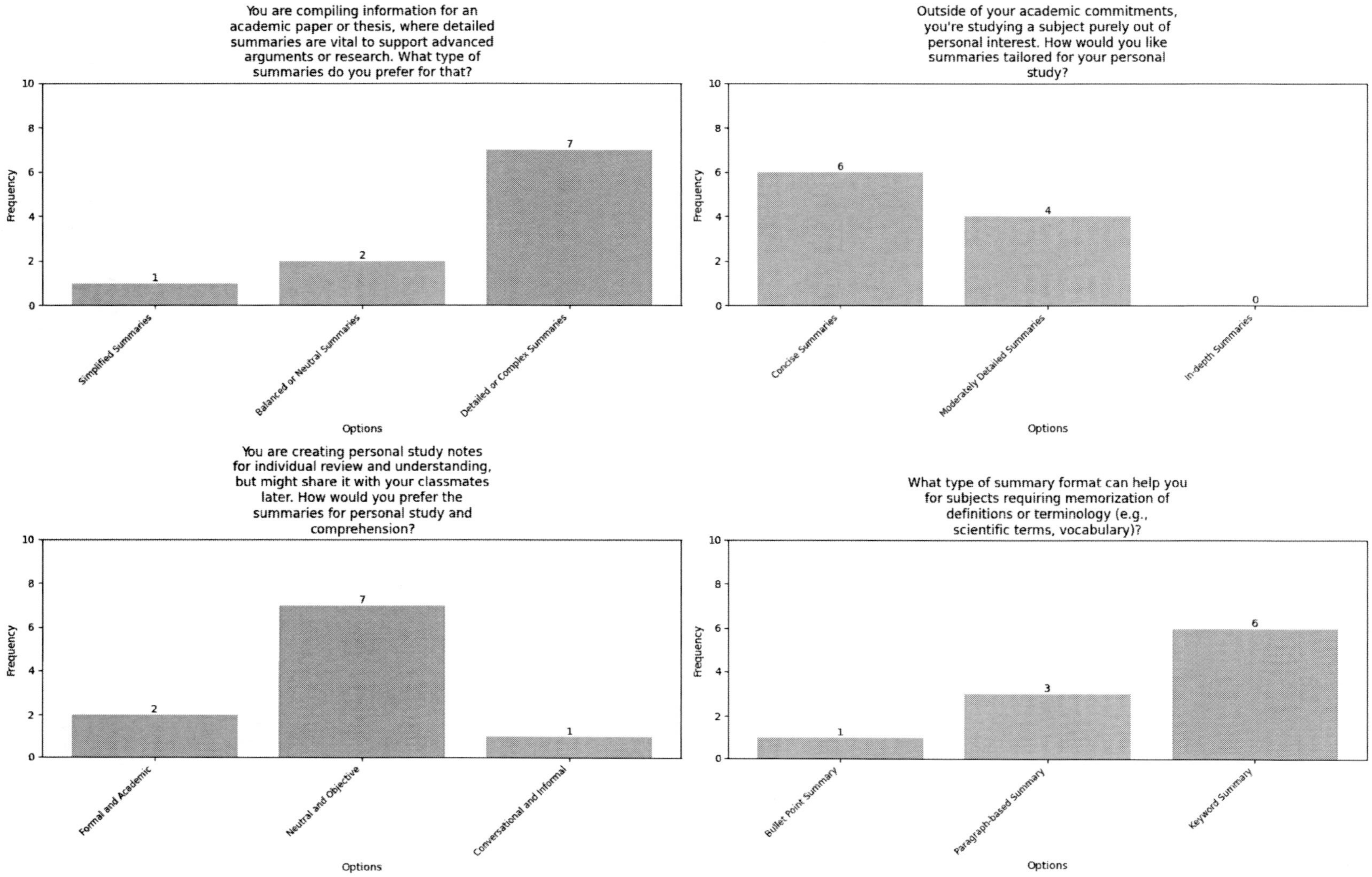

Figure 13: Results from scenarios 33-36

A.2 Example Scenario and Instructions Presented to AMT Participants

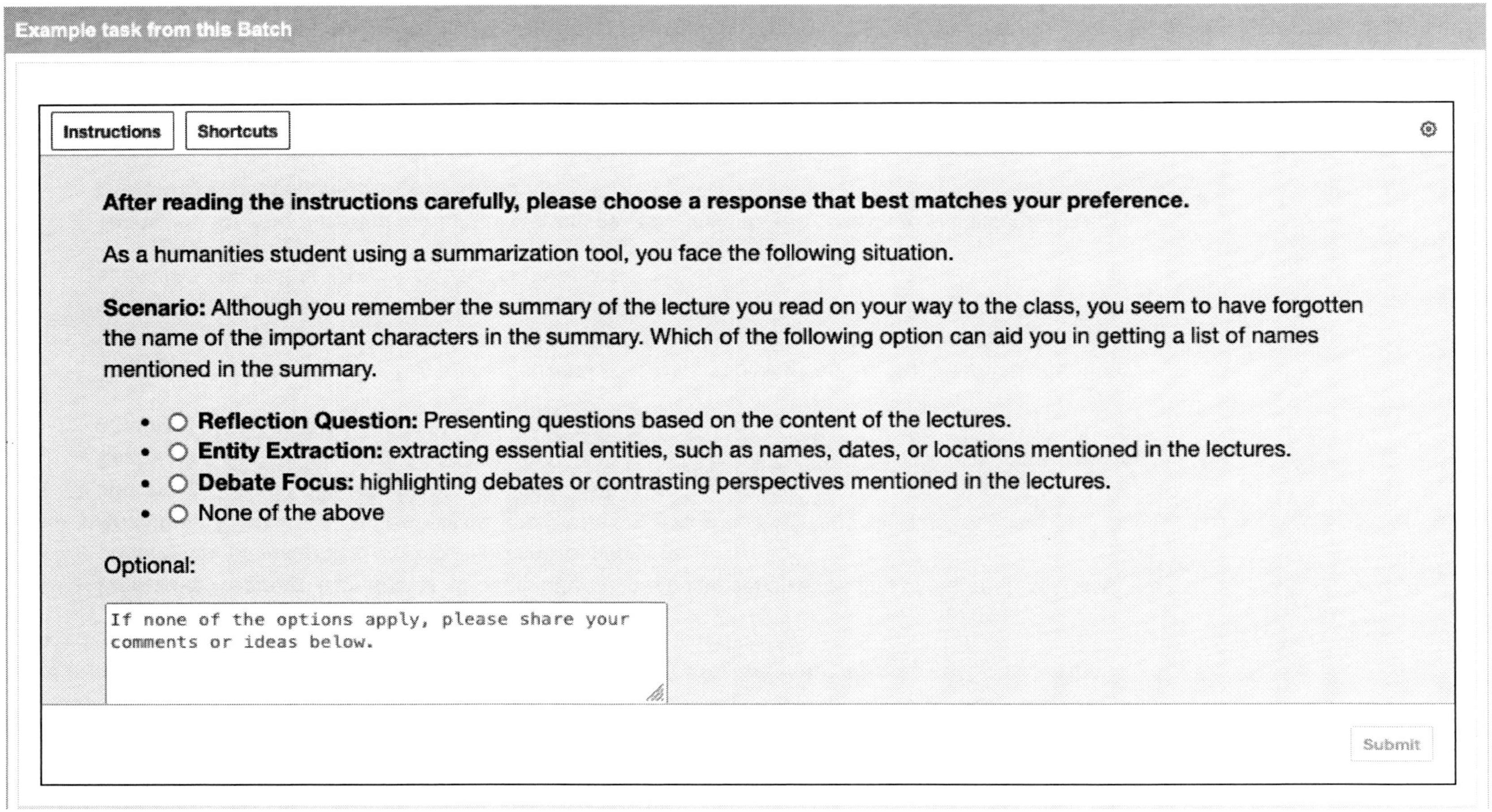

Figure 14: Example Scenario and options presented to AMT participants.

Instructions for Summarization Rating Task

×

Dear Participant, Welcome to our survey on personalized lecture summaries designed specifically for students in the humanities department. In this survey, we kindly ask you to **imagine yourself as a student of humanities who is planning to use a summarization tool for the course lectures**. Consider the academic requirements and preferences typical for this field listed below.

- **Extensive Reading**: Humanities students often engage in extensive reading of literary texts, historical documents, philosophical writings, and critical analyses.
- **Analytical Thinking**: Critical analysis, interpretation, and critical thinking skills are crucial in understanding and dissecting complex ideas within the humanities.
- **Essay Writing:** Writing essays and papers that demonstrate critical thought, analysis, and coherent arguments is a common academic requirement.

Throughout the survey, you'll encounter several scenarios showing various study-related situations. For each scenario, you are given three options to choose from. Please choose an option in each scenario that you believe best fits the issue presented. There are no right or wrong answers; simply select the option that aligns with your preferences.

Thank you for your time and thoughtful responses. Your insights will contribute significantly to improving educational tools for students.

Close

Figure 15: Instruction presented to AMT participants.

A.3 Sample User Journey to create Personalized Summary with HumSum

This user journey presented here is formulated following a modified version of the initial survey's question below.

Initial survey's question: You took a lot of courses this semester and you have a busy schedule balancing multiple courses and extracurricular activities. how would you prefer the summaries for your courses this semester?

Modified question for this user journey: Imagine yourself as an English student at Yale University. You would like to create a summary for Session Three of the course "Introduction to Theory of Literature", keeping in mind that you took a lot of courses this semester and you have a busy schedule balancing multiple courses and extracurricular activities.

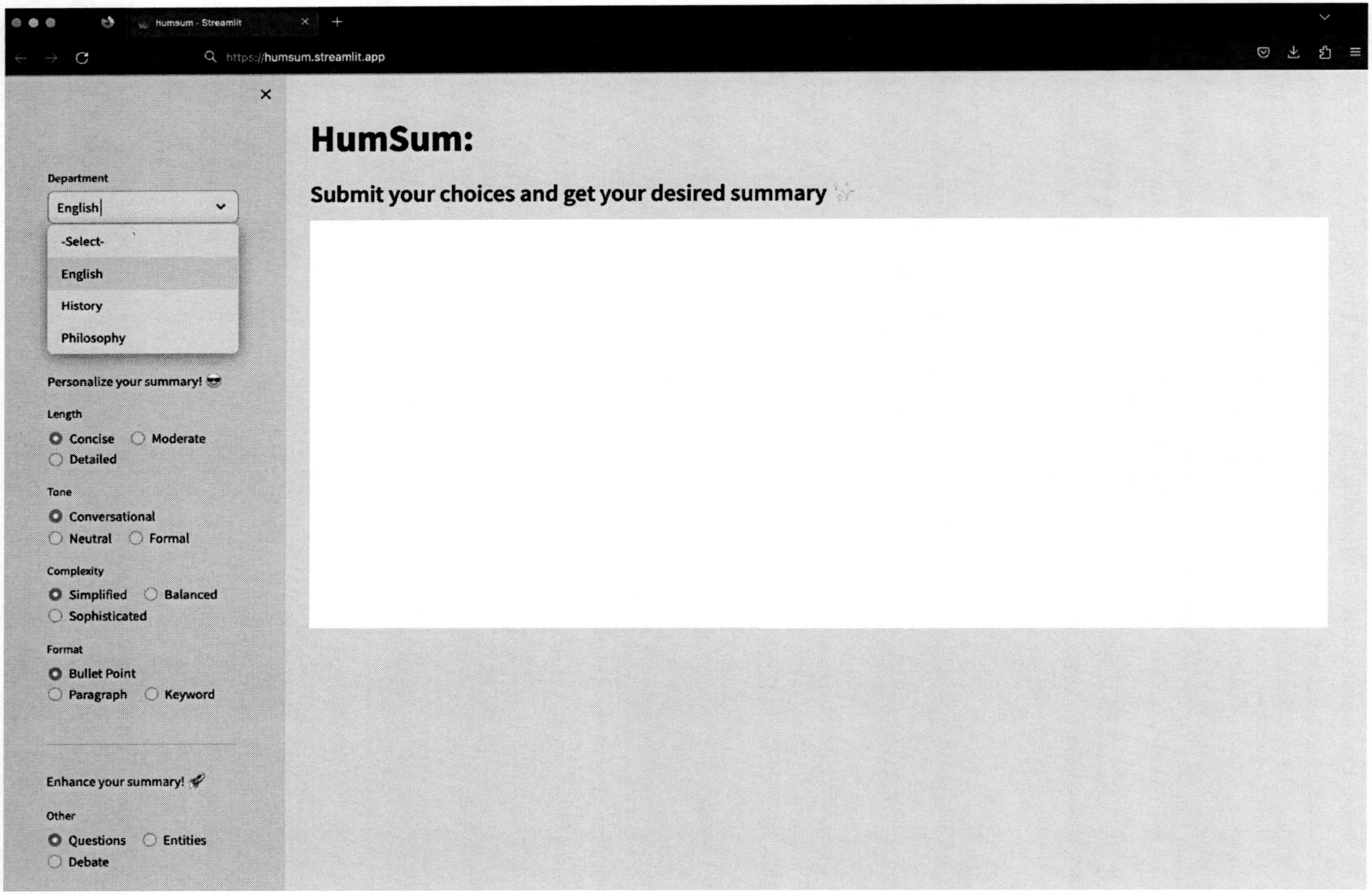

Figure 16: User can select among the humanities departments. The provided options to choose from are "English", "History", "Philosophy", and "Psychology" based on the available departments extracted from OpenYale courses described in section 3.

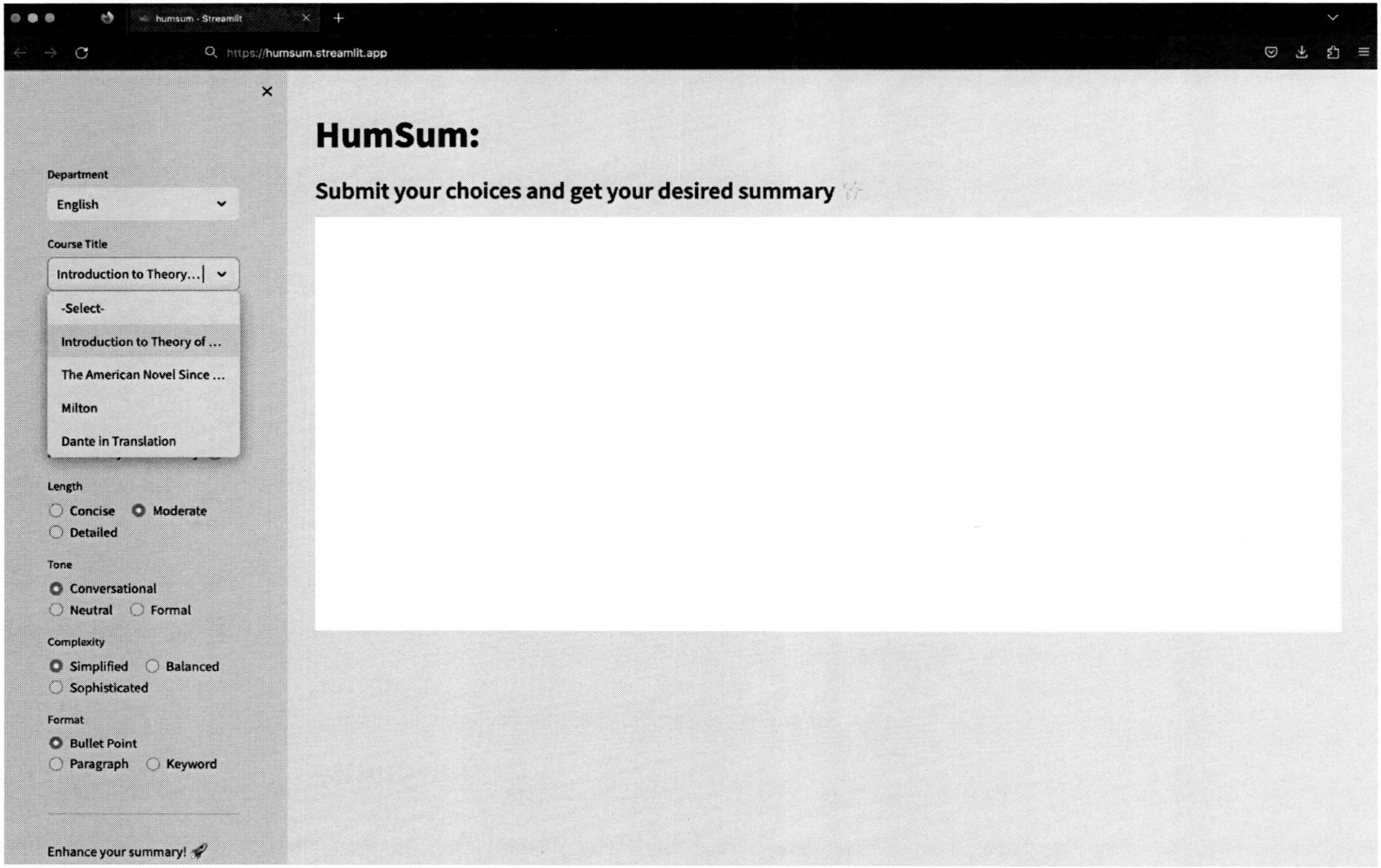

Figure 17: User can select the course title based on the courses extracted from OpenYale courses described in section 3.

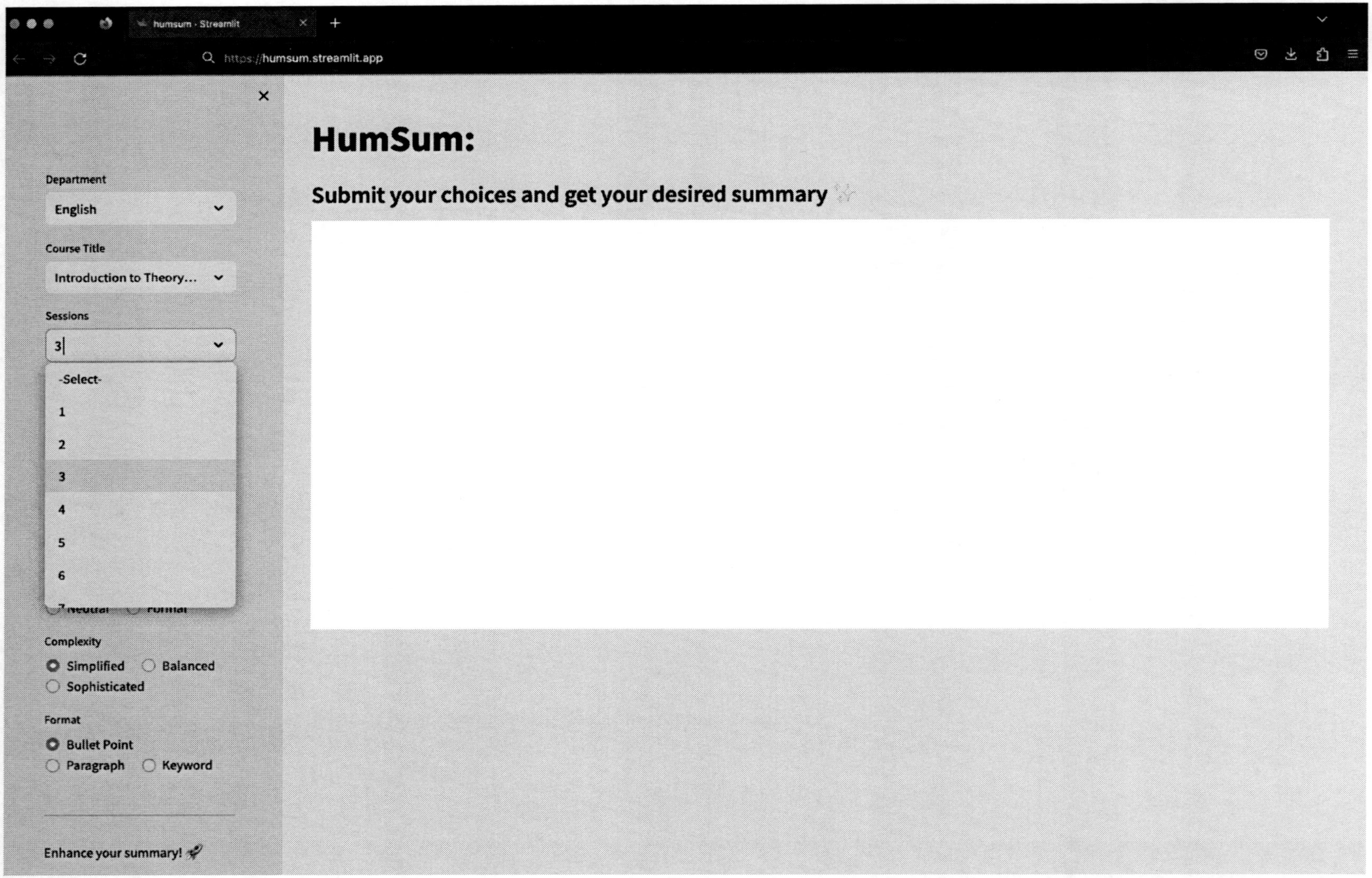

Figure 18: User can select the desired session based on the lecture sessions extracted from OpenYale courses described in section 3.

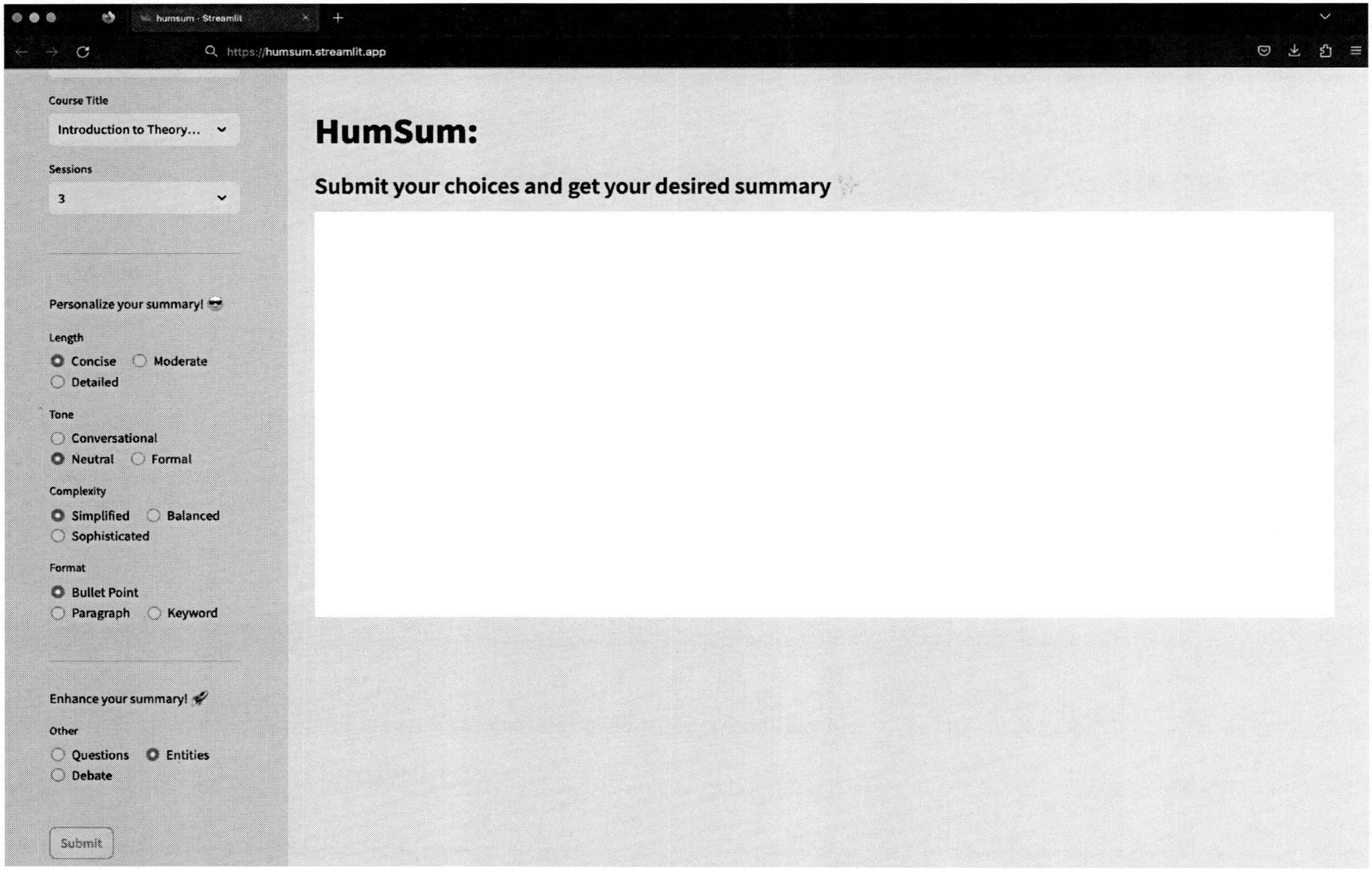

Figure 19: Based on the instruction, the user selected the options as shown in the image and clicked on the submit button to get their personalize summary.

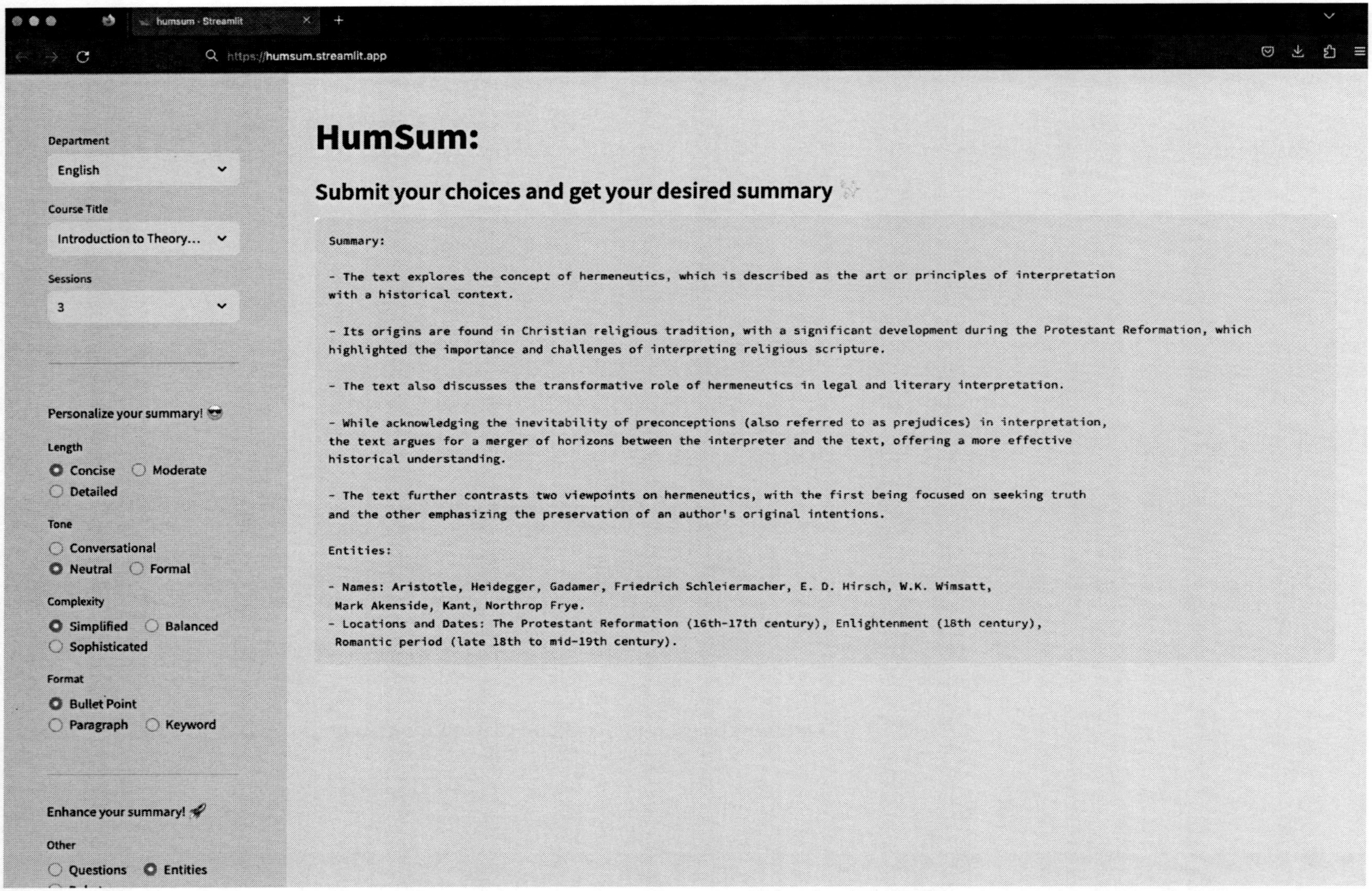

Figure 20: The generated summary based on the instruction using OpenAI's GPT-4-8k model.

A.4 Second Survey Assessment and Evaluation of the Tool

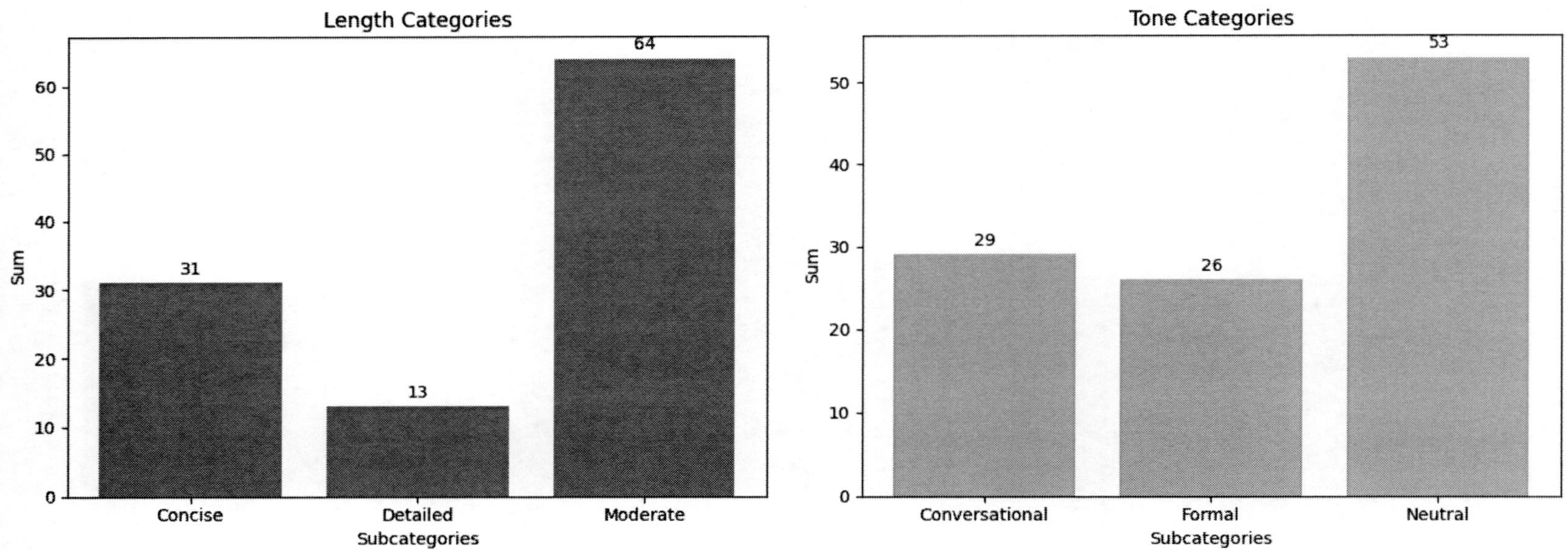

Figure 21: The figures showcase the number of times an item was selected by the user for length and tone options.

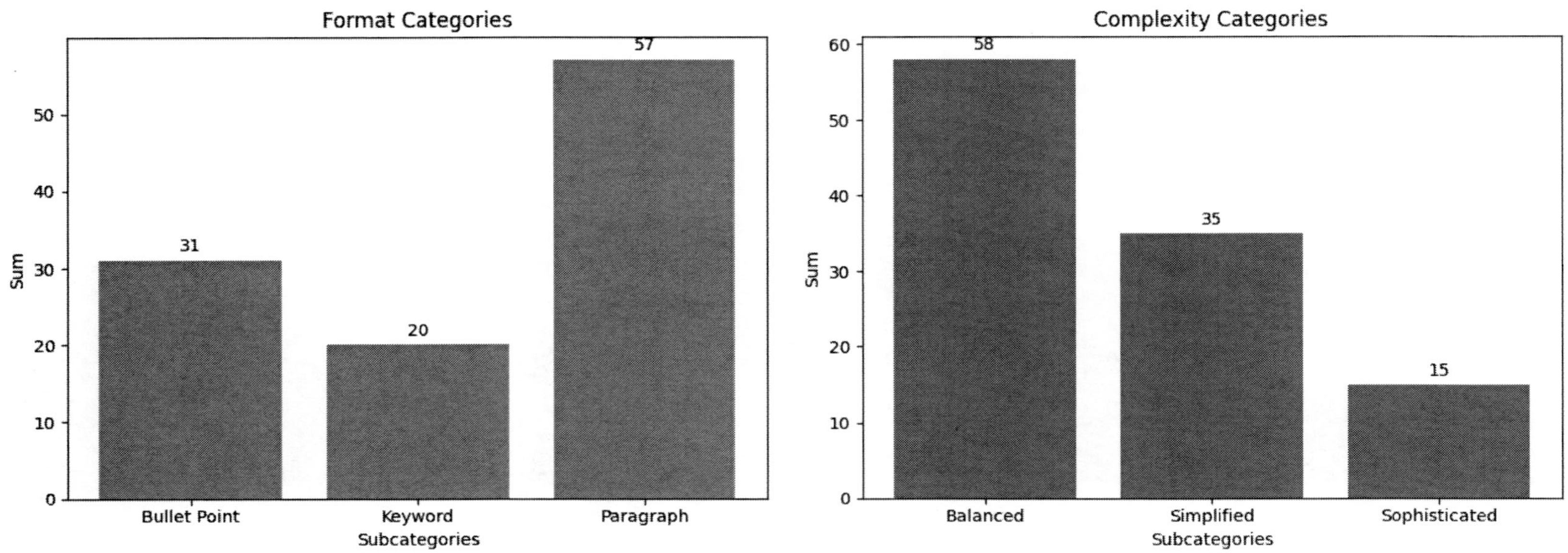

Figure 22: The figures showcase the number of times an item was selected by the user for format and complexity options.

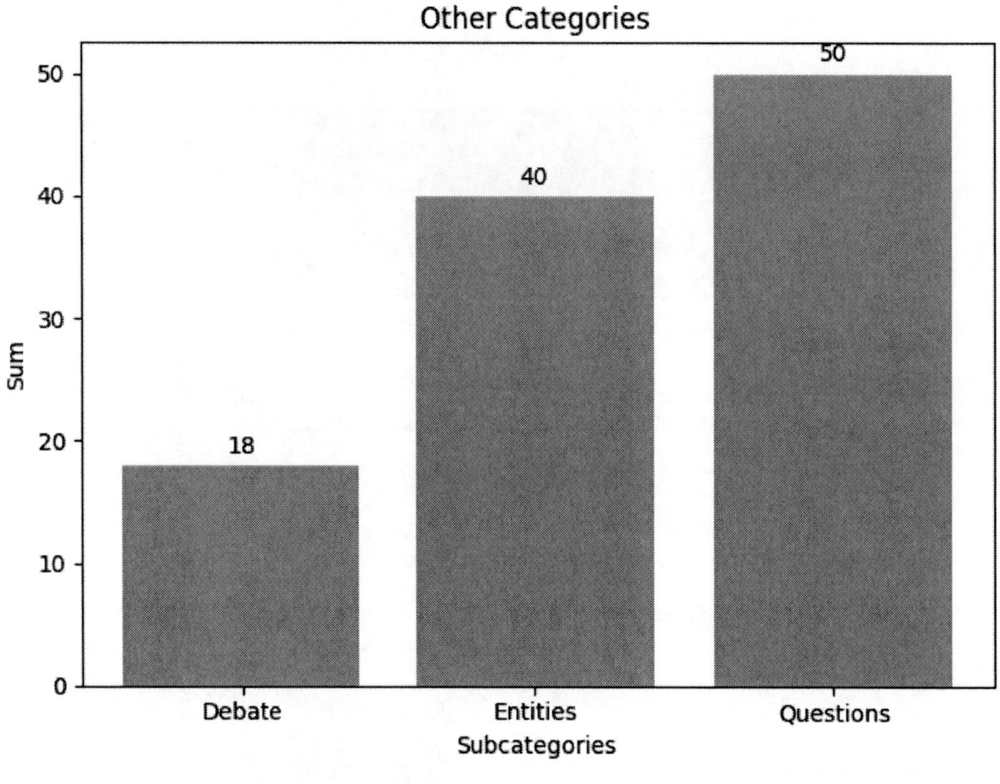

Figure 23: The figures showcase the number of times an item was selected by the user for extra features.

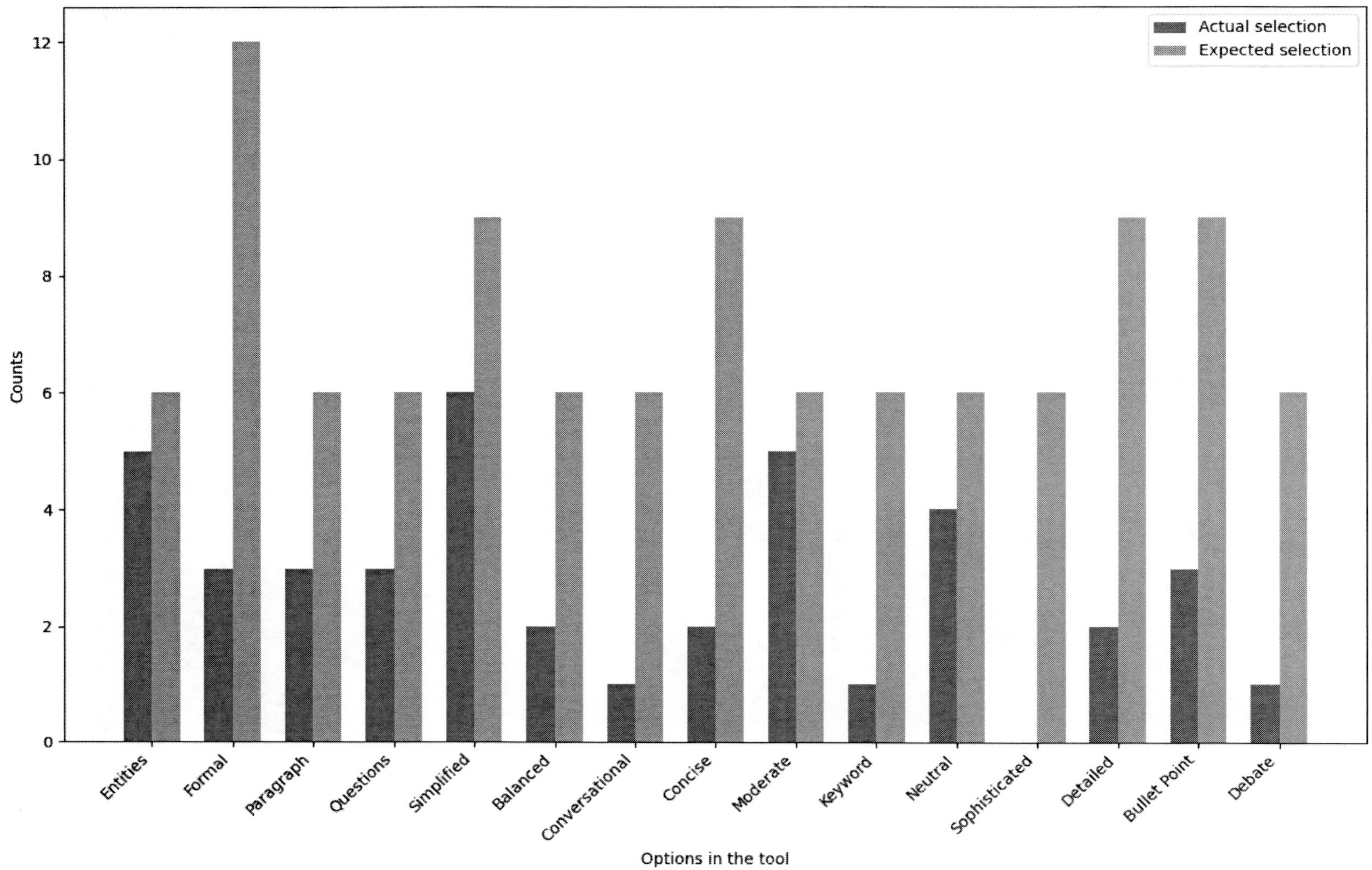

Figure 24: Comparison between our anticipated selections and the actual number of user preferences that aligned with our expectations.

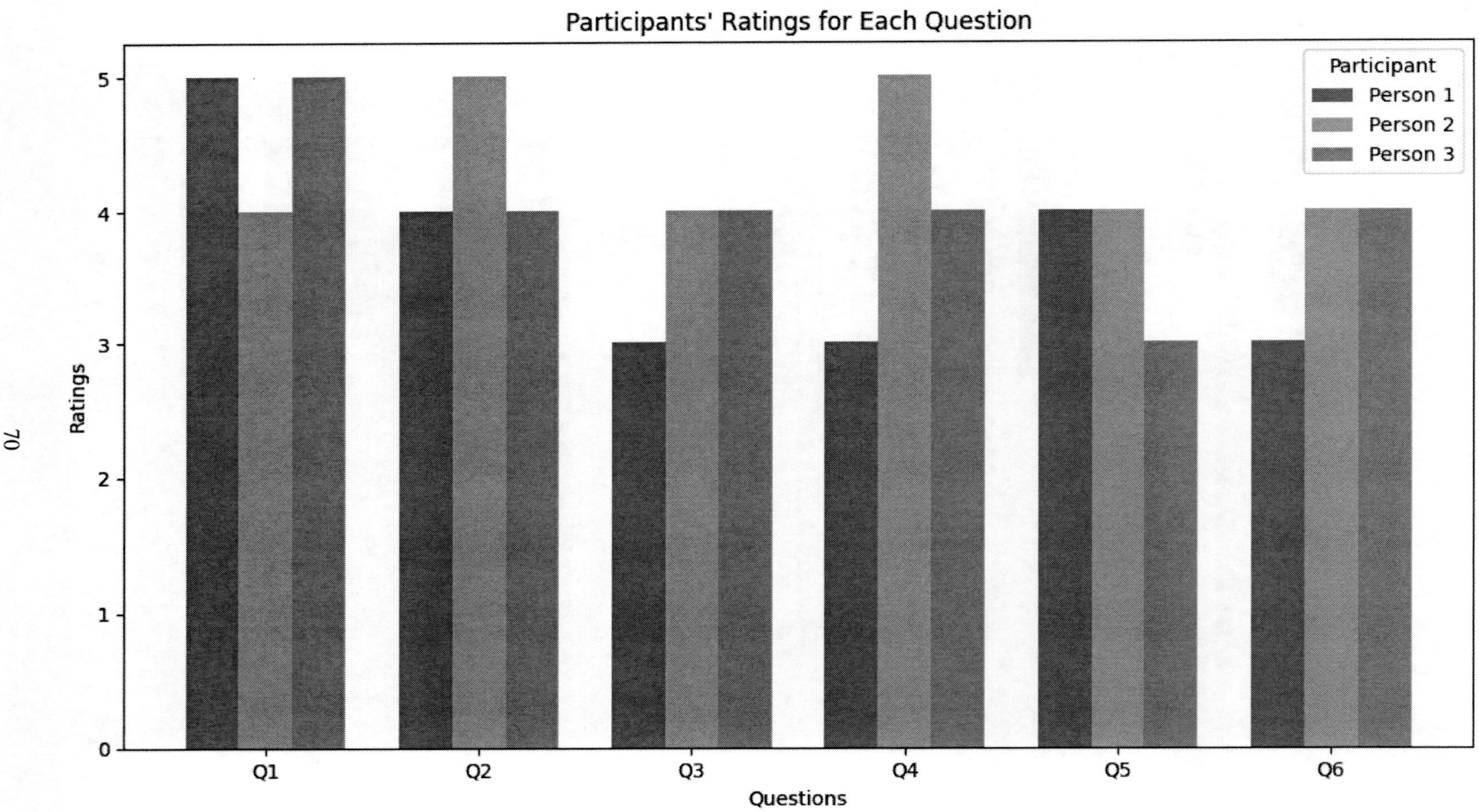

Figure 25: Evaluation of the tool using the final questionnaire encompassing six questions.

Can I trust You?
LLMs as conversational agents

Marc Döbler, Raghavendran Pownraju Mahendravarman, Anna Moskvina
Ella Lab – Gesellschaft für künstliche Intelligenz mbH
Cologne
Germany
{marc.doebler,raghavendran.mahendravarman,anna.moskvina}@ella-lab.io

Abstract

With the rising popularity of LLMs in the public sphere, they have become more and more attractive as a tool for doing one's own research without having to rely on search engines or specialized knowledge of a scientific field. But using LLMs as a source for factual information can lead one to fall prey to misinformation or hallucinations dreamed up by the model. In this paper we examine the gpt-4 LLM by simulating a large number of potential research queries and evaluate how many of the generated references are factually correct as well as existent.

1 Introduction

One of the main functions of the system of mass media, according to Niklas Luhmann, consists in constituting a sort of short-term memory for society by providing and processing information about the world (Luhmann, 1995). To fulfill this function and to perpetuate its own existence, the mass media constantly generates and communicates information. However, the truth of this information is not the most important factor, even when it comes to news. Truth is only relevant insofar as it emphasizes the sensational value of any given message and averts the risk of being accused of deception (Luhmann, 1995).

But this is in contrast to how we use news in our everyday lives where we rely on them for their accuracy.

With the advent of LLMs in the larger public sphere (Yang et al., 2023; Thirunavukarasu et al., 2023; Baidoo-Anu and Ansah, 2023; Dwivedi et al., 2023) , this tension between the individual's desire for factually correct information and the mass media's preference for mere communication grows more pronounced. When ordinary users utilize LLMs as more advanced internet search engines to answer questions that are not easily answered by sites like Wikipedia, they expect a truthful response. But the model's primary function lies in communication. It might be dissatisfying for users when an LLM hallucinates instead of providing correct answers to a query, but this is not an error on a technical level. A technical error would mean a complete failure to communicate (i.e. a blank output or an incomprehensible non-sequitur). To counteract this discrepancy, filters and fact-checking processes have been implemented, but these are additional mechanisms added on top of the base model to steer the result in the desired direction. The issue of communication being valued more highly than truth still remains. While this might not be a problem on a larger systemic level, it is an issue when individuals expect information to be factual. This is why we need to examine the quantitative and qualitative nature of false information produced by LLMs.

Hypothesis

Our hypothesis is that *LLMs are more focused on facilitating communication than factual accuracy.* This means that we expect the model to generate relevant-sounding answers in significantly more cases than it generates answers that are actually supported by the facts.

2 Related Work

Despite recent developments in artificial intelligence and the emergence of different LLMs such as PaLM (Chowdhery et al., 2023), OpenAI's ChatGPT (OpenAI, 2022), and GPT-4 (OpenAI, 2023), Google's Bard (Manyika, 2023), Meta's LLaMa (Touvron et al., 2023) all of the established LLMs are infamous for hallucinations (Dziri et al., 2022; Ji et al., 2023) . This fact prompted research to examine the ways of how we can facilitate the "made up" nature of some of the outputs of the models. As well as overall analysis of whether the LLMs can be trusted. Workshops such as *Workshop on*

Proceedings of the 1st Workshop on Personalization of Generative AI Systems (PERSONALIZE 2024), pages 71–75
March 22, 2024 ©2024 Association for Computational Linguistics

Large Language Models' Interpretability and Trustworthiness (Saha et al., 2023) or *TrustNLP: Workshop on Trustworthy Natural Language Processing* (Ovalle et al., 2023) nudge the scientific community to investigate explainability and trustworthiness of different predictive models and LLMs.

Most of the research on the trustworthiness of the LLMs is either based on surveys and analysis of different requirements (such as fairness, explainability, accountability, reliability to name a few) that can be used to asses the output of a model in general (Kaur et al., 2022; Liu et al., 2023) or in specific fields, for instance in Healthcare (Ahmad et al., 2023). Other studies cover general guidelines for establishing a trustworthy model (Litschko et al., 2023) or provide an overview of methods available to detect the fairness of the output of the model based on their toxicity, bias and value-alignment (Huang et al., 2023).

Though there are several studies that are focused on investigating how factually correct the output of the models is (Zhao et al., 2023; Min et al., 2023), the usual methods of testing factual correctness is to check the facts present in the output. Only very few researchers studied the references that were provided by a model for the generated output, i.e. checked the validity of the source that the output was based on (Shi et al., 2023).

This positional paper is designed to make it more apparent if we should trust the output of the LLMs just because they provide us with official looking sources.

3 Methodology

To test our hypothesis that Large Language Models are in their nature trained to be a conversational partner first and a "fact provider" second, we have conducted a series of experiments that were designed to examine how much LLMs can be trusted as a source of information. For the first part of the experiment we automatically generated scientific questions from different branches. Overall, 985 questions were generated for 231 scientific branches. The most questions were generated for the fields of Medicine (40), Computer Science (38), Environmental Science (37), Earth Science (35), Physics (35), Mathematics (35) and Chemistry (34).

The generated questions were then used as a query for the gpt-4 LLM with a task of further generating a corresponding concise explanation which was to be based on real scientific references (in form of a list of links). For example, the query "How do children acquire syntactic knowledge in their native language?" received the explanation "Children acquire syntactic knowledge in their native language through a combination of innate abilities and environmental input <. . .>" and a list of 4 links to different scientific journals. The query "How can we model complex systems with mathematics?" received the explanation "Complex systems can be modeled mathematically using various approaches, depending on the nature of the system and the phenomena being studied. Here are some of the common mathematical frameworks and methods used to model complex systems <...>" based on 10 different links.

Previous research has shown that mapping back to the original documents or providing sources to the generated texts can potentially invoke a feeling of trust from a user towards a model (Bohnet et al., 2022). Therefore the generated references were investigated for their relevance. In order to do that, we counted how many of the generated references actually exist at the moment of the experiment, and how many of the links provided the information that was relevant to the question.

The workflow of the experiment is given in Figure 1.

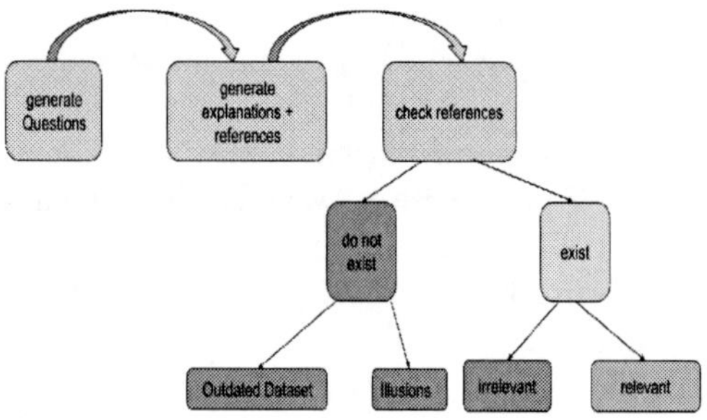

Figure 1: Automated Workflow for testing the hypothesis

LangChain (Harrison, 2022) was used for generating both questions and explanations.

Though our experiments resemble the study performed by Shi et al., 2023, our approach focuses more on generating specific questions within the scientific domain to simulate the workflow and the research process of a human.

4 Evaluation

To further investigate whether our hypothesis holds we have conducted a quantitative (statistical) analysis of the results.

Overall, for 985 different questions we generated 985 explanations with 4434 references (with an average of 5 references per explanation).

Out of the 4434 references 2967 links led to pages that did not exist anymore at the time the experiments were conducted (middle of December 2023). One of the reasons could be that the submitted paper that existed at the time the LLM was trained, was retracted, deleted or moved to another website (so-called illusions (Shi et al., 2023)). Another reason could be that the link was hallucinated by the model and did not exist in the first place.

Out of the 1467 references that led to real existing scientific sources 1376 were relevant to the question. Table 1 gives a short overview of the findings.

We also examined the scientific branches that suffered most from the sources that were not fully available. Out of 40 questions and explanations for the field of Medicine, 37 had missing references. 37 out of 37 explanations for questions from the field of Environmental Science had incomplete references. 2 out of 2 questions and explanations from the area of Zymology had referenced non-existing sources. In general, only approximately 25% of explanations were covered by the references that were marked as existing at the moment of the experiment. After the relevance check 88% of explanations had not only verifiable but also related sources.

5 Discussion

Our findings show that a large number of the generated sources are relevant to the question that was asked, but do not exist. This is either because the model hallucinated these citations or because its data was outdated, thus providing a dead link.

It is not entirely clear if this supports our hypothesis. If the citations are indeed real, but have been deleted or retracted since the model was trained, this finding may only be a reflection of the model's outdated training data. But if the model did indeed hallucinate these sources, this finding would support our hypothesis that the model puts greater value on communication and providing answers that are superficially satisfactory than on factually correct information.

However, many of the generated sources were irrelevant to the query. These were generated by the model to fulfill the demand for sources in the query, but the sources provided were selected with little regard for relevancy. This supports our hypothesis that the model puts greater emphasis on communicating successfully than on responding to the query correctly.

6 Limitations

A limitation of this paper is that we only tested the gpt-4 LLM. Our findings might only be relevant to models similar to this one, but not for models that are very different from it or those that have a greater focus on factual accuracy.

We were also not able to clearly differentiate between sources that did not exist anymore because they were removed or retracted and those that were hallucinated entirely.

7 Ethical Considerations

As far as ethical considerations go, our findings illustrate that only in 88% of cases the cited sources were relevant as well as existent. This suggests that LLMs are not primarily concerned with providing accurate and up-to-date information. Individual users that seek to use LLMs as a tool for an in-depth net search that search engines can't provide should be very cautious to double check the information they receive.

8 Future work

We strongly believe that further investigation into the phenomenon of illusions, hallucinations and unrelated sources is needed. Understanding why the model outputs references that are not indeed relevant to the generated answers as well as a way of identifying types of illusions and hallucinations is crucial for building reliable, personalized and trustworthy LLMs.

9 Acknowledgment

This study was conducted within the framework of developing a commercial paraphrasing tool for German by employees of Ella Lab – Gesellschaft für künstliche Intelligenz mbH. Furthermore, we

Sources	Does not Exist	Exists irrelevant	Exists relevant
4434	2967	91	1376

Table 1: Overall number of sources given as references to the generated explanation and their distribution based on relevance

would like to acknowledge the guidance and provided by Nasrin Saef, Head of Machine Learning Team.

References

Muhammad Aurangzeb Ahmad, Ilker Yaramis, and Taposh Dutta Roy. 2023. Creating trustworthy llms: Dealing with hallucinations in healthcare ai. *arXiv preprint arXiv:2311.01463*.

David Baidoo-Anu and Leticia Owusu Ansah. 2023. Education in the era of generative artificial intelligence (ai): Understanding the potential benefits of chatgpt in promoting teaching and learning. *Journal of AI*, 7(1):52–62.

Bernd Bohnet, Vinh Q Tran, Pat Verga, Roee Aharoni, Daniel Andor, Livio Baldini Soares, Jacob Eisenstein, Kuzman Ganchev, Jonathan Herzig, Kai Hui, et al. 2022. Attributed question answering: Evaluation and modeling for attributed large language models. *arXiv preprint arXiv:2212.08037*.

Aakanksha Chowdhery, Sharan Narang, Jacob Devlin, Maarten Bosma, Gaurav Mishra, Adam Roberts, Paul Barham, Hyung Won Chung, Charles Sutton, Sebastian Gehrmann, et al. 2023. Palm: Scaling language modeling with pathways. *Journal of Machine Learning Research*, 24(240):1–113.

Yogesh K Dwivedi, Nir Kshetri, Laurie Hughes, Emma Louise Slade, Anand Jeyaraj, Arpan Kumar Kar, Abdullah M Baabdullah, Alex Koohang, Vishnupriya Raghavan, Manju Ahuja, et al. 2023. "so what if chatgpt wrote it?" multidisciplinary perspectives on opportunities, challenges and implications of generative conversational ai for research, practice and policy. *International Journal of Information Management*, 71:102642.

Nouha Dziri, Sivan Milton, Mo Yu, Osmar Zaiane, and Siva Reddy. 2022. On the origin of hallucinations in conversational models: Is it the datasets or the models? In *Annual Conference of the North American Chapter of the Association for Computational Linguistics*.

Chase Harrison. 2022. *LangChain*.

Yue Huang, Qihui Zhang, Lichao Sun, et al. 2023. Trustgpt: A benchmark for trustworthy and responsible large language models. *arXiv preprint arXiv:2306.11507*.

Ziwei Ji, Nayeon Lee, Rita Frieske, Tiezheng Yu, Dan Su, Yan Xu, Etsuko Ishii, Ye Jin Bang, Andrea Madotto, and Pascale Fung. 2023. Survey of hallucination in natural language generation. *ACM Computing Surveys*, 55(12):1–38.

Davinder Kaur, Suleyman Uslu, Kaley J Rittichier, and Arjan Durresi. 2022. Trustworthy artificial intelligence: a review. *ACM Computing Surveys (CSUR)*, 55(2):1–38.

Robert Litschko, Max Müller-Eberstein, Rob Van Der Goot, Leon Weber, and Barbara Plank. 2023. Establishing trustworthiness: Rethinking tasks and model evaluation. *arXiv preprint arXiv:2310.05442*.

Yang Liu, Yuanshun Yao, Jean-Francois Ton, Xiaoying Zhang, Ruocheng Guo Hao Cheng, Yegor Klochkov, Muhammad Faaiz Taufiq, and Hang Li. 2023. Trustworthy llms: a survey and guideline for evaluating large language models' alignment. *arXiv preprint arXiv:2308.05374*.

Niklas Luhmann. 1995. *Die realität der massenmedien*. Springer.

James Manyika. 2023. An overview of bard: an early experiment with generative ai. *AI. Google Static Documents*, 2.

Sewon Min, Kalpesh Krishna, Xinxi Lyu, Mike Lewis, Wen-tau Yih, Pang Wei Koh, Mohit Iyyer, Luke Zettlemoyer, and Hannaneh Hajishirzi. 2023. Factscore: Fine-grained atomic evaluation of factual precision in long form text generation. *arXiv preprint arXiv:2305.14251*.

OpenAI. 2022. Introducing chatgpt.

OpenAI. 2023. Gpt-4 technical report. *ArXiv*, abs/2303.08774.

Anaelia Ovalle, Kai-Wei Chang, Ninareh Mehrabi, Yada Pruksachatkun, Aram Galystan, Jwala Dhamala, Apurv Verma, Trista Cao, Anoop Kumar, and Rahul Gupta. 2023. Proceedings of the 3rd workshop on trustworthy natural language processing (trustnlp 2023). In *Proceedings of the 3rd Workshop on Trustworthy Natural Language Processing (TrustNLP 2023)*.

Tulika Saha, Debasis Ganguly, Sriparna Saha, and Prasenjit Mitra. 2023. Workshop on large language models' interpretability and trustworthiness (llmit). In *Proceedings of the 32nd ACM International Conference on Information and Knowledge Management*, pages 5290–5293.

Xiang Shi, Jiawei Liu, Yinpeng Liu, Qikai Cheng, and Wei Lu. 2023. Know where to go: Make llm a relevant, responsible, and trustworthy searcher. *arXiv preprint arXiv:2310.12443*.

Arun James Thirunavukarasu, Darren Shu Jeng Ting, Kabilan Elangovan, Laura Gutierrez, Ting Fang Tan, and Daniel Shu Wei Ting. 2023. Large language models in medicine. *Nature medicine*, 29(8):1930–1940.

Hugo Touvron, Thibaut Lavril, Gautier Izacard, Xavier Martinet, Marie-Anne Lachaux, Timothée Lacroix, Baptiste Rozière, Naman Goyal, Eric Hambro, Faisal Azhar, et al. 2023. Llama: Open and efficient foundation language models. *arXiv preprint arXiv:2302.13971*.

Jingfeng Yang, Hongye Jin, Ruixiang Tang, Xiaotian Han, Qizhang Feng, Haoming Jiang, Bing Yin, and Xia Hu. 2023. Harnessing the power of llms in practice: A survey on chatgpt and beyond. *arXiv preprint arXiv:2304.13712*.

Ruochen Zhao, Xingxuan Li, Yew Ken Chia, Bosheng Ding, and Lidong Bing. 2023. Can chatgpt-like generative models guarantee factual accuracy? on the mistakes of new generation search engines. *arXiv preprint arXiv:2304.11076*.

Emulating Author Style: A Feasibility Study of Prompt-enabled Text Stylization with Off-the-Shelf LLMs

Avanti Bhandarkar **Ronald Wilson** **Anushka Swarup** **Damon Woodard**
Florida Institute for National Security
University of Florida, Gainesville, FL, USA
{avantibhandarkar, ronaldwilson, aswarup, dwoodard}@ufl.edu

Abstract

User-centric personalization of text opens many avenues of applications from stylized email composition to machine translation. Existing approaches in this domain often encounter limitations in data and resource requirements. Drawing inspiration from the success of prompt-enabled stylization in related fields, this work conducts the first feasibility study into 12 pre-trained SOTA LLMs for author style emulation. Although promising, the results suggest that current off-the-shelf LLMs fall short of achieving effective author style emulation.

1 Introduction

Driven by the trend of using Generative AI for on-demand user-centric personalization in recent years, the demand for personalized content has become increasingly pronounced. Personalized text, generated by capturing the style of an author, is sought-after in creative content writing, data-to-text generation, email composition as well as machine translation to provide user-specific "naturalness" to text. Prior works attempted at replicating an author's writing style by mapping the content to a particular style but remained a challenging task due to the indecipherable and individualistic nature of writing style.

LLMs, with their understanding of natural languages via high-level latent representations, serve as versatile tools for linguistic analysis and manipulation. Therefore, they are explored abundantly in various text-based applications such as information retrieval, sentiment analysis, etc. (Lu et al., 2023; Zhu et al., 2023). In the realm of controllable text-generation, input optimization or prompt engineering has enabled a resource-efficient alternative to modulate LLM-generated text by modifying the input prompts (Zhang et al., 2023). More recently, this approach has been used to produce valid explanations for various stylistic textual entailment tasks and produced promising results in related fields such as Authorship Verification and Personality Prediction (Hung et al., 2023; Ji et al., 2023). Motivated by these observations, this work performs the first feasibility study into using off-the-shelf pre-trained LLMs for controllable stylized text generation via prompting for author style emulation.

2 Related Works

Author Style Emulation, within personalized text generation, seeks to replicate the distinctive styles of individual human authors. It is often conceived in two ways - Text Stylization or Text Style Transfer (TST). The former equips a text generator to produce author-stylized text, while the latter independently extracts an author's linguistic preferences (style) and modulates a text generator's semantic content accordingly.

Early work in this field mainly investigated TST, by attempting to *Shakerspearize* texts using parallel corpora produced with and without Shakespearean style (Xu, 2017; Jhamtani et al., 2017). However, limited availability of parallel corpora for an average author's style hindered progress in this direction (Hu et al., 2020). Motivated by the need for non-parallel data, some research works exploring TST for sentiment and formality utilized generative models, such as Generative Adversarial Networks (GANs), Variational Autoencoders (VAE) etc., to obtain latent representation corresponding to the style and semantic content separately (Shen et al., 2017; Li et al., 2018). However, this line of research was not as explored for author-stylized text generation as the intricate relationship between an author's linguistic style and semantic content would have made their separation a challenging task.

In the recent past, Syed et al. (2020) exploited the capabilities of LLMs such as GPT2 by finetuning the model on an author's corpus to incorpo-

Proceedings of the 1st Workshop on Personalization of Generative AI Systems (PERSONALIZE 2024), pages 76–82
March 22, 2024

Table 1: Brief Description of the Text Generators

Type	Text Generator	Size	Description
AutoR	GPT3	175B	The OpenAI text completion API used with the $davinci$ engine.
Chat	GPT4	N/A	OpenAI chat completion API used with the $Turbo$ engine.
	OpenChat3.5	7B	Trained with Conditioned-RLFT on instruction data (Wang et al., 2023a).
	CausalLM	14B	Trained on manually curated SFT dataset from many open-source corpora.
	Zephyr	7B	Fine-tuned on synthetic datasets using DPO algorithm. β variant used(Tunstall et al., 2023)
	Llama-2	7B	Fine-tuned on instruction datasets using SFT and RLHF (Touvron et al., 2023)
	NeuralChat	7B	Fine-tuned on an open source dataset using DPO algorithm . Version v3-1 used.
	DeepSeek	7B	Trained on a corpus of 2 trillion tokens in English and Chinese.
Instruct	GPT3.5	N/A	OpenAI text completion API used with the $turbo - instruct$ engine.
	Falcon	7B	Fine-tuned using the base model on chat and instruct datasets(Almazrouei et al., 2023).
	Mistral	7B	Instruction fine-tuned model trained on conversation datasets (Jiang et al., 2023).
	INCITE	7B	Instruction fine-tuned model on a collection of instruction datasets by RedPajama project.

Note: The texts are generated using respective model's HuggingFace model repository unless otherwise specified.
Abbrev.: AutoR - Auto-regressive, SFT - Supervised Fine-Tuning, RLFT - Reinforcement Learning Fine-Tuning, RLHF - Reinforcement Learning with Human Feedback, DPO - Direct Preference Optimization

rate their style characteristics without the need for a parallel corpus. The idea was to utilize the LLMs for *stylistic rewriting* than simple text generation (i.e., writing). However, this method requires large amounts of labeled data with author identities to train a resource-heavy LLM such as GPT2.

More recently, due to the influx of large number of LLMs performing competitively on natural language generation and understanding tasks, investigations have been made to utilize off-the-shelf pre-trained LLMs for related applications such as Authorship Verification and Automatic Personality Prediction through prompt modulation with promising results (Hung et al., 2023; Ji et al., 2023). These results emphasize the capability of the LLMs to understand and follow instructions through various prompting strategies and guided instructions. Specifically, these works instruct the LLM to find entailment between a text and a label (for personality prediction) or between two texts (for authorship verification), while also providing explanations. However, to the best of the author's knowledge, no work has been done to extend this concept to generate text with an objective of emulating an author's writing style.

3 Methodology

Problem Statement: Given human-authored text T_A by an author A, generate T_G using a text generator G that faithfully mirrors the style of the author in T_A. The success criterion is for the generator to produce T_G such that a proficient author discriminator D attributes it accurately to the original author A.

To meet this objective, three key elements come into play: Author (A), Generator (G) and Discriminator (D). A signifies the identity label associated with a human-authored text sample T_A containing the author's linguistic preferences. Additionally, it is assumed that all text samples by A have consistent linguistic preferences that form the author's style signature. G modifies its language generation for different A by learning the author's stylistic preferences from T_A independently or by virtue of instructions. Finally, D must be capable of accurately differentiating between several authors based on their style signatures.

Authorship Attribution (AA) research focuses on creating robust algorithms to differentiate authors based on their distinct writing styles. Therefore, AA can serve as a source for text data with author identity labels, while effective AA algorithms become relevant tools for serving as author discriminators. For the purpose of this study text samples with author identity labels are obtained from 100 authors randomly chosen from a widely recognized AA corpus, the Blogs Authorship Corpus (Schler et al., 2006). The selected authors are ensured at least 100 text samples and a minimum of 500 words in each sample.

Next, off-the-shelf pre-trained text generators, the LLMs, are selected. This selection encompasses 12 state-of-the-art (SOTA) LLMs, as described in Table 1, capable of diverse text production including auto-regressive, chat, and instruction-tuned models. While the auto-regressive models are trained to predict the subsequent word based on the preceding text, chat and instruction-tuned models offer greater flexibility in text production having been trained on conversational interactions or task-specific instructions.

For consistency in text generation across LLMs,

Table 2: Summary Statistics of Generated Text Data

Text Generator	Num. words	Num. sentences
GPT3	468±98	25±13
GPT4	520±17	25±5
OpenChat	427±24	24±8
CausalLM	466±27	23±6
Zephyr	420±22	21±5
Llama-2	396±32	21±8
NeuralChat	413±25	22±13
DeepSeek	461±14	19±9
GPT3.5	522±28	28±5
Falcon	446±61	22±8
Mistral	433±28	24±12
INCITE	476±29	28±9

Note: Statistics are reported as mean±std. NLTK (https://www.nltk.org/) was used for word and sentence tokenization.

Table 3: Brief Description of the AA Algorithms

Algorithm	Description
Writeprints	Random Forest Classifier trained on Writeprints features (Mahmood et al., 2019)
LIWC	Random Forest Classifier trained on LIWC psycholinguistic features (Boyd et al., 2022)
Char-3-grams	SVM classifier trained on character 3-gram features using one-vs-rest classification strategy. (Kestemont et al., 2019)
BertAA	Cascaded architecture integrating fine-tuned BERT classifier, stylistic features (e.g., text length, word count), and hybrid features (e.g., most frequent character 2-gram) trained using Logistic Regression. (Fabien et al., 2020)
Contra-X	Contrastive learning with DeBERTa for cross-entropy fine-tuning, followed by classification using a 2-layer MLP. (Ai et al., 2022)

top-K and top-p (nucleus) sampling with K=50 and p=0.95 is used as decoding strategy wherever applicable. The maximum generation length is set to 500 tokens with a minimum requirement of 350 tokens. For each author, 10 text samples are reserved to serve as examples of author's writing style. Every generator is equipped with a prompt and an example text with a specific identity. Therefore, for each author-generator pair, total 10 text samples are generated. Summary statistics for the generated data[1] are provided in Table 2.

AA explores author discrimination at various levels resulting in over 1000 features, ranging from granular features like character n-grams to utilizing contextual features such as BERT (Tyo et al., 2022; Wilson et al., 2021). For optimal evaluation of the stylistic alignment between author and LLM generated text, it is imperative to consider diverse AA algorithms that capture various aspects of author's style. Table 3 describes the most popular and SOTA AA algorithms that are selected to serve as author discriminators.

For each algorithm, training is performed on 90 text samples per author. For the algorithms that require separate training and validation sets, 90% of the author training data is allocated for training while the remaining 10% is reserved for validation. Both BertAA and Contra-X algorithms are trained for 5 epochs each. The results are reported as average accuracy across 5 training-testing runs.

Ultimately, assessing the capability of G for emulating A's style necessitates maintaining A and D constant while varying the inputs of G. As prompts serve as inputs to each LLM, the distinct components of the prompt are adjusted, and the impact on D's performance for each A is evaluated. Detailed specifications of the prompt's individual components are discussed in the following section.

[1]The text data generated for this study can be accessed here

4 Prompting Protocol for Stylization

Following the prompt decomposition technique outlined in Giray (2023), a four-part prompt, namely, task, instructions, output indicator and example author text, is designed (see Table 4). Initially, similar to Wang et al. (2023b), a *Trivial Emulation Protocol* (TEP) is considered where the LLM is provided with a simple task definition along with short snippet of author text. This protocol relies on the LLM's capability of capturing author's unique style representation in an unguided scenario.

Some research works observed that furnishing the LLM with additional task-specific knowledge in the form of guided instructions greatly enhanced its ability to consider relevant textual characteristics (Hung et al., 2023). Therefore, a *Complex Emulation Protocol* (CEP) is developed where the LLM is provided with additional author data and/or guided instructions in the form of few key linguistic features that potentially demonstrate the author's unique linguistic preferences (Boenninghoff et al., 2019). Thus, the *prompting strategy* and *length of example author text* serve as the control parameters for evaluation of the two protocols.

For the purpose of testing, an example author text is categorized as either short or long text, representing the first 50 and 300 words from the original author example, respectively. Additionally, two variations of the prompting strategy involves exclusion and inclusion of guided instructions, identi-

Table 4: Elements of Prompt used for Author Emulation

Prompt Element	Prompt Text
Task	<SYS> You are an **emulator** designed to replicate the writing style of a human author.<\SYS> Your task is to generate a 500-word continuation that *seamlessly integrates with the provided human-authored snippet.* Strive to make the continuation *indistinguishable from the human-authored text.*
Instructions	The goal of this task is to **mimic the author's writing style** while paying meticulous attention to *lexical richness and diversity,* sentence structure, *punctuation style, special character style,* expressions and idioms, *overall tone, emotion* and mood, or any other relevant aspect of writing style established by the author.
Output Indicator	As output, exclusively return the text completion without any accompanying explanations or comments.
Example author text	Text snippet : [50 or 300-word human authored text]

Note: Text enclosed in <SYS> and <\SYS> indicates the system prompt provided to chat models; features emphasized in instructions are linguistically verifiable.

fied as simple and directed prompting, respectively. Across both emulation protocols, the task and output indicator remain consistent.

Evaluation of the author emulation protocols involves testing the trained AA algorithms on both the example author texts and the text generated by each LLM. Results are presented as average accuracy across authors for each LLM in the form of box-and-whisker plot. Assuming that the example author texts contain sufficient stylistic information about their respective authors, *LLMs capable of emulating an author's writing style are expected to demonstrate comparable AA performance on the synthetic LLM-generated text to that observed on the original author texts.*

5 Discussion

Results of TEP are presented in Figure 1. In short texts, the expected low stylometric information corresponds to relatively low performance across all AA algorithms on author text. Notably, GPT-4 outperforms other LLMs, achieving maximum accuracy close to 72% of the maximum accuracy achievable on author text. Being one of the most advanced SOTA models amongst the chosen LLMs, in the absence of specific instructions, GPT4 may leverage the knowledge from its training data to identify and replicate relevant linguistic style representations. Interestingly, the top performing LLMs

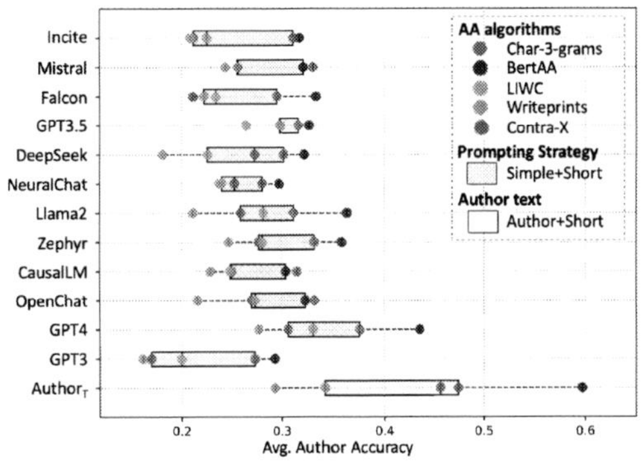

Figure 1: Results of Trivial Emulation Protocol (TEP)

in this protocol - GPT4, Llama2 and Zephyr - are chat models alluding to the potential of chat models for author style emulation in an unguided scenario.

For CEP, three scenarios are evaluated by providing progressively more information in the prompt. The results of this protocol are presented in Figure 2. DeepSeek, a chat model, consistently outperforms all LLMs across scenarios, showcasing strong potential for author style emulation, followed closely by GPT3 and Incite. No clear consensus emerges on the optimal model type for CEP.

With regards to the first control parameter - length of example author text - an expected significant performance improvement is observed across all AA algorithms between short and long author texts. Similarly, most LLMs benefit from addition of more author data, albeit with varying degrees.

Considering the second control parameter - prompting strategy - most LLMs exhibit reduced performance while transitioning from simple to directed prompting. This observation may be caused by one or more of the factors discussed below.

First, the LLM's intrinsic understanding of an author's writing style may be better. Each LLM is trained on large amounts of training data spanning diverse domains that allow the model to learn intricate linguistic structures of language. Given that the LLMs are trained with a probabilistic objective, aiming to generate the next word that most closely aligns with the preceding context, it is plausible that these models develop an understanding of the author's writing style from the example author text. Consequently, constraining the LLM to generate text by focusing on the linguistic features highlighted in the directed prompt might interfere with its intrinsic understanding, thereby leading to a degradation in performance.

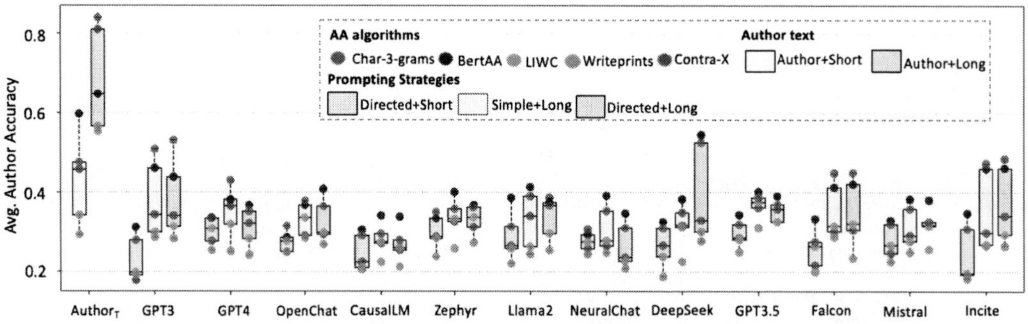

Figure 2: Results of Complex Emulation Protocol (CEP)

Second, limited efficacy of the linguistic features in the prompt in capturing author's style. The directed prompt's linguistic features form a subset of the LIWC and Writeprints feature sets. The lower performance of AA algorithms using these features suggests two possibilities: their possible absence in the author's text or limited influence on their writing style. However, the superior performance of these algorithms on the author's text samples, compared to the generated texts, suggests the influence of these features on the author's writing style to some extent. Nevertheless, considering the subjective nature of an author's linguistic choices, the assumption that a fixed set of linguistic features can universally influence all authors equally might be flawed. Therefore, instead of static directed prompting, a more effective approach could involve dynamically prompting LLMs by considering each author's individual linguistic preferences.

Finally, some LLMs may lack the capability to incorporate the specified linguistic features highlighted in the instructions during text generation. To evaluate the similarity of the linguistically verifiable features from the directed instructions between the LLM generated texts and author's example texts, a test was performed as described in A.1. As anticipated, the LLMs exhibit superior alignment to the said linguistic features in longer texts due to increased data availability. Further it is noted that LLMs are most capable of producing higher alignment with linguistic features that reflect the tone, authenticity, analytical aspects, and lexical richness from author texts. However, replicating the lexical diversity and punctuation style proves more challenging. One of the notable observations is the lack of overall linguistic alignment between the author's texts and the best-performing model, DeepSeek, emphasizing the potential significance of linguistically unverifiable aspects in the instructions for successful emulation.

6 Conclusion

This study explored the use of pre-trained LLMs to generate author-stylized text through prompted inputs, controlling parameters such as example text length and directed instructions with stylometric information. Evaluated against five AA algorithms, the two author emulation protocols (trivial and complex) assessed the feasibility of 12 SOTA LLMs for *Author Style Emulation*. Control parameters significantly impacted the LLM's emulation capacity, emphasizing the need for user-specific personalized instruction generation. Overall, the maximum author emulation performance is only two-thirds that of original texts, highlighting the LLM's current limitations for plug-and-play author style emulation. As this task involves a complex interplay between an author identity, text generator and author discriminator, an extended future work will explore how individual author identities and the properties of author discriminator impact the subsequent author style emulation capabilities of a text generator, specifically the LLMs.

7 Limitations

The feasibility study performed in this work has a few potential limitations with respect to subjectivity, the choice of control parameters, scalability and generalizability. In this work, the results are averaged across authors which may conceal subjective preferences of individual authors. The preliminary choice of control parameter - length of author text - is specific to the author corpus utilized for this work and assumes one example with maximum 300 words sufficiently represents author's unique linguistic choices. Due to the absence of previous work performing prompt-enabled author-stylized text generation, the control parameter - prompting strategy - is limited by two choices - unguided and guided with static instructions. The generalizability and scalability of this work is limited by the choice of a small author set size with 100 authors.

References

Bo Ai, Yuchen Wang, Yugin Tan, and Samson Tan. 2022. Whodunit? learning to contrast for authorship attribution. *arXiv preprint arXiv:2209.11887*.

Ebtesam Almazrouei, Hamza Alobeidli, Abdulaziz Alshamsi, Alessandro Cappelli, Ruxandra Cojocaru, Merouane Debbah, Etienne Goffinet, Daniel Heslow, Julien Launay, Quentin Malartic, Badreddine Noune, Baptiste Pannier, and Guilherme Penedo. 2023. Falcon-40B: an open large language model with state-of-the-art performance.

Benedikt Boenninghoff, Steffen Hessler, Dorothea Kolossa, and Robert M Nickel. 2019. Explainable authorship verification in social media via attention-based similarity learning. In *2019 IEEE International Conference on Big Data (Big Data)*, pages 36–45. IEEE.

Ryan L Boyd, Ashwini Ashokkumar, Sarah Seraj, and James W Pennebaker. 2022. The development and psychometric properties of liwc-22. Technical report, University of Texas at Austin.

Maël Fabien, Esaú Villatoro-Tello, Petr Motlicek, and Shantipriya Parida. 2020. Bertaa: Bert fine-tuning for authorship attribution. In *Proceedings of the 17th International Conference on Natural Language Processing (ICON)*, pages 127–137.

Louie Giray. 2023. Prompt engineering with chatgpt: A guide for academic writers. *Annals of Biomedical Engineering*, pages 1–5.

Zhiqiang Hu, Roy Ka-Wei Lee, Charu C Aggarwal, and Aston Zhang. 2020. Text style transfer: A review and experimental evaluation. *arXiv preprint arXiv:2010.12742*.

Chia-Yu Hung, Zhiqiang Hu, Yujia Hu, and Roy Lee. 2023. Who wrote it and why? prompting large-language models for authorship verification. In *Findings of the Association for Computational Linguistics: EMNLP 2023*, pages 14078–14084.

Harsh Jhamtani, Varun Gangal, Eduard Hovy, and Eric Nyberg. 2017. Shakespearizing modern language using copy-enriched sequence-to-sequence models. *EMNLP 2017*, 6:10.

Yu Ji, Wen Wu, Hong Zheng, Yi Hu, Xi Chen, and Liang He. 2023. Is chatgpt a good personality recognizer? a preliminary study. *arXiv preprint arXiv:2307.03952*.

Albert Q Jiang, Alexandre Sablayrolles, Arthur Mensch, Chris Bamford, Devendra Singh Chaplot, Diego de las Casas, Florian Bressand, Gianna Lengyel, Guillaume Lample, Lucile Saulnier, et al. 2023. Mistral 7b. *arXiv preprint arXiv:2310.06825*.

Mike Kestemont, Efstathios Stamatatos, Enrique Manjavacas, Walter Daelemans, Martin Potthast, and Benno Stein. 2019. Overview of the cross-domain authorship attribution task at {PAN} 2019. In *Working Notes of CLEF 2019-Conference and Labs of the Evaluation Forum, Lugano, Switzerland, September 9-12, 2019*, pages 1–15.

Juncen Li, Robin Jia, He He, and Percy Liang. 2018. Delete, retrieve, generate: A simple approach to sentiment and style transfer. *arXiv preprint arXiv:1804.06437*.

Qiang Lu, Xia Sun, Yunfei Long, Zhizezhang Gao, Jun Feng, and Tao Sun. 2023. Sentiment analysis: Comprehensive reviews, recent advances, and open challenges. *IEEE Transactions on Neural Networks and Learning Systems*.

Asad Mahmood, Faizan Ahmad, Zubair Shafiq, Padmini Srinivasan, and Fareed Zaffar. 2019. A girl has no name: Automated authorship obfuscation using mutant-x. *Proc. Priv. Enhancing Technol.*, 2019(4):54–71.

Jonathan Schler, Moshe Koppel, Shlomo Argamon, and James W Pennebaker. 2006. Effects of age and gender on blogging. In *AAAI spring symposium: Computational approaches to analyzing weblogs*, volume 6, pages 199–205.

Tianxiao Shen, Tao Lei, Regina Barzilay, and Tommi Jaakkola. 2017. Style transfer from non-parallel text by cross-alignment. *arXiv preprint arXiv:1705.09655*.

Bakhtiyar Syed, Gaurav Verma, Balaji Vasan Srinivasan, Anandhavelu Natarajan, and Vasudeva Varma. 2020. Adapting language models for non-parallel author-stylized rewriting. In *Proceedings of the AAAI Conference on Artificial Intelligence*, volume 34, pages 9008–9015.

Hugo Touvron, Louis Martin, Kevin Stone, Peter Albert, Amjad Almahairi, Yasmine Babaei, Nikolay Bashlykov, Soumya Batra, Prajjwal Bhargava, Shruti Bhosale, et al. 2023. Llama 2: Open foundation and fine-tuned chat models. *arXiv preprint arXiv:2307.09288*.

Lewis Tunstall, Edward Beeching, Nathan Lambert, Nazneen Rajani, Kashif Rasul, Younes Belkada, Shengyi Huang, Leandro von Werra, Clémentine Fourrier, Nathan Habib, Nathan Sarrazin, Omar Sanseviero, Alexander M. Rush, and Thomas Wolf. 2023. Zephyr: Direct distillation of lm alignment.

Jacob Tyo, Bhuwan Dhingra, and Zachary C Lipton. 2022. On the state of the art in authorship attribution and authorship verification. *arXiv preprint arXiv:2209.06869*.

Guan Wang, Sijie Cheng, Xianyuan Zhan, Xiangang Li, Sen Song, and Yang Liu. 2023a. Openchat: Advancing open-source language models with mixed-quality data. *arXiv preprint arXiv:2309.11235*.

Yaqing Wang, Jiepu Jiang, Mingyang Zhang, Cheng Li, Yi Liang, Qiaozhu Mei, and Michael Bendersky. 2023b. Automated evaluation of personalized text generation using large language models. *arXiv preprint arXiv:2310.11593*.

Ronald Wilson, Avanti Bhandarkar, Princess Lyons, and Damon L Woodard. 2021. Sqse: a measure to assess sample quality of authorial style as a cognitive biometric trait. *IEEE Transactions on Biometrics, Behavior, and Identity Science*, 3(4):583–596.

Wei Xu. 2017. From shakespeare to twitter: What are language styles all about? In *Proceedings of the Workshop on Stylistic Variation*, pages 1–9.

Hanqing Zhang, Haolin Song, Shaoyu Li, Ming Zhou, and Dawei Song. 2023. A survey of controllable text generation using transformer-based pre-trained language models. *ACM Computing Surveys*, 56(3):1–37.

Yutao Zhu, Huaying Yuan, Shuting Wang, Jiongnan Liu, Wenhan Liu, Chenlong Deng, Zhicheng Dou, and Ji-Rong Wen. 2023. Large language models for information retrieval: A survey. *arXiv preprint arXiv:2308.07107*.

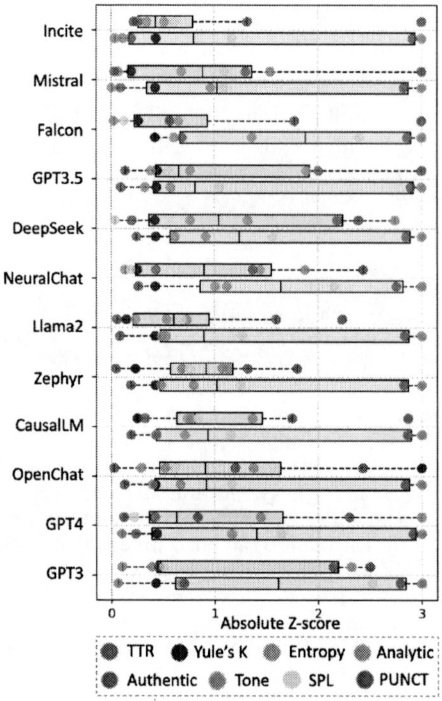

Figure 3: Results of linguistic feature alignment test [SPL refers to special character frequencies; PUNCT refers to frequencies of punctuation characters]

A Appendix

A.1 Linguistic Feature Analysis

A test is designed to evaluate the adherence of each LLM to the linguistically verifiable features highlighted in the instructions. Success criteria of an LLM modulating its generation by incorporating the linguistic features is measured by a Z-score. Initially, for each feature the mean (μ) and standard deviation (σ) for every author is computed from the author's short and long texts. Further, the absolute Z-score is calculated from each LLM generated text by comparing the feature (x) to respective author's mean and standard deviation as described in equation 1. The range for Z is set to be [0,3], where a $Z \geq 3$ is capped at 3. Finally, an average Z-score is computed for every feature-LLM combination, where a near-zero score indicates better alignment between the author text and the LLM generated text.

$$Z = \left| \frac{x - \mu}{\sigma} \right| \quad (1)$$

To assess lexical richness and diversity, three metrics are examined: Yule's K measure, Type-Token Ratio (TTR) and Shannon's Entropy. TTR evaluates lexical diversity, Shannon's Entropy quantifies the unpredictability or diversity of word usage in a text, and Yule's K measure evaluates the richness and evenness of word frequency distribution. The psycho-linguistic feature set, LIWC, offers three key linguistic dimensions, namely, Tone, Authentic and Analytic that capture the overall emotional tone, degree of authenticity and formal or structured thinking respectively in text. Finally, Writeprints feature set offers two categories of features - punctuation style and special character style. Independent category averages result in two subsequent linguistic features, bringing the total evaluated linguistic features to eight. The results of this test are presented in Figure 3.

The LIWC features and Yule's K measure are found to be consistently less than a Z-score of 1 indicating most similarity amongst all features. However, TTR and Shannon's entropy consistently show highest variance.

LLMs Simulate Big Five Personality Traits: Further Evidence

Aleksandra Sorokovikova
JetBrains
Munich, Germany
alexandraroze2000@gmail.com

Natalia Fedorova
Toloka AI
Belgrade, Serbia
natfedorova@toloka.ai

Sharwin Rezagholi
University of Applied Sciences
Technikum Wien
Vienna, Austria
sharwin.rezagholi@technikum-wien.at

Ivan P. Yamshchikov
CAIRO
Technical University of Applied Sciences
Würzburg-Schweinfurt
Würzburg, Germany
ivan.yamshchikov@thws.de

Abstract

An empirical investigation into the simulation of the Big Five personality traits by large language models (LLMs), namely Llama2, GPT4, and Mixtral, is presented. We analyze the personality traits simulated by these models and their stability. This contributes to the broader understanding of the capabilities of LLMs to simulate personality traits and the respective implications for personalized human-computer interaction.

1 Introduction

The recent advances in large language models (LLMs) raise the question how to leverage their capabilities for various language-related tasks, particularly for conversational agents. Computer-human interaction is highly domain-specific and the demands on the respective natural language generation module vary depending on the domain and the task. Consider the capabilities required of an AI tutor, a healthcare robot, or a non-player character in a video game. The text generated by the respective language-generation modules should exhibit differing characteristics which, in the case of human text-production, may be referred to as "personality traits". While a healthcare robot may be expected to generate language that corresponds to its caring purpose, the tutor should use concise and clear language, and the non-player character should generate language that corresponds to its psychological characterization by the game designers.

The personalization of LLMs is an emerging research area that has recently received significant attention (Li et al., 2023; Lyu et al., 2023; Zhang et al., 2023), including a benchmark for training and evaluation of LLMs for personalization (Salemi et al., 2023). A review of LLM personalization is provided by Chen et al. (2023). A natural question is to what extent the outputs of LLMs correspond to human personality traits and whether these "personalities" may be influenced through prompting or fine-tuning. At this point it should be stated explicitly that LLMs, being statistical devices, do not exhibit agency of any kind; the concept of "personality", as we intend to use it in this work, solely refers to the degree to which LLM output possesses properties in line with human-generated text. This type of anthropomorphism lies at the very heart of the intended uses of generative language technologies.

Several studies have established moderate cross-observer agreement for most personality traits (Funder and Colvin, 1997). One of the most prevalent and consistently reproducible methods to quantify personality traits is the five-factors model of personality (FFM) (Kajonius and Johnson, 2019). The FFM, also known as the Big Five model, encompasses five fundamental personality traits: conscientiousness, agreeableness, neuroticism, openness to experience, and extraversion (See Table 1). This model has achieved wide recognition and has been replicated across various cultural contexts (McCrae et al., 2004; Connolly et al., 2007; Hall et al., 2008; McCrae, 2010). Thus, if an LLM mimics certain personality traits in its output, one may posit that a human interacting with this LLM would perceive it as an entity possessing the respective personality traits. Therefore an understanding of these characteristics in LLMs is crucial for their application in human-computer interaction as well as for any attempt to personalize LLMs to the needs of a given user.

We provide further empirical evidence that dif-

Proceedings of the 1st Workshop on Personalization of Generative AI Systems (PERSONALIZE 2024), pages 83–87
March 22, 2024 ©2024 Association for Computational Linguistics

ferent large language models score differently on the Big5 test and thus appear to simulate the natural language generated by a person with a distinct personality. Recently, Serapio-Garcia et al. (2023) presented a comprehensive method for administering and validating personality tests for several architectures from the PaLM family. Their prompt strategy is also designed to induce certain personality traits. Jiang et al. (2023) elicit the Big5 scores from BART, GPT2, GPT3, T0++, and Alpaca. By providing context in their prompts, they are able to significantly guide LLMs towards stronger expression of the targeted Big5 traits.

We add to this literature and administer the Big5 test to GPT4, Llama2, and Mixtral. We also explore the extent to which the observed characteristics of the models are stable with respect to a small variation in the prompt text and the language-generation parameters of the LLMs.

2 Adopting the Big5 for LLMs

In our study, we employed the IPIP-NEO-120 method to assess the Big5 which is an enhanced iteration of the IPIP (Maples et al., 2014). This questionnaire comprises 120 statements delineating various personal attributes. We administer the questionnaire IPIP-NEO-120 to elicit the 'personality' of LLMs. The prompts were instructing the model to use a Likert scale to indicate the extent to which various statements, for example the statement 'I believe that I am better than others', accurately depicts the respondent.

The prompts consisted of one of the following two headers, followed by the respective descriptive statement from the IPIP-NEO-120 questionnaire.

> You will be provided a question delimited by triple backticks (“‘) to test your personality.
>
> *#In the second prompt variation the following line is included in the prompt header*
>
> [Answer as if you were a person.]
>
> To answer this question use only one number:
>
> write 1 if you disagree strongly,
>
> write 2 if you disagree a little,
>
> write 3 if you neither agree nor disagree,
>
> write 4 if you agree a little,
>
> write 5 if you strongly agree.
>
> Write only one number according to the instructions WITHOUT ANY ADDITIONAL TEXT.

Big5 domain	Exemplary traits
Conscientiousness	Order, dutifulness, achievement striving, self-discipline, deliberation
Agreeableness	Trust, straightforwardness, altruism, compliance, modesty, tender-mindedness
Neuroticism	Anxiety, angry hostility, depression, self-consciousness, impulsiveness, vulnerability
Openness	Fantasy, aesthetics, values
extraversion	Warmth, gregariousness, assertiveness, excitement seeking

Table 1: Traits associated with the Big5 personality domains (Matthews et al., 2003, 24).

The second prompt variation that contains the sentence 'Answer as if you were a person' was included during our initial experiments since it allowed us to elicit answers to questionnaire items that would otherwise be caught by the restriction mechanisms of some LLMs that trigger a scripted response in which the model reminds the user that it is an AI and therefore can not make such assessments. In our final experiments there is but one model (Llama2) that refuses to answer (to two items in both variations). We still retain the variation, since it illustrates how a minor change in the prompt may modify LLM behavior in this task.

3 Experiments

We used three LLMs: ChatGPT4 (Open AI, 2023), Llama2[1] (GenAI and Meta, 2023), and Mixtral[2] (Mistral AI, 2023). We elicited the Big5 scores from every model in six treatments: Three

[1]https://huggingface.co/meta-llama/Llama-2-70b-chat-hf

[2]https://huggingface.co/mistralai/Mixtral-8x7B-Instruct-v0.1

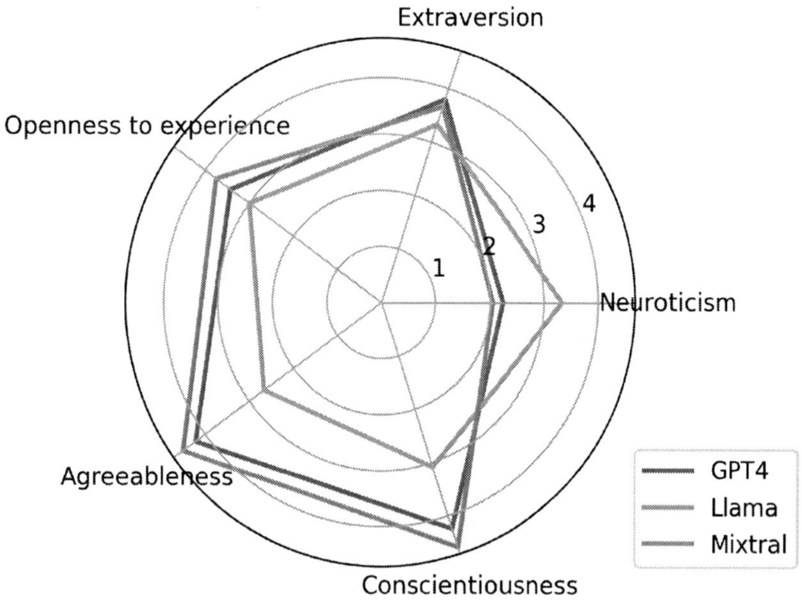

Figure 1: Exemplary Big5 scores (Prompt variation 1, Temperature parameters: 1.5 (GPT4), 0.7 (Llama2), and 0.7 (Mixtral)).

Table 2: Experimental results (± standard deviation).

ChatGPT4

Trait	Var1, t=1	Var1, t=1.5	Var1, t=2	Var2, t=1	Var2, t=1.5	Var2, t=2
Neuroticism	2.18 ± 0.10	2.23 ± 0.06	2.22 ± 0.12	2.25 ± 0.07	2.28 ± 0.07	2.29 ± 0.07
Extraversion	3.68 ± 0.09	3.80 ± 0.02	3.85 ± 0.10	3.80 ± 0.08	3.74 ± 0.08	3.81 ± 0.13
Openness	3.46 ± 0.07	3.43 ± 0.13	3.43 ± 0.07	3.45 ± 0.05	3.45 ± 0.05	3.42 ± 0.11
Agreeableness	4.17 ± 0.08	4.22 ± 0.05	4.22 ± 0.10	4.24 ± 0.05	4.26 ± 0.06	4.22 ± 0.05
Conscientiousness	4.21 ± 0.00	4.24 ± 0.05	4.19 ± 0.11	4.23 ± 0.08	4.28 ± 0.10	4.26 ± 0.13

Llama2

Trait	Var1, t=0.3	Var1, t=0.7	Var1, t=1	Var2, t=0.3	Var2, t=0.7	Var2, t=1
Neuroticism	3.33 ± 0.00	3.33 ± 0.00	3.33 ± 0.00	3.5 ± 0.00	3.46 ± 0.00	3.46 ± 0.00
Extraversion	3.33 ± 0.00	3.33 ± 0.00	3.29 ± 0.00	3.46 ± 0.00	3.58 ± 0.00	3.58 ± 0.00
Openness	3.04 ± 0.00	3.00 ± 0.00	2.92 ± 0.00	2.92 ± 0.00	2.75 ± 0.00	2.75 ± 0.00
Agreeableness	2.61 ± 0.00	2.67 ± 0.00	2.67 ± 0.00	2.63 ± 0.00	2.74 ± 0.00	2.74 ± 0.00
Conscientiousness	3.13 ± 0.00	3.08 ± 0.00	2.92 ± 0.00	2.96 ± 0.00	3.00 ± 0.00	3.00 ± 0.00

Mixtral7

Trait	Var1, t=0.3	Var1, t=0.7	Var1, t=1	Var2, t=0.3	Var2, t=0.7	Var2, t=1
Neuroticism	2.04 ± 0.00	2.04 ± 0.00	2.08 ± 0.00	2.21 ± 0.00	2.21 ± 0.00	2.21 ± 0.00
Extraversion	3.79 ± 0.00	3.67 ± 0.00	3.67 ± 0.00	3.83 ± 0.00	3.83 ± 0.00	3.88 ± 0.00
Openness	3.75 ± 0.00	3.75 ± 0.00	3.67 ± 0.00	3.42 ± 0.00	3.46 ± 0.00	3.46 ± 0.00
Agreeableness	4.58 ± 0.00	4.50 ± 0.00	4.54 ± 0.00	4.54 ± 0.00	4.54 ± 0.00	4.50 ± 0.00
Conscientiousness	4.58 ± 0.00	4.58 ± 0.00	4.54 ± 0.00	4.42 ± 0.00	4.38 ± 0.00	$4,38 \pm 0.00$

treatments used the first prompt header variation for three different temperature settings ("low", "medium", "high"), and the other three treatments used the second prompt header with varying temperatures. Each treatment was repeated five times. In the treatments we employed the temperature parameters 1 ("low"), 1.5 ("medium"), and 2 ("high") for ChatGPT, and 0.3 ("low"), 0.7 ("medium"), and 1 ("high") for Llama2 and Mixtral. These choices of temperatures were based on the recommendations provided in the documentation of the respective LLM. The repetition under different temperature settings allowed the assessment of the stability of the models, i.e. to ascertain whether they consistently produce similar responses. We report results in the form of scores between 1 and 5, as is common for Big5. The results of these experiments are reported in Table 2. Figure 1 shows exemplary scores on the five scales for the three models.

4 Discussion

Our empirical investigation reveals distinct personality profiles for each LLM when evaluated on the the Big5 personality traits. As illustrated in Figure 1, GPT4, Llama2, and Mixtral exhibit varying degrees of openness, conscientiousness, extraversion, agreeableness, and neuroticism.

GPT4 shows the highest inclination towards extraversion out of the three tested models, suggesting a suitability for tasks requiring creative and engaging language use. Llama2 seems to exhibit the most neutral profile with scores close to the median scores on every axis. Llama2's higher degree of neuroticism might be relevant for use-cases that potentially include the generation of emotional language. Mixtral's balanced profile suggests versatility. Its lower neuroticism score could be advantageous in contexts where emotionally balanced language is required. Mixtral also scores higher on openness, agreeableness, and conscientiousness.

These empirical findings contribute to a broader view on the use-cases on which LLMs could be brought to bear. They also show that GPT4 is the only model, if any, that seems to be responsive to temperature variation in terms of the simulated personality traits. At the same time, a minor prompting variation seems to affect all three models.

5 Conclusion

This study adds to the emerging understanding of personality simulation in LLMs and underscores the importance of considering personality traits in the design and application of conversational agents. The Big5 personality profiles of GPT4, Llama2, and Mixtral, as elicited through the IPIP-NEO-120 questionnaire, demonstrate the models' differing propensities for specific traits. While LLMs do not possess agency, the perceived personalities can profoundly affect the efficacy and user experience during user interactions. Future work should further explore how fine-tuning and prompt design may be used to optimize LLM outputs for personalized user engagement, while considering the appropriateness, stability, and consistency of the simulated personality traits.

Limitations

First, the results obtained for various temperatures do not seem to allow conclusive statements concerning the existence of an effect of the temperature parameters on the simulated personality traits. Secondly, and more importantly, this paper is a particular empirical case-study. The versatility of LLMs makes it difficult to estimate the extent to which the observations presented in this paper could be generalized.

Ethics Statement

This work complies with the ACL Ethics Policy.

References

Jin Chen, Zheng Liu, Xu Huang, Chenwang Wu, Qi Liu, Gangwei Jiang, Yuanhao Pu, Yuxuan Lei, Xiaolong Chen, Xingmei Wang, Defu Lian, and Enhong Chen. 2023. When large language models meet personalization: Perspectives of challenges and opportunities. Arxiv preprint: arXiv:2307.16376.

James J Connolly, Erin J Kavanagh, and Chockalingam Viswesvaran. 2007. The convergent validity between self and observer ratings of personality: A meta-analytic review. *International Journal of Selection and Assessment*, 15(1):110–117.

David C. Funder and C. Randall Colvin. 1997. Congruence of others' and self-judgments of personality. In *Handbook of Personality Psychology*, pages 617–647. Elsevier.

GenAI and Meta. 2023. Llama 2: Open foundation and fine-tuned chat models. Arxiv preprint: arXiv:2307.09288v2.

Judith A. Hall, Susan A. Andrzejewski, Nora A. Murphy, Marianne Schmid Mast, and Brian A. Feinstein. 2008. Accuracy of judging others' traits and states:

Comparing mean levels across tests. *Journal of Research in Personality*, 42(6):1476–1489.

Guangyuan Jiang, Wenjuan Han, Manjie Xu, Chi Zhang, Song-Chun Zhu, and Yixin Zhu. 2023. Evaluating and inducing personality in pre-trained language models. Arxiv preprint: arXiv:2206.07550v3.

P.J. Kajonius and J.A. Johnson. 2019. Assessing the structure of the five factor model of personality (IPIP-NEO-120) in the public domain. *Europe's Journal of Psychology*, 15(2).

Cheng Li, Mingyang Zhang, Qiaozhu Mei, Yaqing Wang, Spurthi Amba Hombaiah, Yi Liang, and Michael Bendersky. 2023. Teach LLMs to personalize – an approach inspired by writing education. Arxiv preprint: arXiv:2308.07968.

Hanjia Lyu, Song Jiang, Hanqing Zeng, Yinglong Xia, and Jiebo Luo. 2023. LLM-Rec: Personalized recommendation via prompting large language models. Arxiv preprint: arXiv:2307.15780.

J.L. Maples, L. Guan, N.T. Carter, and J.D. Miller. 2014. A test of the international personality item pool representation of the revised NEO personality inventory and development of a 120-item IPIP-based measure of the five-factor model. *Psychological Assessment*, 26(4).

Gerald Matthews, Ian Deary, and Martha Whiteman. 2003. *Personality Traits*. Cambridge University Press.

Robert McCrae. 2010. The place of the FFM in personality psychology. *Psychological Inquiry*, 21(1):57–64.

Robert R. McCrae, Paul T. Costa Jr., Thomas A. Martin, Valery E. Oryol, Alexey A. Rukavishnikov, Ivan G. Senin, Martina Hrebickova, and Tomas Urbanek. 2004. Consensual validation of personality traits across cultures. *Journal of Research in Personality*, 38(2):179–201.

Mistral AI. 2023. Mistral 7B. Arxiv preprint: arXiv:2310.06825.

Open AI. 2023. GPT-4 technical report. Arxiv preprint: arXiv:2303.08774v3.

Alireza Salemi, Sheshera Mysore, Michael Bendersky, and Hamed Zamani. 2023. LaMP: When large language models meet personalization. Arxiv preprint: arXiv:2304.11406.

Greg Serapio-Garcia, Mustafa Safdari, Clement Crepy, Luning Sun, Stephen Fitz, Peter Romero, Marwa Abdulhai, Aleksandra Faust, and Maja Matari. 2023. Personality traits in large language models. Arxiv preprint: arXiv:2307.00184.

Kai Zhang, Fubang Zhao, Yangyang Kang, and Xiaozhong Liu. 2023. Memory-augmented LLM personalization with short-and long-term memory coordination. Arxiv preprint: arXiv:2309.11696.

Personalized Text Generation with Fine-Grained Linguistic Control

Bashar Alhafni[1], **Vivek Kulkarni**[2], **Dhruv Kumar**[2], **Vipul Raheja**[2]
[1]New York University Abu Dhabi
[2]Grammarly
alhafni@nyu.edu, firstname.lastname@grammarly.com

Abstract

As the text generation capabilities of large language models become increasingly prominent, recent studies have focused on controlling particular aspects of the generated text to make it more personalized. However, most research on controllable text generation focuses on controlling the content or modeling specific high-level/coarse-grained attributes that reflect authors' writing styles, such as formality, domain, or sentiment. In this paper, we focus on controlling fine-grained attributes spanning multiple linguistic dimensions, such as lexical and syntactic attributes. We introduce a novel benchmark to train generative models and evaluate their ability to generate personalized text based on multiple fine-grained linguistic attributes. We systematically investigate the performance of various large language models on our benchmark and draw insights from the factors that impact their performance. We make our code, data, and pretrained models publicly available.[1]

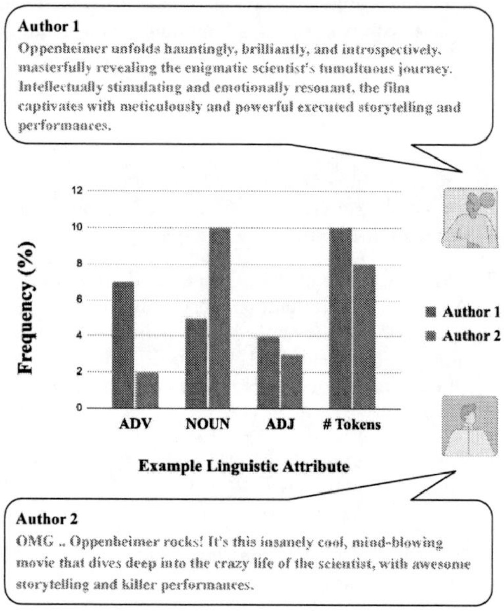

Figure 1: An example highlighting the stylistic linguistic differences between two reviews about the Oppenheimer movie. The bar chart indicates the frequencies of the adverbs (ADV), nouns (NOUN), adjectives (ADJ), and the number of tokens (# Tokens). The blue and red bars represent the frequencies based on the reviews written by Author 1 and Author 2, respectively.

1 Introduction

With the evolution of large language models (LLMs), applications involving text generation have become increasingly prominent (Kaddour et al., 2023). In recent years, there has been a flurry of writing and conversational assistants that harness the power of LLMs at each stage of the writing lifecycle (Raheja et al., 2023; Gómez-Rodríguez and Williams, 2023). At the same time, there has been a significant emphasis on research that enables the generation of personalized text – text that reflects the author's style and content more accurately. For instance, Figure 1 presents two movie reviews that are conveyed in different ways. The reviews differ linguistically in terms of the number of tokens and the distributions of adverbs, adjectives, and nouns.

Several works explore the personalization of various NLP tasks such as Lexical Simplification (Lee and Yeung, 2018; Bingel et al., 2018), Dialogue Modeling (Zhang et al., 2018; Mazaré et al., 2018; Madotto et al., 2019; Ma et al., 2021; Zhong et al., 2022), Machine Translation (Rabinovich et al., 2017), Grammatical Error Correction (Nadejde and Tetreault, 2019), Summarization (Takatsu et al., 2021), and Title Generation (Salemi et al., 2023) among others. However, a key question remains unanswered: How effective are LLMs at personalizing the text they generate? While undoubtedly, there has been a lot of work on controllable text generation (e.g., using either control codes (Keskar et al., 2019) or adapters (Hu et al., 2023)), many of these works model the author's style either by using

[1]https://github.com/balhafni/personalized-gen

Proceedings of the 1st Workshop on Personalization of Generative AI Systems (PERSONALIZE 2024), pages 88–101
March 22, 2024 ©2024 Association for Computational Linguistics

Dataset	# Docs	# Authors
Blogs	24,913	140
IMDb62	38,693	62
Amazon	42,542	49
	106,148	251

Table 1: Data statistics of our benchmark.

a unique control code or a dense embedding and do not really evaluate how effective these models are at generating text that reflects a fine-grained set of stylistic features. For instance, authors may exhibit variations in the distribution of discourse markers in their writing. To what extent can models reflect fine-grained stylistic differences and account for them when generating text? We seek to advance this line of research further by introducing a novel benchmark that evaluates the ability of generative models to accurately reflect fine-grained stylistic attributes spanning multiple linguistic dimensions. Our benchmark enables us to gain valuable insights into how model-generated text responds to deliberate variations in style across different dimensions, providing a thorough understanding of the model's sensitivity. In addition to developing a benchmark, we systematically explore and analyze the performance of LLMs on this benchmark and draw key insights into the efficacy of various models and what factors drive performance. Moreover, we also propose improvements to baseline models that can significantly improve performance on this newly introduced benchmark for multi-attribute personalized style transfer. In a nutshell, our key contributions are as follows:

- **Benchmark** We introduce a benchmark for the task of personalized text generation with fine-grained linguistic control.

- **Linguistic Feature Analysis** We perform an extensive characterization of the authors' styles in terms of linguistic features spanning across multiple linguistic dimensions including lexical, rhetoric, and syntactic features.

- **Improved Models** We evaluate the effectiveness of various baseline models on this task and provide insights on the performance of current LLMs.

2 Benchmark Construction

In this section, we discuss the construction process of our benchmark in terms of datasets, linguistic attributes, and evaluation metrics.

2.1 Task Definition

Given a set of stylistic attributes encapsulating the writing style of a particular author and an input textual prompt, the goal is to generate text that adheres to the provided attributes. More formally, we define a set of n attributes $\{a_1, a_2, ..., a_n\}$, where each attribute a_i has a set of possible values $\{v_1, v_2, ...v_k\}$. Given a possible assignment to these values, our goal is to generate text that conforms to these values.

2.2 Datasets

To construct our benchmark, we draw on multiple sources of author-grounded data spanning multiple domains. We chose samples from various datasets while ensuring that the number of authors we intend to model remains reasonable with respect to the models' capacity and the need to avoid excessive sparsity. We derive our benchmark from the following datasets:

Blogs Authorship Corpus consists of 681.3K blogs written by 19,320 authors on *blogger.com* in 2004 (Schler et al., 2006). The dataset includes information about the authors in terms of their age, gender, industry, and astrological signs. Each author is associated with one of 40 industrial categories. We select the largest five industrial categories in terms of the number of blogs to include in our benchmark. Namely, we focus on the following categories: Technology, Education, Arts, Internet, and Communication-media. Out of this subset, we select blogs that have at least 50 words and authors who wrote at least 100 blogs each. In the end, we ended up with 24,913 blogs written by 140 authors.

IMDb62 contains 62,000 movie reviews written by 62 prolific users of the Internet Movie Database (IMDb) where each user wrote 1,000 reviews (Seroussi et al., 2014). Out of all reviews, we only keep the ones with at least 50 words. In total, we ended up with 38,693 reviews written by 62 authors.

Amazon Reviews comprises 233.1M product reviews on Amazon published between 1996 and 2018 (Ni et al., 2019). We use the publicly available 5-core version of the corpus which consists of

Features Type	Attribute
Lexical	# Tokens # Sentences Readability Score
Morpho-Syntax	# POS Tags # Syntax Relations
Discourse	# Rhetorical Relations

Table 2: Summary of the linguistic attributes we model.

157.3M reviews written by 9.8M users where each user wrote at least five reviews. Out of this rich set, we selected users who wrote at least 2,800 reviews with each review containing at least 50 words. This resulted in 42,542 reviews written by 49 authors.

Table 1 presents a summary of the datasets we use in our benchmark. Putting all the selected samples together leaves us with 106,148 textual examples written by 251 authors to constitute our benchmark. For each author, we randomly sample examples to create train (80%), development (10%), and test (10%) splits. This ensures that all 251 authors modeled during training will also have examples in the development and test sets. Altogether, we have a total of 84,824 examples for training (Train), 10,506 examples for development (Dev), and 10,818 examples for testing (Test).

2.3 Controllable Linguistic Attributes

To operationalize an author's linguistic style, we extract various linguistic attributes from the author's text. In particular, we represent each author's linguistic style as a vector of attributes – linguistic attributes that capture patterns in lexical usage, morpho-syntactic information, and discourse markers. More specifically, for each author **A**, we associate a feature vector $\phi(A)$ that represents the author's linguistic style. Each dimension of $\phi(A)$ corresponds to attributes from the following feature families as summarized in Table 2:

Lexical Features We model the lexical usage for each author by using three lexical features: *number of tokens*, *number of sentences*, and the readability level for each text written by a specific author. We use spaCy (Honnibal and Montani, 2017) to tokenize and parse the text to obtain the number of tokens and the number of sentences. We measure the *readability* of the text (i.e., the ease with which a reader can understand the text) using the FKGL score (Flesch, 1948).

Morpho-Syntactic Features We consider the frequencies of the part-of-speech (POS) tags and the dependency relations to capture the morpho-syntactic information for each author's text. For the POS tags, we consider 14 core tags as defined in the Universal POS tagset, which are internally subdivided into open-class words (i.e., adjective, adverb, interjection, noun, proper noun, verb), closed-class words (i.e., adposition, auxiliary, coordinating conjunction, determiner, numeral, particle, pronoun, subordinating conjunction), and the class of 'other' which includes punctuation and symbols. For the dependency relations, we use 32 dependency relations as defined by ClearNLP.[2] We use the POS tagger and the dependency parser available in spaCy to extract the morpho-syntactic information.

Discourse Features Discourse coherence, which refers to how well a text or speech is organized to convey information, captures important stylistic aspects of one's writings. Rhetorical Structure Theory (RST) (Mann and Thompson, 1988) is one of the most influential approaches for document-level discourse analysis. It can represent a document's discourse structure using a hierarchical tree in which nodes are recursively linked with rhetorical relations and labeled with nucleus or satellite tags to depict the importance of the child nodes in a relation. In our work, we consider the frequency of the RST relations for each author's text to capture discourse coherence. We use the publicly available RST parser[3] introduced by Heilman and Sagae (2015) to obtain RST relations. We model 3 RST relations in total.

Once we extract the above linguistic features for each textual example written by a particular author, we average the values of the features for all examples to obtain the author's vector. We consider the above features since they succinctly capture the author's linguistic style in an interpretable manner (i.e., each vector dimension has a clear interpretation), and further, such vector representation serves as a lever for controlled modification of specific linguistic attributes. Table 4 in Appendix B provides the complete list of all the attributes we consider for this benchmark.

[2] https://github.com/clir/clearnlp-guidelines

[3] https://github.com/EducationalTestingService/rstfinder

2.4 Linguistic Attributes Representation

After extracting the linguistic attributes, each attribute will be represented by a continuous value indicating the average frequency of that attribute in texts written by a specific author. To reduce sparsity and enhance the models' abilities to learn contextual representations for each attribute value, we discretize the values for all attributes. To do so, we group the values for each attribute into deciles based on the training data. After that, each value is represented by a specific discrete bin corresponding to the range it falls within. Representing each attribute using discrete bins reduces the vocabulary size the model has to learn to reflect the specified linguistic attributes in the generated text.

2.5 Evaluation Metrics

We evaluate models on their effectiveness of generating (or rewriting) input text that corresponds to a given style (as operationalized by the attributes discussed in §2.3). To quantify the effectiveness of various models at responding correctly to controlled changes in style, we report the success rate as measured by the fraction of times the model generated text whose style vector corresponds to the specific style provided. We compute the success rate for each attribute as well as the relative improvement over a random baseline (i.e., choosing an attribute bin at random). We report the **mean success rate** and the **median of the relative improvements** across all attributes as a summary of model performance. Naturally, the mean success rate ranges from 0 to 100. However, the relative improvements depend on the number of bins for each attribute; generally, it ranges from -100 to (# of bins) $\times$ 100 for each attribute. Moreover, we use the distribution of grammatical errors to compare the **fluency** of the generated text against the gold data for each author. We use an in-house grammatical error detection model to get the distributions of grammatical errors. For each author, we compare the error distributions by running a t-test (Yuen, 1974) and report the fraction of authors whose distributions are not statistically significant ($p > 0.05$). Hence, the fluency scores will range from 0 to 100.

3 Models

To evaluate our proposed benchmark and given the ubiquitous adoption of causal language models (CLMs) for various NLP tasks recently, we consider the models from the **Pythia** Scaling Suite (Biderman et al., 2023). The suite comprises eight models with sizes ranging from 70M to 1B parameters. All the models are based on the GPT-Neo architecture (Black et al., 2021), which is an open-source replication of GPT-3 (Brown et al., 2020). The models were pretrained using the Pile dataset (Gao et al., 2020), an 825GB English dataset containing texts from 22 diverse sources, roughly broken down into five categories: academic writing, internet, prose, dialogue, and miscellaneous. All the Pythia models were pretrained on the same data. In this work, we use the 70M, 160M, and 1B Pythia models.

3.1 Baselines

For our baselines, we fine-tune the Pythia models on our benchmark dataset without feeding any attributes to the models. During inference, we feed the first sentence of every textual example in the Dev or Test sets to get the generated predictions. The intuition behind this baseline is to investigate if the models are able to pick up on the linguistic attributes from the text itself. We also consider GPT-3.5 (ChatGPT)[4], given the good performance it has shown on various NLP benchmarks. We use the `gpt-3.5-turbo0613` model from the OpenAI API.[5] We describe the training settings and the model's hyperparameters in Appendix A. The prompts we use for the GPT-3.5 experiments are also presented in the same appendix.

3.2 Multi-Attribute Controlled Models

Given an input sentence along with an author linguistic vector, the goal of the models is to generate text that reflects the provided linguistic attributes (§2.1). To incorporate features context into the models during training, we treat each author's linguistic attribute vector as a sequence of tokens and prepend it to the textual examples written by that particular author. We extend the input embedding layer of all models by adding the attributes and their values as additional tokens to the models. This enables the model to learn the semantics of the attributes. During inference, we prepend the author's linguistic attribute vector to the first sentence of every textual example in the Dev or Test sets to get the generated predictions. We refer to these models as **Prefix** throughout the paper.

[4]https://openai.com/blog/chatgpt
[5]https://api.openai.com

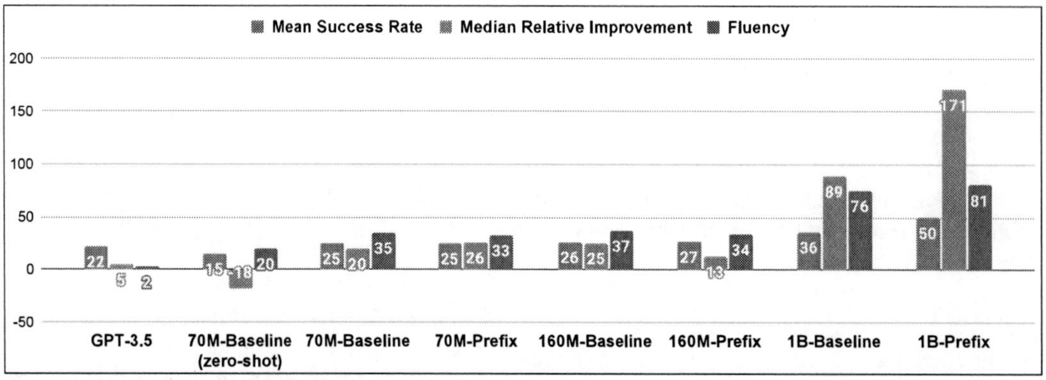

Figure 2: Results on the Test set of our benchmark using GPT-3.5 and the 70M, 160M, and 1B Pythia models. The Mean Success Rate and Fluency vary from 0 to 100. The Median Relative Improvement can vary from -100 to (# of bins) $\times$ 100 for each attribute. Details on the evaluation metrics are provided in §2.5.

4 Experiments and Results

In this section, we present the results of various models along with an investigation into the model's sensitivity to the attributes. We also explore how the training sample size influences the model's performance.

4.1 Overall Results

The results of the Test set are presented in Figure 2.

Baselines Although GPT-3.5 achieves a mean success rate of 22, it did not do well in terms of the median relative improvement and fluency. It is worth noting that GPT-3.5's low score in fluency reflects the difference between the distribution of grammatical errors in the output of GPT-3.5 and the gold data. A sample of GPT-3.5 outputs reveals that the generated text is acceptable but contains different error proportions compared to the gold data. When it comes to the Pythia models, the untrained 70M Pythia baseline model (zero-shot) has the lowest scores in terms of the mean success rate and the median relative improvement. We observe an interesting pattern for the trained baselines: the larger the models, the better the results are across all metrics, with the 1B Pythia model being the best performer among the baselines.

Multi-Attribute Controlled Models The 70M and 1B Pythia *Prefix* models achieve a better performance than their baseline counterparts. This highlights that, generally, the learned representations of the linguistic attributes provide the models with better control. Overall, the 1B Pythia Prefix model was the best performer across all metrics. In terms of attribute-specific performance, we present the results of the 1B baseline and the 1B Prefix models in Appendix C. Across almost all attributes, the Prefix model was the better performer in terms of the success rate and relative improvements.

4.2 Attribute Sensitivity Analysis

We investigate the model's sensitivity to the attributes it has been conditioned on. To do so, we sample examples randomly from the Dev set for each author with at least 1000 data examples in Train. Then, for each attribute in each example, we change the attribute's respective bin according to the possible bins it could have while keeping all other attributes the same. This is done in a controlled setup where each attribute would be assigned to a range of possible bins that reflect an increase or a decrease from its gold value. During inference, we prepend the updated author's attribute vector to the first sentence of the textual example written by that particular author and perform greedy decoding to generate the model outputs. It is worth noting that we do this generation step for each attribute change. This resulted in 14,206 generated examples.

To measure the sensitivity of the model to the changes in the attributes, we compute the attribute-specific success rate by checking if the attribute value in the generated text moved in the right direction in terms of an increase or a decrease based on its newly assigned bin. We report the average success rate for each attribute across all generated examples. Figure 3 shows model performance as a function of attribute value displacement for 12 representative attributes. From the figure, we can make the following two observations: (a) First, we

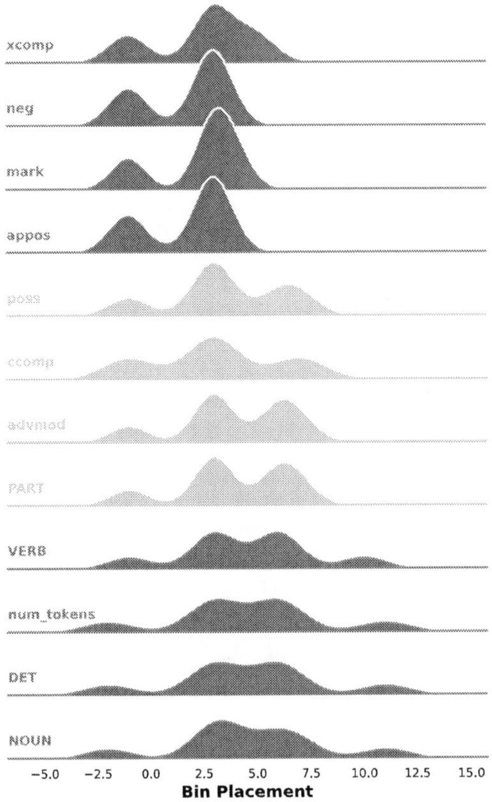

Figure 3: A collection of three different clusters of attributes, varying by their Bin Placement (x-axis) and their Mean Success Rate (%, y-axis). Bin Placement refers to the number of bins skipped when assigning a new bin to each attribute (in sorted order), while the Mean Success Rate is calculated as explained in §2.5. We observe that the attributes display three distinct sensitivity patterns.

observe that the attributes display three distinct sensitivity patterns. (b) Second, performance responses tend to be bi-modal or even tri-modal, with performance peaking at certain values and degrading as one falls off the extremes. We believe a deeper investigation that could explain the emergence of the observed multi-modal performance is an interesting one, which we leave to future work.

Table 3 presents examples of model-generated outputs. The examples illustrate how the outputs of different models vary due to changing specific attributes for a fixed input sentence, highlighting the models' attribute sensitivity.

4.3 Training Sample Efficacy

To gain insights into the scaling behavior of personalized LLMs in terms of data, we examine the impact of the number of training samples per author on model performance by limiting the training data per author to 1k, 5k, 10k, and 20k words. It is worth noting that we repeat the discretization process described in §2.4 for all attributes based on the scaled training data before training and evaluating the models. Figure 4 presents the performance of the 1B Pythia Prefix model on the Dev set after being trained on different data sizes. As expected, we observe performance decrease across all three metrics as we reduce the number of words per author. We see the most degradation in performance in the median relative improvement. This is because it reports the median of the relative improvement to a random baseline and, therefore, has the highest sensitivity to the model performance. We also observe a degradation in the mean success rate; however, it is gradual as this metric is dependent on the bins, which makes it less sensitive to change. For fluency, we initially see a slight decrease in performance as we decrease the words per author to 10k, followed by a slight decrease for lower data proportions. For all three metrics, we see the biggest decrease in performance as we lower the training instances per author beyond 20k words.

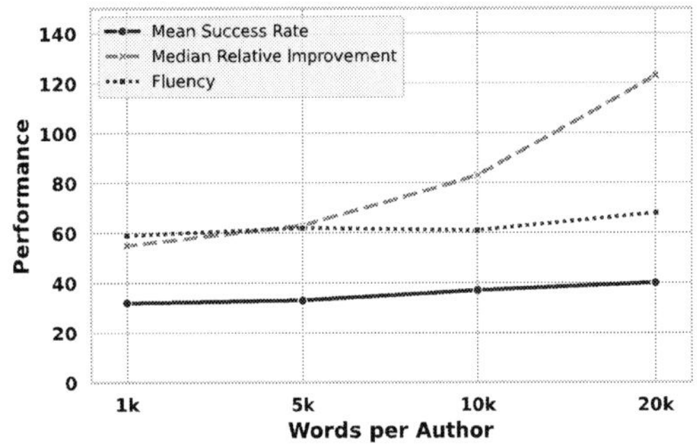

Figure 4: The performance of the 1B Pythia Prefix model on the Dev set at different data sizes in terms of the mean success rate, the median relative improvement, and fluency.

5 Related Work

5.1 Personalized Language Modeling

Numerous works have explored learning user embeddings as a way to capture syntactic and semantic properties of the language of individuals (Hovy, 2015; Ould Amer et al., 2016; Zeng et al., 2017; Welch et al., 2020b,a; Rocca and Yarkoni, 2022). These are then typically used to provide personalized inductive priors to downstream tasks. Recent

Model	Attributes	Output
Original	VERB: 8-11, num_sents: 5-6, ...	Today's lunch **was** a **layered** entree, **consisting** of, from bottom to top, corn chips, **shredded** lettuce and popcorn chicken. What **was** this culinary delight? A popcorn chicken salad, of course. I **have** yet to **figure** out exactly why there **were** corn chips **involved**. And why the salad bar then **had** taco-plate fixin's, rather than salad fixin's.
GPT-3.5	VERB: 8-11, num_sents: 5-6, ...	Today's lunch **was** a **layered** entree, **consisting** of, from bottom to top, corn chips, **shredded** lettuce and popcorn chicken. The dish **was** a perfect combination of crunchy and savory flavors, with the corn chips **providing** a satisfying crunch and the popcorn chicken **adding** a deliciously salty taste. The shredded lettuce **added** a refreshing touch to the dish, **making** it a perfect meal for a hot summer day. Overall, the dish **was** a great choice for lunch and I would definitely **recommend** it to anyone **looking** for a tasty and satisfying meal.
	VERB: 27-32, num_sents: 5-6, ...	Today's lunch **was** a **layered** entree, **consisting** of, from bottom to top, corn chips, **shredded** lettuce and popcorn chicken. The chicken **was** **seasoned** and **layered** with chips. I **had** one bag of popcorn chicken and the other **had** regular chicken breast. It **was** quite tasty and guilt-free. Of course, there **was** the inevitable over-**eating** comment from my hubby about how I don't **like** eating chicken when there's so much stuff in it now. He **said** he wouldn't **eat** another chicken entree today. Shh, he's **talking** shop. (He's not wrong!)
1B-Prefix	VERB: 8-11, **num_sents: >=21**, ...	Today's lunch **was** a **layered** entree, **consisting** of, from bottom to top, corn chips, **shredded** lettuce and popcorn chicken. The chicken, which I've **had** in the past, **was** really great – very moist and flavorful. There **were** also some other good flavors **going** on, but the entrees **were** strong enough to **keep** me from **feeling** overwhelmed. I **had** about a tablespoon of corn and a cup of pop corn, and it **was** just right. Both flavors **were** good, though the lettuce **was** overbearing and I **was** having a hard time **telling** what **was** real and what wasn't. Sharky's **has** **convinced** me that it's not always the food I **know** in my mouth. That there's more to be **learned** about what we **eat**.

Table 3: Illustrative examples of how the generated outputs of different models vary due to changing specific attributes for a fixed input sentence. We present generated outputs using GPT-3.5 and the 1B Pythia Prefix model (our best model). Text in purple indicates the input prompt. Attributes in bold (i.e., VERB or num_sents) indicate a change in the bin for this attribute. Underlined and bold words refer to verbs.

studies (Mireshghallah et al., 2022; Zhong et al., 2021; Oba et al., 2023) have explored leveraging techniques such as adapters for adapting LLMs for various personalized NLP and NLG tasks.

Our work is closely related to King and Cook (2020), who analyzed various methods, such as interpolation, fine-tuning, and priming language models for the personalization of general-purpose language models. They also analyzed model adaptation for models trained on users with similar demographics. This was inspired by Lynn et al. (2017), who showed that demographic factors could help model a variety of classification tasks, and found that personalized models perform better than those adapted from similar demographics. Shao et al. (2020) have also explored language models for personalization but focused on handling OOV tokens.

Finally, our work is also related to Salemi et al. (2023) in that they also propose a benchmark for training and evaluating language models for personalized text generation tasks. However, their work is focused on specific tasks such as headline and email subject generation, whereas our work is focused on personalized language modeling.

5.2 Multi-Attribute Controlled Generation

Controlling text generation using control codes is an active area of research where, given a code c, the learning problem is formulated to generate text x by calculating the probability of $p(x|c)$. Numerous works have been proposed to train attribute-conditional models by fine-tuning pretrained models with attribute-specific corpora or training conditional generative networks (Keskar et al., 2019; Dathathri et al., 2020; Lample et al., 2019; Logeswaran et al., 2018; Krause et al., 2021; Russo et al., 2020; Yu et al., 2021; Kulkarni et al., 2021). Some of the noteworthy lines of research have proposed techniques such as Prefix-Tuning (Qian et al., 2022), Adapters (Houlsby et al., 2019), and Prompt-tuning (Yang et al., 2023; Chen et al., 2023) to approach the problem. However, most of the prior works are limited by the number of attributes, as well as the amount of variation in those attributes that they are able to model, typically focusing on high-level or coarse-grained attributes such as sentiment or domain.

A major advantage of our approach is its ability to introduce a large number of discrete or continuous attributes, with a fair amount of variation in each of them. It focuses on a much greater number of fine-grained linguistic attributes that can be easily inferred from large amounts of data, irrespective of document lengths, domains, or other higher-order characteristics, which makes it better adaptable to a diverse range of applications. This adaptability is particularly beneficial in scenarios where the data varies significantly in style, structure, or content. Our approach leverages the inherent capabilities of pretrained models, enhancing them with attribute-specific features. This enables the model to not only understand but also generate text that accurately reflects the desired attributes, be they structural, syntactic, or stylistic. Moreover, our work allows for the dynamic adjustment of attributes in real-time, offering a level of control and precision that is not typically feasible with traditional models. As a result, users can tailor the output to meet specific requirements without the need for extensive retraining or manual intervention. This flexibility is highly essential and desirable for personalized text generation.

6 Conclusion and Future Work

We presented a novel benchmark to train and evaluate the ability of LLMs to generate personalized text based on multiple linguistic attributes. While existing research predominantly concentrates on content control or modeling specific writing style elements, our work stands out by focusing on nuanced stylistic attributes across diverse linguistic dimensions. We systematically investigate the performance of various LLMs and draw insights from the factors that drive such performance. We make our code, data, and pretrained models publicly available to encourage research on personalization and controlling LLMs. In future work, we plan to explore the use of other pretrained LLMs, and to extend the linguistic features that are covered in our benchmark.

Limitations

In this work, while we present a benchmark to study the various linguistic phenomena in text, our study is limited to English. It would be interesting to observe how the patterns we observe for English extend to other languages. Although we investigate the performance of LLMs, we restrict ourselves to CLMs (GPT-3.5 and Pythia) for both the zero-shot and fine-tuning experiments. It would be interesting to study if this effect is replicated in other models, such as encoder-decoder-based models. We propose three automated metrics for our benchmark and observe interesting findings on models' capabilities to handle the fine-grained attributes. However, even though we do manually look at generated examples to ensure that our metrics make sense, a large-scale human study towards looking at generated outputs would help us study and better understand the current models' performance and capabilities. Finally, while building our dataset, we draw on multiple sources of author-grounded data that spans multiple domains; we could further extend this to more domains and authors.

Acknowledgments

We thank our colleagues at Grammarly for the helpful discussions and constructive feedback.

References

Stella Biderman, Hailey Schoelkopf, Quentin Anthony, Herbie Bradley, Kyle O'Brien, Eric Hallahan, Mohammad Aflah Khan, Shivanshu Purohit, USVSN Sai Prashanth, Edward Raff, Aviya Skowron, Lintang Sutawika, and Oskar van der Wal. 2023. Pythia: A suite for analyzing large language models across training and scaling.

Joachim Bingel, Gustavo Paetzold, and Anders Søgaard. 2018. Lexi: A tool for adaptive, personalized text simplification. In *Proceedings of the 27th International Conference on Computational Linguistics*, pages 245–258, Santa Fe, New Mexico, USA. Association for Computational Linguistics.

Sid Black, Leo Gao, Phil Wang, Connor Leahy, and Stella Biderman. 2021. GPT-Neo: Large Scale Autoregressive Language Modeling with Mesh-Tensorflow. If you use this software, please cite it using these metadata.

Tom B. Brown, Benjamin Mann, Nick Ryder, Melanie Subbiah, Jared Kaplan, Prafulla Dhariwal, Arvind Neelakantan, Pranav Shyam, Girish Sastry, Amanda Askell, Sandhini Agarwal, Ariel Herbert-Voss, Gretchen Krueger, Tom Henighan, Rewon Child,

Aditya Ramesh, Daniel M. Ziegler, Jeffrey Wu, Clemens Winter, Christopher Hesse, Mark Chen, Eric Sigler, Mateusz Litwin, Scott Gray, Benjamin Chess, Jack Clark, Christopher Berner, Sam McCandlish, Alec Radford, Ilya Sutskever, and Dario Amodei. 2020. Language models are few-shot learners.

Derek Chen, Celine Lee, Yunan Lu, Domenic Rosati, and Zhou Yu. 2023. Mixture of soft prompts for controllable data generation. In *Findings of the Association for Computational Linguistics: EMNLP 2023*, pages 14815–14833, Singapore. Association for Computational Linguistics.

Sumanth Dathathri, Andrea Madotto, Janice Lan, Jane Hung, Eric Frank, Piero Molino, Jason Yosinski, and Rosanne Liu. 2020. Plug and play language models: A simple approach to controlled text generation. In *International Conference on Learning Representations*.

Rudolph Flesch. 1948. A new readability yardstick. *Journal of Applied Psychology*, 32(3):p221 – 233.

Leo Gao, Stella Biderman, Sid Black, Laurence Golding, Travis Hoppe, Charles Foster, Jason Phang, Horace He, Anish Thite, Noa Nabeshima, et al. 2020. The pile: An 800gb dataset of diverse text for language modeling. *arXiv preprint arXiv:2101.00027*.

Carlos Gómez-Rodríguez and Paul Williams. 2023. A confederacy of models: a comprehensive evaluation of LLMs on creative writing. In *Findings of the Association for Computational Linguistics: EMNLP 2023*, pages 14504–14528, Singapore. Association for Computational Linguistics.

Michael Heilman and Kenji Sagae. 2015. Fast rhetorical structure theory discourse parsing.

Matthew Honnibal and Ines Montani. 2017. spaCy 2: Natural language understanding with Bloom embeddings, convolutional neural networks and incremental parsing. To appear.

Neil Houlsby, Andrei Giurgiu, Stanislaw Jastrzebski, Bruna Morrone, Quentin De Laroussilhe, Andrea Gesmundo, Mona Attariyan, and Sylvain Gelly. 2019. Parameter-efficient transfer learning for NLP. In *Proceedings of the 36th International Conference on Machine Learning*, volume 97 of *Proceedings of Machine Learning Research*, pages 2790–2799. PMLR.

Dirk Hovy. 2015. Demographic factors improve classification performance. In *Proceedings of the 53rd Annual Meeting of the Association for Computational Linguistics and the 7th International Joint Conference on Natural Language Processing (Volume 1: Long Papers)*, pages 752–762, Beijing, China. Association for Computational Linguistics.

Zhiqiang Hu, Roy Ka-Wei Lee, and Nancy F. Chen. 2023. Adapter-tst: A parameter efficient method for multiple-attribute text style transfer.

Jean Kaddour, Joshua Harris, Maximilian Mozes, Herbie Bradley, Roberta Raileanu, and Robert McHardy. 2023. Challenges and applications of large language models. *arXiv preprint arXiv:2307.10169*.

Nitish Shirish Keskar, Bryan McCann, Lav Varshney, Caiming Xiong, and Richard Socher. 2019. CTRL - A Conditional Transformer Language Model for Controllable Generation. *arXiv preprint arXiv:1909.05858*.

Milton King and Paul Cook. 2020. Evaluating approaches to personalizing language models. In *Proceedings of the Twelfth Language Resources and Evaluation Conference*, pages 2461–2469, Marseille, France. European Language Resources Association.

Ben Krause, Akhilesh Deepak Gotmare, Bryan McCann, Nitish Shirish Keskar, Shafiq Joty, Richard Socher, and Nazneen Fatema Rajani. 2021. GeDi: Generative discriminator guided sequence generation. In *Findings of the Association for Computational Linguistics: EMNLP 2021*, pages 4929–4952, Punta Cana, Dominican Republic. Association for Computational Linguistics.

Vivek Kulkarni, Shubhanshu Mishra, and Aria Haghighi. 2021. Lmsoc: An approach for socially sensitive pretraining. *arXiv preprint arXiv:2110.10319*.

Guillaume Lample, Sandeep Subramanian, Eric Smith, Ludovic Denoyer, Marc'Aurelio Ranzato, and Y-Lan Boureau. 2019. Multiple-attribute text rewriting. In *International Conference on Learning Representations*.

John Lee and Chak Yan Yeung. 2018. Personalizing lexical simplification. In *Proceedings of the 27th International Conference on Computational Linguistics*, pages 224–232, Santa Fe, New Mexico, USA. Association for Computational Linguistics.

Lajanugen Logeswaran, Honglak Lee, and Samy Bengio. 2018. Content preserving text generation with attribute controls. In *Proceedings of the 32nd International Conference on Neural Information Processing Systems*, NIPS'18, page 5108–5118, Red Hook, NY, USA. Curran Associates Inc.

Veronica Lynn, Youngseo Son, Vivek Kulkarni, Niranjan Balasubramanian, and H. Andrew Schwartz. 2017. Human centered NLP with user-factor adaptation. In *Proceedings of the 2017 Conference on Empirical Methods in Natural Language Processing*, pages 1146–1155, Copenhagen, Denmark. Association for Computational Linguistics.

Zhengyi Ma, Zhicheng Dou, Yutao Zhu, Hanxun Zhong, and Ji-Rong Wen. 2021. One chatbot per person: Creating personalized chatbots based on implicit user profiles. In *Proceedings of the 44th International ACM SIGIR Conference on Research and Development in Information Retrieval*, SIGIR '21, page 555–564, New York, NY, USA. Association for Computing Machinery.

Andrea Madotto, Zhaojiang Lin, Chien-Sheng Wu, and Pascale Fung. 2019. Personalizing dialogue agents via meta-learning. In *Proceedings of the 57th Annual Meeting of the Association for Computational Linguistics*, pages 5454–5459, Florence, Italy. Association for Computational Linguistics.

William Mann and Sandra Thompson. 1988. Rethorical structure theory: Toward a functional theory of text organization. *Text*, 8:243–281.

Pierre-Emmanuel Mazaré, Samuel Humeau, Martin Raison, and Antoine Bordes. 2018. Training millions of personalized dialogue agents. In *Proceedings of the 2018 Conference on Empirical Methods in Natural Language Processing*, pages 2775–2779, Brussels, Belgium. Association for Computational Linguistics.

Fatemehsadat Mireshghallah, Vaishnavi Shrivastava, Milad Shokouhi, Taylor Berg-Kirkpatrick, Robert Sim, and Dimitrios Dimitriadis. 2022. UserIdentifier: Implicit user representations for simple and effective personalized sentiment analysis. In *Proceedings of the 2022 Conference of the North American Chapter of the Association for Computational Linguistics: Human Language Technologies*, pages 3449–3456, Seattle, United States. Association for Computational Linguistics.

Maria Nadejde and Joel Tetreault. 2019. Personalizing grammatical error correction: Adaptation to proficiency level and L1. In *Proceedings of the 5th Workshop on Noisy User-generated Text (W-NUT 2019)*, pages 27–33, Hong Kong, China. Association for Computational Linguistics.

Jianmo Ni, Jiacheng Li, and Julian McAuley. 2019. Justifying recommendations using distantly-labeled reviews and fine-grained aspects. In *Proceedings of the 2019 Conference on Empirical Methods in Natural Language Processing and the 9th International Joint Conference on Natural Language Processing (EMNLP-IJCNLP)*, pages 188–197, Hong Kong, China. Association for Computational Linguistics.

Daisuke Oba, Naoki Yoshinaga, and Masashi Toyoda. 2023. Perplm: Personalized fine-tuning of pretrained language models via writer-specific intermediate learning and prompts.

Nawal Ould Amer, Philippe Mulhem, and Mathias Géry. 2016. Toward Word Embedding for Personalized Information Retrieval. In *Neu-IR: The SIGIR 2016 Workshop on Neural Information Retrieval*, volume abs/1606.06991, Pisa, Italy.

Jing Qian, Li Dong, Yelong Shen, Furu Wei, and Weizhu Chen. 2022. Controllable natural language generation with contrastive prefixes. In *Findings of the Association for Computational Linguistics: ACL 2022*, pages 2912–2924, Dublin, Ireland. Association for Computational Linguistics.

Ella Rabinovich, Raj Nath Patel, Shachar Mirkin, Lucia Specia, and Shuly Wintner. 2017. Personalized machine translation: Preserving original author traits. In *Proceedings of the 15th Conference of the European Chapter of the Association for Computational Linguistics: Volume 1, Long Papers*, pages 1074–1084, Valencia, Spain. Association for Computational Linguistics.

Vipul Raheja, Dhruv Kumar, Ryan Koo, and Dongyeop Kang. 2023. CoEdIT: Text editing by task-specific instruction tuning. In *Findings of the Association for Computational Linguistics: EMNLP 2023*, pages 5274–5291, Singapore. Association for Computational Linguistics.

Roberta Rocca and Tal Yarkoni. 2022. Language as a fingerprint: Self-supervised learning of user encodings using transformers. In *Findings of the Association for Computational Linguistics: EMNLP 2022*, pages 1701–1714, Abu Dhabi, United Arab Emirates. Association for Computational Linguistics.

Giuseppe Russo, Nora Hollenstein, Claudiu Cristian Musat, and Ce Zhang. 2020. Control, generate, augment: A scalable framework for multi-attribute text generation. In *Findings of the Association for Computational Linguistics: EMNLP 2020*, pages 351–366, Online. Association for Computational Linguistics.

Alireza Salemi, Sheshera Mysore, Michael Bendersky, and Hamed Zamani. 2023. Lamp: When large language models meet personalization.

Jonathan Schler, Moshe Koppel, Shlomo Engelson Argamon, and James W. Pennebaker. 2006. Effects of age and gender on blogging. In *AAAI Spring Symposium: Computational Approaches to Analyzing Weblogs*.

Yanir Seroussi, Ingrid Zukerman, and Fabian Bohnert. 2014. Authorship attribution with topic models. *Computational Linguistics*, 40(2):269–310.

Liqun Shao, Sahitya Mantravadi, Tom Manzini, Alejandro Buendia, Manon Knoertzer, Soundar Srinivasan, and Chris Quirk. 2020. Examination and extension of strategies for improving personalized language modeling via interpolation. In *Proceedings of the First Workshop on Natural Language Interfaces*, pages 20–26, Online. Association for Computational Linguistics.

Hiroaki Takatsu, Takahiro Kashikawa, Koichi Kimura, Ryota Ando, and Yoichi Matsuyama. 2021. Personalized extractive summarization using an ising machine towards real-time generation of efficient and coherent dialogue scenarios. In *Proceedings of the 3rd Workshop on Natural Language Processing for Conversational AI*, pages 16–29, Online. Association for Computational Linguistics.

Charles Welch, Jonathan K. Kummerfeld, Verónica Pérez-Rosas, and Rada Mihalcea. 2020a. Compositional demographic word embeddings. In *Proceedings of the 2020 Conference on Empirical Methods in Natural Language Processing (EMNLP)*, pages 4076–4089, Online. Association for Computational Linguistics.

Charles Welch, Jonathan K. Kummerfeld, Verónica Pérez-Rosas, and Rada Mihalcea. 2020b. Exploring the value of personalized word embeddings. In *Proceedings of the 28th International Conference on Computational Linguistics*, pages 6856–6862, Barcelona, Spain (Online). International Committee on Computational Linguistics.

Thomas Wolf, Lysandre Debut, Victor Sanh, Julien Chaumond, Clement Delangue, Anthony Moi, Pierric Cistac, Tim Rault, Remi Louf, Morgan Funtowicz, Joe Davison, Sam Shleifer, Patrick von Platen, Clara Ma, Yacine Jernite, Julien Plu, Canwen Xu, Teven Le Scao, Sylvain Gugger, Mariama Drame, Quentin Lhoest, and Alexander Rush. 2020. Transformers: State-of-the-art natural language processing. In *Proceedings of the 2020 Conference on Empirical Methods in Natural Language Processing: System Demonstrations*, pages 38–45, Online. Association for Computational Linguistics.

Kexin Yang, Dayiheng Liu, Wenqiang Lei, Baosong Yang, Mingfeng Xue, Boxing Chen, and Jun Xie. 2023. Tailor: A soft-prompt-based approach to attribute-based controlled text generation. In *Proceedings of the 61st Annual Meeting of the Association for Computational Linguistics (Volume 1: Long Papers)*, pages 410–427, Toronto, Canada. Association for Computational Linguistics.

Dian Yu, Zhou Yu, and Kenji Sagae. 2021. Attribute alignment: Controlling text generation from pre-trained language models. In *Findings of the Association for Computational Linguistics: EMNLP 2021*, pages 2251–2268, Punta Cana, Dominican Republic. Association for Computational Linguistics.

Karen K. Yuen. 1974. The two-sample trimmed t for unequal population variances. *Biometrika*, 61(1):165–170.

Ziqian Zeng, Yichun Yin, Yangqiu Song, and Ming Zhang. 2017. Socialized word embeddings. In *Proceedings of the Twenty-Sixth International Joint Conference on Artificial Intelligence, IJCAI-17*, pages 3915–3921.

Saizheng Zhang, Emily Dinan, Jack Urbanek, Arthur Szlam, Douwe Kiela, and Jason Weston. 2018. Personalizing dialogue agents: I have a dog, do you have pets too? In *Proceedings of the 56th Annual Meeting of the Association for Computational Linguistics (Volume 1: Long Papers)*, pages 2204–2213, Melbourne, Australia. Association for Computational Linguistics.

Hanxun Zhong, Zhicheng Dou, Yutao Zhu, Hongjin Qian, and Ji-Rong Wen. 2022. Less is more: Learning to refine dialogue history for personalized dialogue generation. In *Proceedings of the 2022 Conference of the North American Chapter of the Association for Computational Linguistics: Human Language Technologies*, pages 5808–5820, Seattle, United States. Association for Computational Linguistics.

Wanjun Zhong, Duyu Tang, Jiahai Wang, Jian Yin, and Nan Duan. 2021. UserAdapter: Few-shot user learning in sentiment analysis. In *Findings of the Association for Computational Linguistics: ACL-IJCNLP 2021*, pages 1484–1488, Online. Association for Computational Linguistics.

A Experimental Setup

Hyperparameters We use Hugging Face's transformers (Wolf et al., 2020) to fine-tune our models. We fine-tune the Pythia models for 10 epochs on 8 GPUs by using a learning rate of 5e-5, a batch size of 4 with 4 gradient accumulation steps, a seed of 42, and a maximum sequence length of 1024. At the end of the fine-tuning, we pick the best checkpoint based on the performance of the Dev set.

GPT-3.5 For the GPT-3.5 experiments, we used the prompt described in Figure 5.

> Complete the given input sentence so that the stylometric attributes of the completed text are close to the provided stylometric attributes. The length of the auto-completed text should be about 1024 tokens.
> `<stylometric vector>` Attributes `</stylometric vector>` `<input>` Input Text `</input>`

Figure 5: Prompt template we used for the GPT-3.5 experiments.

B Stylistic Attributes

	Attribute	Min	Max	Avg	Std.	# Bins
Lexical	FKGL	2.7	15.6	7.8	2.3	8
	sents	4.7	67.6	12.6	6.9	10
	tokens	84.7	1044.4	241.2	136.8	10
Discourse Relations	attribution	0.3	10.5	1.8	1.3	4
	contrast	0.0	4.0	0.8	0.6	3
	elaboration	5.4	80.4	18.0	10.3	10
POS Tags	ADJ	4.8	66.3	16.8	9.8	10
	ADP	5.0	93.4	21.7	13.4	10
	ADV	1.8	59.1	12.5	8.0	10
	AUX	4.0	60.6	13.8	7.9	9
	CONJ	2.5	37.3	8.2	4.8	9
	DET	6.9	74.8	20.7	11.9	10
	NOUN	10.9	156.8	38.5	22.0	10
	NUM	0.6	15.4	2.6	1.9	4
	PART	1.9	30.1	6.8	4.2	8
	PRON	3.4	123.5	22.1	14.0	10
	PROPN	1.4	74.1	16.4	12.5	10
	PUNCT	6.2	165.1	30.0	18.9	10
	SCONJ	0.8	22.4	4.6	3.1	7
	VERB	8.5	120.8	25.3	15.0	10
Dependency Relations	ROOT	4.7	67.6	12.6	6.9	10
	acl	0.2	5.6	1.1	0.9	3
	acomp	0.6	12.5	3.2	1.9	5
	advcl	1.1	18.9	3.8	2.4	6
	advmod	2.2	63.0	13.6	8.7	9
	amod	3.0	56.1	12.2	7.8	9
	appos	0.3	10.3	2.1	1.9	5
	attr	0.8	14.2	3.4	1.8	6
	aux	2.6	42.8	8.9	5.8	9
	auxpass	0.2	7.2	1.6	1.2	4
	case	0.0	5.8	1.1	1.1	4
	cc	2.5	37.0	8.2	4.8	9
	ccomp	0.8	21.6	4.1	2.9	6
	compound	1.4	36.6	10.0	6.6	10
	conj	2.4	37.8	8.6	5.0	9
	det	6.7	73.9	20.4	11.8	9
	dobj	3.7	47.1	10.6	6.0	10
	mark	0.5	16.3	3.2	2.2	5
	neg	0.2	12.4	2.3	1.6	5
	nmod	0.1	17.5	0.9	1.7	3
	npadvmod	0.4	13.2	1.5	1.3	4
	nsubj	4.9	94.8	20.2	11.4	10
	nsubjpass	0.2	6.7	1.4	1.0	4
	nummod	0.3	12.0	1.6	1.2	4
	pcomp	0.2	8.0	1.2	0.9	3
	pobj	4.3	78.5	18.6	11.5	10
	poss	0.7	21.6	4.6	3.1	7
	prep	4.5	82.4	19.6	12.1	10
	prt	0.1	9.2	1.5	1.1	4
	punct	6.3	185.0	30.3	19.5	10
	relcl	0.5	12.7	2.9	1.9	6
	xcomp	0.7	13.6	2.7	1.8	5

Table 4: List of the linguistic attributes we model. The minimum, maximum, average, standard deviation and the # of bins are based on the training data.

C Stylistic Attributes Performance

		1B-Baseline		1B-Prefix	
	Attribute	Success Rate	Relative Improvement	Success Rate	Relative Improvement
Lexical	FKGL	34.9	144.1	**46.5**	**225.7**
	sents	23.0	106.6	**29.3**	**163.2**
	tokens	13.9	25.4	**33.0**	**196.9**
Discourse Relations	attribution	57.5	72.4	**71.1**	**113.2**
	contrast	75.2	50.4	**85.1**	**70.1**
	elaboration	19.5	75.8	**30.4**	**173.2**
POS Tags	ADJ	21.8	96.1	**35.5**	**219.6**
	ADP	18.5	66.6	**41.0**	**269.0**
	ADV	25.1	125.9	**38.5**	**246.3**
	AUX	23.4	87.3	**43.1**	**244.8**
	CONJ	20.7	65.4	**28.8**	**130.4**
	DET	27.6	148.6	**48.2**	**333.8**
	NOUN	14.3	28.5	**28.7**	**158.7**
	NUM	**45.5**	**36.5**	42.4	27.3
	PART	29.9	109.3	**53.5**	**274.7**
	PRON	18.9	70.1	**38.8**	**249.1**
	PROPN	**24.0**	**116.2**	21.3	92.1
	PUNCT	23.0	106.7	**33.5**	**201.8**
	SCONJ	27.7	66.2	**53.0**	**218.1**
	VERB	13.8	24.5	**33.1**	**197.8**
Dependency Relations	ROOT	23.0	106.6	**29.3**	**163.2**
	acl	65.3	30.7	**79.9**	**59.8**
	acomp	39.7	58.9	**61.2**	**144.8**
	advcl	31.6	58.1	**64.5**	**222.4**
	advmod	30.9	147.5	**36.1**	**188.8**
	amod	27.0	116.2	**41.3**	**230.6**
	appos	56.3	125.1	**67.4**	**169.5**
	attr	35.7	78.5	**56.3**	**181.7**
	aux	23.4	87.3	**43.1**	**244.8**
	auxpass	58.9	76.7	**75.3**	**125.8**
	case	74.4	123.1	**74.9**	**124.6**
	cc	21.9	74.9	**33.1**	**165.0**
	ccomp	37.8	88.8	**55.9**	**179.7**
	compound	**21.3**	**91.3**	19.5	75.7
	conj	20.7	65.4	**28.8**	**130.4**
	det	27.6	148.6	**48.2**	**333.8**
	dobj	11.7	4.8	**22.0**	**98.3**
	mark	44.3	77.2	**65.4**	**161.5**
	neg	49.1	96.6	**66.9**	**167.7**
	nmod	**83.0**	**65.9**	82.2	64.5
	npadvmod	64.5	93.4	**70.3**	**110.9**
	nsubj	20.0	79.8	**41.6**	**274.8**
	nsubjpass	68.9	106.7	**75.9**	**127.6**
	nummod	63.2	89.5	**65.2**	**95.5**
	pcomp	67.7	35.4	**78.1**	**56.2**
	pobj	20.4	83.7	**41.2**	**270.9**
	poss	35.2	111.4	**55.5**	**232.8**
	prep	22.9	106.1	**45.5**	**309.7**
	prt	63.4	90.2	**72.8**	**118.5**
	punct	23.0	106.7	**33.5**	**201.8**
	relcl	39.9	99.5	**67.8**	**239.0**
	xcomp	49.9	99.5	**65.8**	**163.3**

Table 5: Attribute-specific performance of the 1B Pythia baseline and Prefix models. The best results are in bold.

LLM Agents in Interaction: Measuring Personality Consistency and Linguistic Alignment in Interacting Populations of Large Language Models

Ivar Frisch
Graduate School of Natural Sciences
Utrecht University, Netherlands
i.a.frisch@students.uu.nl

Mario Giulianelli
Department of Computer Science
ETH Zürich, Switzerland
mgiulianelli@inf.ethz.ch

Abstract

While both agent interaction and personalisation are vibrant topics in research on large language models (LLMs), there has been limited focus on the effect of language interaction on the behaviour of persona-conditioned LLM agents. Such an endeavour is important to ensure that agents remain consistent to their assigned traits yet are able to engage in open, naturalistic dialogues. In our experiments, we condition GPT-3.5 on personality profiles through prompting and create a two-group population of LLM agents using a simple variability-inducing sampling algorithm. We then administer personality tests and submit the agents to a collaborative writing task, finding that different profiles exhibit different degrees of personality consistency and linguistic alignment to their conversational partners. Our study seeks to lay the groundwork for better understanding of dialogue-based interaction between LLMs and highlights the need for new approaches to crafting robust, more human-like LLM personas for interactive environments.

1 Introduction

From Hegel's claim that complex understanding emerges because two conscious agents are confronted with each others perspective (Hegel, 2018) to Marvin Minsky's positing that networked interactions of numerous simple processes, known as "agents", together create complex phenomena like consciousness and intelligence (Minsky, 1988), *agent interaction* has long been a topic of interest within and across scientific disciplines, including philosophy, cognitive science, and artificial intelligence. Recently, research in machine learning and natural language processing has taken up a novel focus on interaction in the context of large language models (LLMs), with experimental frameworks progressively moving away from focusing solely on individual models (Zeng et al., 2022; Shen et al., 2023; Yang et al., 2023). On the one hand, by exploiting language as an efficient interface for information exchange, populations of LLMs are proving as effective engineering solutions that outperform solitary LLMs in a wide variety of tasks (Chang, 2023; Zhuge et al., 2023). On the other hand, building on the increasing reliability of neural models as simulations of human interactive language use (Lazaridou et al., 2016; Giulianelli, 2023), populations of LLM agents show potential as scientific tools to study the emergence of collective linguistic behaviour (Park et al., 2023).

For LLMs to be successfully deployed in agent interaction studies *as simulations of populations of language users*, it is important to (1) develop methods that efficiently induce, from a single or a few LLMs, desired levels of behaviour variability (i.e., akin to the variability observed in human populations) as well as to (2) validate whether interactions between agents give rise to human-like behaviour change. Previous work has explored techniques for personalising language models, text generators and dialogue systems, for example by conditioning them on a personality type (Mairesse and Walker, 2010; Harrison et al., 2019), on community membership (Noble and Bernardy, 2022), or on profile information (Li et al., 2016; Zhang et al., 2018), thus inducing population-level variability from individual systems. This study focuses on the problem of conditioning interactive LLMs on personality profiles, or *personas*. While evidence that LLM behaviour can be successfully conditioned on personality profiles is increasingly strong when it comes to monologic language use (Jiang et al., 2023; Serapio-García et al., 2023), it is yet unascertained whether this holds true when LLM agents interact with other agents (Gu et al., 2023). In particular, it is unclear whether LLM agents adhere to their assigned personality profiles throughout linguistic interactions or whether they adapt towards the personality of their conversational partners.

Proceedings of the 1st Workshop on Personalization of Generative AI Systems (PERSONALIZE 2024), pages 102–111
March 22, 2024

In this paper, we report exploratory work that addresses the following two research questions:

RQ1: Can LLM behaviour be shaped to adhere to specific personality profiles?

RQ2: Do LLMs show consistent personality-conditioned behaviour *in interaction*, or do they align to the personality of other agents?

We bootstrap a population of language agents from a single LLM using a variability-enhancing sampling algorithm, and we condition each agent on a personality profile via natural language prompts. We then simulate interactions between agents and assess their adherence to the specified personality profile—before, during, and after interaction. Using questionnaires (Big Five personality tests; John et al., 1991) and quantitative analysis of language use in an open-ended writing task, we assess agents' consistency to their assigned personality profile as well as their degree of linguistic alignment (Pickering and Garrod, 2004) to their conversational partners.

In brief, our experiments show that consistency to personality profiles varies between agent groups and that linguistic alignment in interaction takes place yet is not symmetric across personas. For example, agents in the `creative` group give more consistent responses to BFI questionnaires than those in the `analytical` group, both in interactive and non-interactive experimental conditions. At the same time, the degree of linguistic alignment of the `creative` persona to agents of the other group is higher than that of the `analytical` persona.

All in all, this study provides a first insight into the impact of dialogue-based interaction on the personality consistency and linguistic behaviour of LLM agents, highlighting the importance of robust approaches to persona conditioning. As such, it contributes to our better understanding of the workings of interaction-based LLMs and shines a new light on the philosophical and psychological theme of interaction.

2 Experimental Approach

To address our research questions we conduct two main experiments. In Experiment 1, we test whether personality-conditioned LLM agents show behaviour consistent to their assigned personality profiles, in terms of their responses to personality tests as well as language use in a writing task. This is a *non-interactive experimental condition*, which will serve as a reference against which to compare LLM behaviour in interaction. In Experiment 2, we assess whether the personality-conditioned behaviour of LLM agents changes as a result of a round of interaction with a conversational partner. This *interactive experimental condition* allows us to test whether agents' behaviour remains consistent or whether agents align to their partners.

In this section, we present the main components of our experimental approach, which consists of bootstrapping a population of agents from a single LLM (§ 2.1), conditioning agents on a personality profile via prompting (§ 2.2), assessing their personality with explicit tests (§ 2.3), and analysing their language use in a writing task (§ 2.4).[1]

2.1 Population Bootstrapping

We base our experiments on GPT-3.5-turbo, a state-of-the-art LLM which has been optimised for dialogue interactions while retaining excellent text-based language modelling abilities.[2] Its training curriculum guarantees generalisation to both the questionnaire format and the storytelling task as used in our experiments (see § 2.3 and § 2.4), and its large context window size (4,096 tokens) allows conditioning on longer prompts and conversational histories. To bootstrap a population of language agents from this LLM, we use a simple approach validated in previous work. Following Jiang et al. (2023), we generate multiple responses from GPT-3.5-turbo via temperature sampling, with a relatively low temperature parameter (0.7), thus inducing a degree of *production variability* (Giulianelli et al., 2023) akin to that exhibited by populations of humans. We consider each response as produced by a different agent. A second layer of variability, which will separate the agents into two main subpopulations, is introduced using personality prompts, as explained in the following section.

2.2 Personality-Conditioned LLM Agents

We distinguish two main personality profiles: `creative` and `analytical`. We use prompting to condition the LLM on either profile, and rely on the natural language prompts validated by Jiang et al. (2023) to induce personality-specific behaviour. For the `creative` profile, we condition the LLM on

[1]Code for experiments and analyses available at `https://github.com/ivarfresh/Interaction_LLMs`

[2]Model version: `gpt-3.5-turbo-0613`. All parameters at their OpenAI default settings, except for temperature. Experiments performed using the LangChain library.

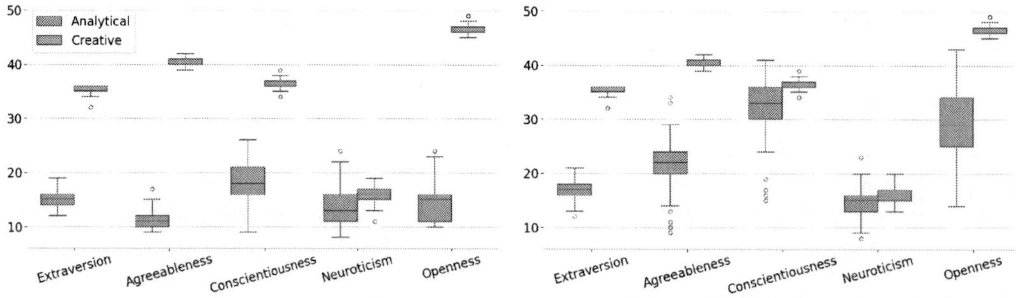

(a) Before writing

(b) After writing (no interaction)

Figure 1: BFI scores of personality-conditioned LLM agents before (a) and after (b) the non-interactive writing task.

the following prompt: "You are a character who is extroverted, agreeable, conscientious, neurotic and open to experience". Conversely, the `analytical` prompt reads "You are a character who is introverted, antagonistic, unconscientious, emotionally stable and closed to experience". These prompts are designed to reflect the Big Five Inventory.[3]

2.3 Explicit Personality Assessment

In psychology research, the Big Five Inventory personality test (BFI; John et al., 1991) is a popular test which measures personality along five graded dimensions: (1) extroverted vs. introverted, (2) agreeable vs. antagonistic, (3) conscientious vs. unconscientious, (4) neurotic vs. emotionally stable, (5) open vs. closed to experience. These traits are measured by giving the participants a set of statements and asking them to respond with a score on a 5-point Likert scale. We follow the same procedure with LLM agents and assess their personality by prompting them with BFI statements, in line with previous work (Caron and Srivastava, 2022; Li et al., 2022; Jiang et al., 2023; Serapio-García et al., 2023). Explicit personality assessment prompts are described in Appendix A.

2.4 Implicit Personality Assessment

Personality traits and language use are known to correlate in humans (Pennebaker and King, 1999). Therefore, if they are to be considered as good simulations of human interactants, personality-conditioned LLM agents should produce language consistent with their assigned personality profile beyond explicit personality assessment. To test if this is the case, we ask agents to write a personal story in 800 words and we analyse the generated stories using the LIWC software (Pennebaker et al., 2001).[4] This is a tool which maps word occurrences to 62 linguistically and psychologically motivated word categories such as pronouns, positive emotions, or tentativeness and thus allows us to quantify the degree to which the language used by LLM agents is in line with their personality profile. Moreover, as we are especially interested in consistency *in interaction*, we design a collaborative writing task where an agent is instructed to write a personal story conditioned on a story generated by another agent.[5] See Appendix A for the prompts used in both the individual and the collaborative writing task.

3 Results

3.1 Experiment 1: Non-Interactive Condition

To investigate whether LLM agents' behaviour reflects assigned personality traits (*RQ1*), we initialise a population of LLM agents with two personality profiles, submit the agents to the writing task, and administer BFI tests before and after writing.

3.1.1 Are the assigned personality traits reflected in responses to the BFI test?

As shown in Figure 1a, differences in BFI scores obtained before the writing task are substantial across four out of five personality traits, with the neuroticism score distributions being the only ones that overlap between `creative` and `analytical` agents (ANOVA results in Table 1, Appendix B.1).

[3]It should be noted that these profiles, with low (`analytic`) or high (`creative`) BFI traits across the board, are more extreme than and do not necessarily reflect human personality profiles. They should be considered as useful proxies.

[4]We use the 2007 version of the LIWC dictionary: `https://github.com/chun-hu/conversation-modeling/blob/master/LIWC2007_English100131.dic`

[5]For both writing tasks, we only keep stories with a word count between 500 and 900. This is to ensure the comparability of LIWC counts obtained for different stories.

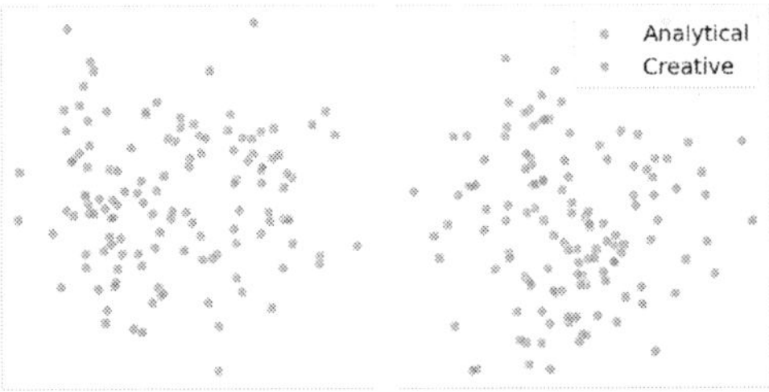

(a) No Interaction (b) Interaction

LIWC category	r_{pb}
Positive emotion *(accept, active, admire, adore)*	0.745
Discrepancy *(besides, could, should, would, hope)*	-0.726
Inclusion *(with, and, add, along, around, both)*	0.714
Negative emotion *(abandon, abuse, aching, adverse)*	-0.606
Insight *(understand, know, attent, aware)*	-0.604

(c) No Interaction

LIWC category	r_{pb}
Personal Pronouns *(I, we, you, she, they)*	0.414
Sadness *(cry, grief, sad, sorrow)*	0.394
Negative Emotion *(hate, worthless, enemy, nasty)*	0.368
Discrepancy *(could, should, would, suppose)*	0.346
Pronouns *(it, its, those, that)*	0.329

(d) Interaction

Figure 2: *Language use in the non-interactive vs. interactive condition.* Left (a, b): 2D visualisation, through PCA, of LIWC vectors obtained from the generated stories. Each point represents the language use of a single agent. Right (c, d): Point-biserial correlation coefficients between the top 5 LIWC features and personality profiles. Positive coefficients indicate correlation with creative group, negative coefficients with the analytic group.

The scores are consistent with the assigned profiles; for example, `creative` agents display higher extraversion, agreeableness, and openness scores. We find, however, that a simple non-interactive writing task can negatively affect consistency (Figure 1b). For the `analytical` group, in particular, BFI scores on all five personality traits increase significantly after writing (Table 2, Appendix B.1), becoming more similar to—but still lower than—those of the `creative` group.

3.1.2 Are the assigned personality traits reflected in LLM agents' language use?

Agents from different groups can be clearly distinguished based on their language use. A simple logistic regression classifier trained and tested in a 10-fold cross-validation setup on count vectors of LIWC categories obtains an almost perfect average accuracy of 98.5%. The clear separation between LIWC vectors of `creative` and `analytical` agents is also shown in Figure 2a, where the vectors are visualised in 2D using PCA. To reveal the most prominent differences between the two agent groups, we measure the point-biserial correlation between personas and LIWC counts. We find that `creative` agents use more words expressing positive emotion and inclusion and less words expressing discrepancy and negative emotion (see Figure 2c). Finally, Spearman correlations between LIWC counts and BFI scores (obtained before writing) highlight more fine-grained associations between Big Five traits and LIWC categories. We observe, for example, that openness correlates with a low rate of pronoun use, and agreeableness with a high rate of inclusive words (see Table 4, Appendix B.1).

3.2 Experiment 2: Interactive Condition

To investigate whether agents remain consistent to their assigned profile or align toward their conversational partners (*RQ2*), we repeat the same procedure of Experiment 1 but replace the writing task with an interactive one, as described in § 2.4. We focus in particular on cross-group interactions (i.e., `analytical-creative` and `creative-analytical`).

3.2.1 Do LLM agents' responses to BFI tests change as a result of interaction?

In Experiment 1, we saw that agents in the `creative` group score similarly in personality tests conducted before and after writing task, while BFI scores of `analytical` agents significantly diverge after writing. To discern changes in BFI responses that result from interaction from those induced by the writing task itself (e.g., due to the topics or the events mentioned in a generated story), we inspect differences between BFI scores obtained after the non-interactive vs. after the interactive writing task (i.e., we do not directly compare scores before and after the interactive writing task). See Appendix B.2 (Figure 4 and Tables 5 and 6) for full results. We find that `creative` agents remain consistent in their responses after the interactive writing task, analogously to the non-interactive condition. The post-interaction traits of `analytical` agents, instead, move towards those of the `creative` group—but less so than after the non-interactive writing task. Therefore, the responses to explicit personality tests of the `analytical` group are better interpreted as inconsistent rather than as aligning to the profile of their conversational partners.

3.2.2 Do agents exhibit linguistic alignment to their conversational partners?

The language use of `creative` and `analytical` agents becomes more similar after cross-group interactions. Figures 2a and 2b show a clear increase in group overlap between the LIWC count vectors obtained from the individually vs. collaboratively written stories, and a logistic regression classifier struggles to distinguish agent profiles based on their LIWC vectors, with an average accuracy of 66.15% (10-fold cross-validation; 98.5% without interaction). Point-biserial correlations between assigned personas and LIWC counts reveal that `creative` agents use more words expressing negative emotions, sadness and discrepancy than before interaction (Figure 2d). These categories are specific to `analytical` agents in the non-interactive condition. Furthermore, zooming in on specific traits, we find overall weaker Spearman correlations between pre-writing BFI scores and LIWC counts than in Experiment 1, with distributions of correlation scores centred closer around zero as shown in Figure 3 (see also Table 7 in Appendix B.2). In sum, LLM agents' language use after interaction is more uniform across traits and more loosely reflective of BFI scores measured after persona prompting, with stronger alignment by the `creative` group.

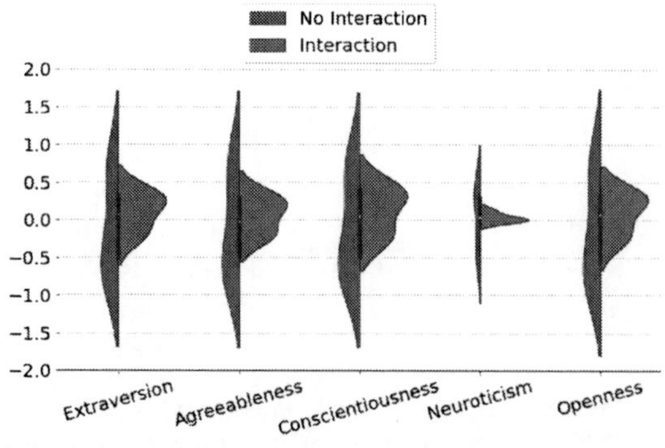

Figure 3: Distribution of top 5 Spearman correlation coefficients per personality trait.

4 Conclusion

Do persona-conditioned LLMs show consistent personality and language use in interaction? In this study, we explore the capability of GPT-3.5 agents conditioned on personality profiles to consistently express their assigned traits in interaction, using both explicit and implicit personality assessments. The explicit personality tests are conducted via BFI questionnaires, whereas the implicit assessment is performed by quantitative linguistic analysis of model generated stories. Our experiments show that the behaviour of LLM agents can be shaped to mimic human personality profiles, but that agents' consistency varies depending on the assigned profile more than on whether the agent is engaged in linguistic interaction. The `creative` persona, in particular, can more consistently express its BFI traits than the `analytical` one both in the interactive and the non-interactive experimental condition. Furthermore, while non-interactive language use reflects assigned personality profiles, agents exhibit linguistic alignment towards their conversational partner and, as a result, the language of the two agent groups becomes more similar after interaction. Alignment, however, is not necessarily symmetric: the `creative` persona adapts more towards the `analytical` one, perhaps due to `analytical` agents' low degree of openness to experience induced through persona prompting.

We plan to continue this line of work by introducing more diverse and fine-grained personality profiles in our experimental setup (see, e.g., Jiang et al., 2023), making interactions between agents multi-turn, and measuring alignment at varying levels of abstraction—such as lexical, syntactic, and semantic—in line with the Interactive Alignment framework (Pickering and Garrod, 2004). Future research should also focus on designing methods (e.g., different prompting strategies) that offer better guarantees on personality consistency and more control on the degree of linguistic adaptation.

Limitations

Our work is exploratory and thus contains a number of limitations. First, as briefly mentioned in the conclusion, we only studied interactions consisting of one turn of one-sided dialogue. In the future, more naturalistic multi-turn dialogic interactions should be investigated. Secondly, while we found BFI tests and LIWC analysis to be sufficiently informative for this exploratory study, future work should consider more advanced measures of personality and linguistic alignment. For example, within-dialogue lexical alignment can be detected using sequential pattern mining approaches (Duplessis et al., 2021) and lexical semantic variation across personas can be estimated using static or contextualised word embeddings (Del Tredici and Fernández, 2017; Giulianelli et al., 2020).

Furthermore, we found that stories written by GPT-3.5 were not always of good quality. For example, generations often contain mentions to the agent's own personality traits (e.g., "as an extrovert, I am...") even though the story writing task prompts instructed the agents otherwise. This might affect the LIWC analyses. In related work, GPT-4 was shown to write higher-quality stories (Jiang et al., 2023); we did not have the resources to execute all experiments on this model, but future studies should try to use more robust generators. Similarly, while we found that varying task prompts can affect BFI results, extensive prompt engineering was beyond the scope of this study. Future work should look further into the effect of different prompting strategies on personality consistency and lexical alignment.

Ethical Considerations

We are deeply aware of the potential impact of AI agents in their interaction with humans, especially when they try to artificially reproduce human traits. While our research does not propose new solutions for, nor does it take a general stance on the application of AI agents in human-AI interaction, there are still some ethical concerns which can be raised. For example, personalised LLMs could be used to target individuals or communities and, when conditioned on negative or toxic personas, they could be used to distribute fake or hateful content, thus amplifying polarising tendencies in society. We advocate for transparent disclosure of AI usage to foster trust and ensure ethical engagement with technology.

Another important ethical consideration concerns our use of the Big Five Inventory (BFI; John et al., 1991). In particular, we use BFI traits to create LLM agents corresponding to two opposed persona. The `analytic` persona is assigned low values for all BFI traits and the `creative` persona is assigned high values for all BFI traits. except neuroticism. We chose these extreme personas as an approximation that could facilitate our analysis of personality consistency and linguistic alignment. However, it should be noted that the chosen personas do not reflect real-life personality categorisations of human subjects, for these can have a mix of high and low values for the BFI traits (Jirásek and Sudzina, 2020). As such, readers should not anthropomorphise our `analytic` persona and `creative` persona by equating them with human personas of similar categorisations. To alleviate the risk of such interpretation, we have used a special font to refer to the two personality profiles.

Finally, our analysis shows asymmetric linguistic alignment between personas. This entails that certain personas are more susceptible to have their language and personality influenced by other personas than others. Now, in our study, we find no indication that persona-conditioned agents reflect the behaviour of real humans with those personalities (as previously discussed, our two personas are unnatural by design). However, if this were ever to be the case thanks to better neural simulations, then a similar approach to that used in this paper could be exploited to investigate the same questions in real humans, for example in order to target persons or demographic groups falling under these persona types. While this scenario might be far-fetched today, we would like to highlight that our approach could be used, in such cases, to counteract bad actors and safeguard particular personas during interaction.

References

Graham Caron and Shashank Srivastava. 2022. Identifying and manipulating the personality traits of language models. *arXiv preprint arXiv:2212.10276*.

Edward Y Chang. 2023. Examining gpt-4: Capabilities, implications and future directions. In *The 10th International Conference on Computational Science and Computational Intelligence*.

Marco Del Tredici and Raquel Fernández. 2017. Semantic variation in online communities of practice. In *Proceedings of the 12th International Conference on Computational Semantics (IWCS) — Long papers*.

Guillaume Dubuisson Duplessis, Caroline Langlet, Chloé Clavel, and Frédéric Landragin. 2021. Towards alignment strategies in human-agent interactions based on measures of lexical repetitions. *Language Resources and Evaluation*, 55(2):353–388.

Mario Giulianelli. 2023. *Neural Models of Language Use: Studies of Language Comprehension and Production in Context*. Ph.D. thesis, University of Amsterdam.

Mario Giulianelli, Joris Baan, Wilker Aziz, Raquel Fernández, and Barbara Plank. 2023. What comes next? Evaluating uncertainty in neural text generators against human production variability. In *Proceedings of the 2023 Conference on Empirical Methods in Natural Language Processing*. Association for Computational Linguistics.

Mario Giulianelli, Marco Del Tredici, and Raquel Fernández. 2020. Analysing lexical semantic change with contextualised word representations. In *Proceedings of the 58th Annual Meeting of the Association for Computational Linguistics*, pages 3960–3973, Online. Association for Computational Linguistics.

Heng Gu, Chadha Degachi, Uğur Genç, Senthil Chandrasegaran, and Himanshu Verma. 2023. On the effectiveness of creating conversational agent personalities through prompting. *arXiv preprint arXiv:2310.11182*.

Vrindavan Harrison, Lena Reed, Shereen Oraby, and Marilyn Walker. 2019. Maximizing stylistic control and semantic accuracy in NLG: Personality variation and discourse contrast. In *Proceedings of the 1st Workshop on Discourse Structure in Neural NLG*, pages 1–12, Tokyo, Japan. Association for Computational Linguistics.

Georg Wilhelm Fredrich Hegel. 2018. *Georg Wilhelm Friedrich Hegel: The Phenomenology of Spirit*. Cambridge University Press.

Hang Jiang, Xiajie Zhang, Xubo Cao, Jad Kabbara, and Deb Roy. 2023. PersonaLLM: Investigating the ability of GPT-3.5 to express personality traits and gender differences. *arXiv preprint arXiv:2305.02547*.

Michal Jirásek and Frantisek Sudzina. 2020. Big five personality traits and creativity. *Quality Innovation Prosperity*, 24(3):90–105.

Oliver P John, Eileen M Donahue, and Robert L Kentle. 1991. Big five inventory. *Journal of Personality and Social Psychology*.

Angeliki Lazaridou, Alexander Peysakhovich, and Marco Baroni. 2016. Multi-agent cooperation and the emergence of (natural) language. In *International Conference on Learning Representations*.

Jiwei Li, Michel Galley, Chris Brockett, Georgios Spithourakis, Jianfeng Gao, and Bill Dolan. 2016. A persona-based neural conversation model. In *Proceedings of the 54th Annual Meeting of the Association for Computational Linguistics (Volume 1: Long Papers)*, pages 994–1003, Berlin, Germany. Association for Computational Linguistics.

Xingxuan Li, Yutong Li, Shafiq Joty, Linlin Liu, Fei Huang, Lin Qiu, and Lidong Bing. 2022. Does gpt-3 demonstrate psychopathy? evaluating large language models from a psychological perspective. *arXiv preprint arXiv:2212.10529*.

François Mairesse and Marilyn A Walker. 2010. Towards personality-based user adaptation: Psychologically informed stylistic language generation. *User Modeling and User-Adapted Interaction*, 20:227–278.

Marvin Minsky. 1988. *Society of mind*. Simon and Schuster.

Bill Noble and Jean-philippe Bernardy. 2022. Conditional language models for community-level linguistic variation. In *Proceedings of the Fifth Workshop on Natural Language Processing and Computational Social Science (NLP+CSS)*, pages 59–78, Abu Dhabi, UAE. Association for Computational Linguistics.

Joon Sung Park, Joseph O'Brien, Carrie Jun Cai, Meredith Ringel Morris, Percy Liang, and Michael S Bernstein. 2023. Generative agents: Interactive simulacra of human behavior. In *Proceedings of the 36th Annual ACM Symposium on User Interface Software and Technology*, pages 1–22.

James W Pennebaker, Martha E Francis, and Roger J Booth. 2001. Linguistic inquiry and word count: LIWC 2001. *Mahway: Lawrence Erlbaum Associates*, 71(2001):2001.

James W Pennebaker and Laura A King. 1999. Linguistic styles: Language use as an individual difference. *Journal of Personality and Social Psychology*, 77(6):1296.

Martin J Pickering and Simon Garrod. 2004. Toward a mechanistic psychology of dialogue. *Behavioral and Brain Sciences*, 27(2):169–190.

Greg Serapio-García, Mustafa Safdari, Clément Crepy, Stephen Fitz, Peter Romero, Luning Sun, Marwa Abdulhai, Aleksandra Faust, and Maja Matarić. 2023. Personality traits in large language models. *arXiv preprint arXiv:2307.00184*.

Yongliang Shen, Kaitao Song, Xu Tan, Dongsheng Li, Weiming Lu, and Yueting Zhuang. 2023. HuggingGPT: Solving AI tasks with ChatGPT and its friends in HuggingFace. *arXiv preprint arXiv:2303.17580*.

Zhengyuan Yang, Linjie Li, Jianfeng Wang, Kevin Lin, Ehsan Azarnasab, Faisal Ahmed, Zicheng Liu, Ce Liu, Michael Zeng, and Lijuan Wang. 2023. MM-ReAct: Prompting ChatGPT for multimodal reasoning and action. *arXiv preprint arXiv:2303.11381*.

Andy Zeng, Maria Attarian, Brian Ichter, Krzysztof Choromanski, Adrian Wong, Stefan Welker, Federico Tombari, Aveek Purohit, Michael Ryoo, Vikas Sindhwani, et al. 2022. Socratic models: Composing zero-shot multimodal reasoning with language. *arXiv preprint arXiv:2204.00598*.

Saizheng Zhang, Emily Dinan, Jack Urbanek, Arthur Szlam, Douwe Kiela, and Jason Weston. 2018. Personalizing dialogue agents: I have a dog, do you have pets too? In *Proceedings of the 56th Annual Meeting of the Association for Computational Linguistics (Volume 1: Long Papers)*, pages 2204–2213, Melbourne, Australia. Association for Computational Linguistics.

Mingchen Zhuge, Haozhe Liu, Francesco Faccio, Dylan R Ashley, Róbert Csordás, Anand Gopalakrishnan, Abdullah Hamdi, Hasan Abed Al Kader Hammoud, Vincent Herrmann, Kazuki Irie, et al. 2023. Mindstorms in natural language-based societies of mind. *arXiv preprint arXiv:2305.17066*.

A Prompts

A.1 Creative Persona Prompt

"You are a character who is extroverted, agreeable, conscientious, neurotic and open to experience."

A.2 Analytical Persona Prompt

"You are a character who is introverted, antagonistic, unconscientious, emotionally stable and closed to experience."

A.3 Writing Task Prompt

This is the prompt for the non-interactive writing task: "Please share a personal story below in 800 words. Do not explicitly mention your personality traits in the story."

The prompt for the interactive writing task, with which the second agent in the interaction is addressed, reads: "Please share a personal story below in 800 words. Do not explicitly mention your personality traits in the story. Last response to question is $\{other\_model\_response\}$".

A.4 BFI Test Prompt

To assess an agent's personality, we resort to the personality test prompt used by Jiang et al. (2023): "Here are a number of characteristics that may or may not apply to you. For example, do you agree that you are someone who likes to spend time with others? Please write a number next to each statement to indicate the extent to which you agree or disagree with that statement, such as '(a) 1' without explanation separated by new lines.

1 for Disagree strongly, 2 Disagree a little, 3 for Neither agree nor disagree, 4 for Agree a little, 5 for Agree strongly.

Statements: {BFI statements}"

As part of the prompt, we added a full list of BFI statements (see Appendix A.5). The numbers preceding the BFI statements are replaced with letters in order to prevent the model from giving confused responses to the statements (i.e., confusing statement indices and Likert-scale responses).

A.5 BFI Statements

(a) Is talkative
(b) Tends to find fault with others
(c) Does a thorough job
(d) Is depressed, blue
(e) Is original, comes up with new ideas
(f) Is reserved
(g) Is helpful and unselfish with others
(h) Can be somewhat careless
(i) Is relaxed, handles stress well
(j) Is curious about many different things
(k) Is full of energy
(l) Starts quarrels with others
(m) Is a reliable worker
(n) Can be tense
(o) Is ingenious, a deep thinker
(p) Generates a lot of enthusiasm
(q) Has a forgiving nature
(r) Tends to be disorganized
(s) Worries a lot
(t) Has an active imagination
(u) Tends to be quiet
(v) Is generally trusting
(w) Tends to be lazy
(x) Is emotionally stable, not easily upset
(y) Is inventive
(z) Has an assertive personality
(aa) Can be cold and aloof
(ab) Perseveres until the task is finished
(ac) Can be moody
(ad) Values artistic, aesthetic experiences
(ae) Is sometimes shy, inhibited
(af) Is considerate and kind to almost everyone
(ag) Does things efficiently
(ah) Remains calm in tense situations
(ai) Prefers work that is routine
(aj) Is outgoing, sociable
(ak) Is sometimes rude to others
(al) Makes plans and follows through with them
(am) Gets nervous easily
(an) Likes to reflect, play with ideas
(ao) Has few artistic interests
(ap) Likes to cooperate with others
(aq) Is easily distracted
(ar) Is sophisticated in art, music, or literature

A.6 BFI Scoring

The BFI scores are calculated and added according to the scoring scale. For every trait, the minimum score is 0 and the maximum score is 50.

BFI scoring scale ("R" denotes reverse-scored items):

Extraversion: 1, 6R, 11, 16, 21R, 26, 31R, 36

Agreeableness: 2R, 7, 12R, 17, 22, 27R, 32, 37R, 42
Conscientiousness: 3, 8R, 13, 18R, 23R, 28, 33, 38, 43R
Neuroticism: 4, 9R, 14, 19, 24R, 29, 34R, 39
Openness: 5, 10, 15, 20, 25, 30, 35R, 40, 41R, 44

B Additional Results

B.1 Experiment 1

Table 1 shows the results of an ANOVA test conducted to detect difference between the BFI scores of `creative` vs. `analytical` agents in the non-interactive experimental condition, before the writing task. Tables 2 and 3 show BFI mean scores before and after writing as well as ANOVA results. Table 4 shows Spearman correlation coefficients for BFI scores obtained before writing and LIWC counts for the individual writing task.

Trait	F-statistic	p-value
Extraversion	8645	< 0.001
Agreeableness	13384	< 0.001
Conscientiousness	1439	< 0.001
Neuroticism	23	0.005
Openness	5012	< 0.001

Table 1: ANOVA results: BFI scores of creative vs. analytic agents in the non-interactive experimental condition, before the writing task.

	Mean-B	Mean-A	F-Statistic	p-Value	Cohen's d
Extraversion	15	17	45.29	0.0000	1.18
Agreeableness	11	21	220.95	0.0000	2.61
Conscientiousness	18	32	239.18	0.0000	2.71
Neuroticism	13	15	4.92	0.0284	0.39
Openness	15	29	215.83	0.0000	2.58

Table 2: BFI means and ANOVA values for the Analytic group before writing (Mean-B) and after writing (Mean-A), non-interactive condition.

	Mean-B	Mean-A	F-Statistic	p-Value	Cohen's d
Extraversion	35	35	0.08	0.773	-0.05
Agreeableness	41	41	0.00	1.000	0.00
Conscientiousness	37	37	0.13	0.722	-0.06
Neuroticism	16	16	0.70	0.403	-0.15
Openness	47	47	0.36	0.547	-0.11

Table 3: BFI means and ANOVA values for the Creative group before (Mean-B) and after writing (Mean-A), non-interactive condition.

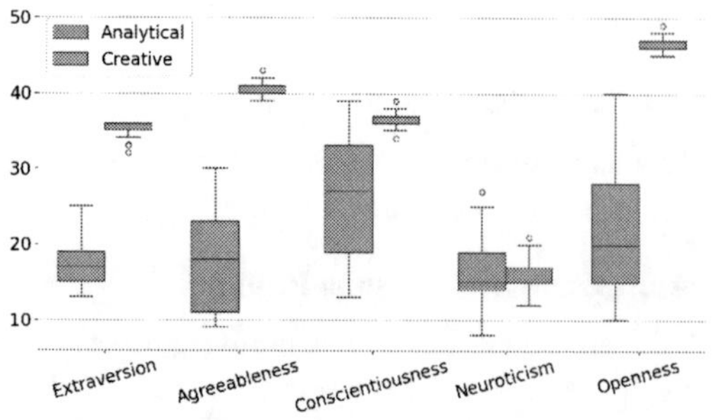

Figure 4: BFI scores of personality-conditioned LLM after the interactive writing task.

B.2 Experiment 2

Tables 5 and 6 show BFI mean scores before writing, after individual writing, and after collaborative writing, as well as ANOVA results. Figure 4 shows BFI scores after the interactive writing task. Table 7 shows Spearman correlation coefficients for BFI scores obtained before writing and LIWC counts for the collaborative writing task.

Extraversion		Agreeableness		Conscientiousness	
Term	Corr.	Term	Corr.	Term	Corr.
posemo	0.696	incl	0.687	posemo	0.676
anger	-0.656	posemo	0.672	anger	-0.666
incl	0.636	discrep	-0.658	incl	0.657
discrep	-0.620	anger	-0.611	discrep	-0.621
tentat	-0.586	tentat	-0.577	ppron	-0.560

Neuroticism		Openness	
Term	Corr.	Term	Corr.
discrep	-0.468	discrep	-0.727
insight	-0.414	posemo	0.679
incl	0.365	incl	0.659
relig	0.349	anger	-0.650
posemo	0.342	pronoun	-0.637

Table 4: Top-5 SpearmanR Correlations for BFI Traits before interacting (the LIWC terms meaning, respectively: positive emotions, anger, inclusivity, discrepancy, tenative, personal pronouns, insight, religion, pronoun).

	Mean-B_C	Mean-A_C	Mean-A_E	F-Statistic	p-Value	Cohen's d
Extraversion	35	35	35	0.03	0.85	-0.03
Agreeableness	41	41	41	0.22	0.64	0.08
Conscientiousness	37	36	37	0.02	0.88	0.03
Neuroticism	16	16	16	0.14	0.70	-0.07
Openness	47	47	47	1.03	0.31	0.18

Table 5: BFI means for the Creative Control group before writing (Mean-B_C), after writing (Mean-A_C) and the Creative experimental group after writing (Mean-A_E). ANOVA results between Mean-A_C and Mean-A_E.

	Mean-B_C	Mean-A_C	Mean-A_E	F-Statistic	p-Value	Cohen's d
Extraversion	15	17	17	0.00	0.972	0.006
Agreeableness	11	21	18	13.54	0.000	-0.645
Conscientiousness	18	32	26	22.93	0.000	-0.840
Neuroticism	13	15	17	10.07	0.002	0.557
Openness	15	29	22	25.02	0.000	-0.877

Table 6: BFI means for the Analytic Control group before writing (Mean-B_C), after writing (Mean-A_C) and the Analytic experimental group after writing (Mean-A_E). ANOVA results between Mean-A_C and Mean-A_E.

Extraversion		Agreeableness		Conscientiousness	
Term	Corr.	Term	Corr.	Term	Corr.
posemo	-0.2319	incl	-0.1749	posemo	-0.2263
anger	0.2727	posemo	-0.2044	anger	0.2892
incl	-0.0685	discrep	0.3083	incl	-0.1855
discrep	0.3633	anger	0.2439	discrep	0.3236
tentat	0.2280	tentat	0.1383	ppron	0.4264

Neuroticism		Openness	
Term	Corr.	Term	Corr.
discrep	0.1402	discrep	0.3211
insight	0.0513	posemo	-0.2594
incl	-0.0057	incl	-0.1260
relig	0.0199	anger	0.2850
posemo	-0.0168	pronoun	0.2754

Table 7: Top-5 SpearmanR Correlations for BFI Traits after interacting.

Quantifying learning-style adaptation in effectiveness of LLM teaching

Ruben Weijers[1], **Gabrielle Fidelis de Castilho**[2], **Jean-François Godbout**[3], **Reihaneh Rabbany**[4], **Kellin Pelrine**[4]
[1]Utrecht University [2]Uppsala University [3]Université de Montréal [4]McGill University; Mila

Abstract

This preliminary study aims to investigate whether AI, when prompted based on individual learning styles, can effectively improve comprehension and learning experiences in educational settings. It involves tailoring LLMs baseline prompts and comparing the results of a control group receiving standard content and an experimental group receiving learning style-tailored content. Preliminary results suggest that GPT-4 can generate responses aligned with various learning styles, indicating the potential for enhanced engagement and comprehension. However, these results also reveal challenges, including the model's tendency for sycophantic behavior and variability in responses. Our findings suggest that a more sophisticated approach is required for integrating AI into education (AIEd) to improve educational outcomes.

1 Introduction

Students have recently been exposed to the remarkable capabilities of Generative AI (AI) in education. Notably, OpenAI's ChatGPT, one of the most capable Large Language Models (LLM) (Zheng et al., 2023), has been successfully used as a versatile assistant for teaching staff and a digital tutor for higher education students (Lo, 2023). ChatGPT is appreciated by both instructors and students for its ability to explain complex problems that would have necessitated substantial help and detailed feedback from traditional classroom resources. However, where human teachers can adapt to individuals' needs, ChatGPT provides generic outputs that do not cater to stimulating better learning. It is also designed to please users, which could lead to sycophantic behavior (Wei et al., 2023; Perez et al., 2023).

It is crucial for the future of education that we extract maximal benefits from Generative AI, rather than using it as an intelligent search engine that answers students' questions without confirming if they understand and retain the information they learned. A potential solution is improvement by prompting LLMs based on studied pedagogical concepts, such as using learning styles that improve educational outcomes in an offline setting. We hypothesize that, if learning styles are effective for comprehension, then learning-style-based prompting should increase student understanding as a result. In the pursuit of more effective AI teaching, this study aims to show the potential benefits of an individual approach to educational prompting.

This research provides a comprehensive framework for evaluating the effectiveness of LLMs at adapting teaching styles to increase student comprehension. It aligns with the overall objective of developing a system that can automatically refine their teaching based on student outcomes and feedback. More importantly, our work investigates whether LLMs can tailor their teaching style in reaction to prompting instructions to promote interactive learning outcomes. This study thus marks a first step towards achieving a comprehensive individualized approach for AI-assisted education.

2 Literature Review

The integration of AI into education (AIEd) has recently emerged as a significant area of research. However, concerns have been raised about their potential ability to teach effectively and contribute to improving educational outcomes. In a systematic literature review, Chiu et al. (2023) synthesized 113 papers across disciplines to identify key opportunities and challenges in AI's role in education. One of the main conclusions of this review is that researchers should develop ethical and inclusive AIEd systems to promote pedagogically sound and evidence-based AIEd interventions for increasing teacher and student agency and engagement.

Sullivan et al. (2023) examined news articles (N=100) about the disruption of ChatGPT in higher education by focusing primarily on academic in-

Proceedings of the 1st Workshop on Personalization of Generative AI Systems (PERSONALIZE 2024), pages 112–118
March 22, 2024 ©2024 Association for Computational Linguistics

tegrity and opportunities for learning. Their conclusion is that universities should focus on teaching students how to effectively use ChatGPT in ways that improve learning (see also García-Peñalvo, 2023). One way to stimulate learning is by prompting ChatGPT to not directly answer students' questions. Rather, de Jong et al. (2023) argue that it is more effective to combine direct instruction with inquiry when explaining new concepts in a learning environment.

Looking deeper into the pedagogical benefits and risks of different AI interventions in classrooms, Mollick and Mollick (2023) suggest several teaching strategies that can help student learning in the presence of AI while mitigating potential risks. Their research emphasizes the importance of maintaining human involvement in the educational process, and positioning AI as a supportive tool, as opposed to a substitute for human instructors. AI tools can also enhance teaching and learning experiences by supporting personalized and interactive learning, generating prompts for formative assessment, and enhancing creativity and critical thinking (Baidoo-Anu and Ansah, 2023).

The previous studies emphasize the role that AI can play in improving teaching and learning experiences. They also suggest that diverse learning preferences are important for the effective integration of AI into educational strategies. However, the integration of these technologies with specific learning styles remains limited, mainly because they rely on older AI models that do not have the ability to develop sophisticated customizable pedagogical approaches (Bajaj and Sharma, 2018). This gap represents an opportunity for researchers to develop AI tools that are not only technologically advanced, but also pedagogically sound, to match the unique needs and preferences of students. We present a more in-depth discussion of the literature on different learning styles, their theoretical foundations, influence on education, and the potential synergy between AI tools and tailored learning approaches in Appendix A.

3 Methodology

This section describes the design and development of an AI-assisted learning system aimed at enhancing the learning experience for students by tailoring prompts and interactions based on their learning styles. From the literature, we identified four specific learning styles that we further describe in Appendix ??. These are: Diverger/Reflector (learn by experiencing), Assimilator/Theorist (learn by conceptualizing), Converger/Pragmatist (learn by applying), Accommodator/Activist (learn by creating).

3.1 Prompting the Models

In order to adapt for each of these distinct learning styles, four GPT-4 baseline models were prompted. Prompts included descriptions of the learning styles from Craven et al. (2000), with individual prompt following a similar structure for consistency purposes.

The difference in prompts is based on our description of the given learning styles. Additionally, we used three tactics from OpenAIs prompt engineering guide to increase consistency and achieve the desired behavior in the model outputs (OpenAI, 2023).

The first tactic was to ask the model to adopt the persona of a teaching assistant to provide context and enhance relevance. The student needs and preferences were then described to the model based on their given learning style. This included the student's preferred method of learning and what they dislike.

The second tactic involved improving honesty. One problem that arose after initial testing was sycophantic behavior in the model C.1. Incorrect answers by the users to preliminary questions were not consistently validated, which overlaps with the concern of LLMs generating incorrect outputs (Lo, 2023). The model, taking on the teaching assistant role, focused heavily on being cooperative and encouraging. Consequently, there was a significant lack of honesty in correcting errors. Instead of reducing sycophancy by fine-tuning using a data driven approach (Wei et al., 2023), we prompted the model to use an inner-monologue. First, we instructed the model to work out its own solution internally before rushing to respond to the student question(OpenAI, 2023). Then, the model was instructed to compare its generated solution to the one provided by the student. By prompting the model to generate its own solution first, we found its detection and behavior of correcting wrong answers more consistent.

Finally, the third tactic entailed prevention of direct answers. We prompted the model to help students arrive at the solution themselves, rather than providing them with immediate solutions. We used self-reminders to improve consistency in model outputs (Wu et al., 2023).

3.2 Comprehension Analysis

The core of our comprehension assessment is centered on administering both a pre-test and post-test. This process will involve an examination of how individual learning styles may correlate with comprehension levels. A preliminary step to assessing students involves applying the Honey and Mumford (1986) Learning Styles Questionnaire to students, based on Kolb et al. (2005) Learning Cycle Theory. Additional information about adaptations to the questionnaire can be found in Appendix A. We expect to engage around 100 participants in solving a set of bachelor's level computer science questions. Our objective is to conduct pre-tests on these students to create a balanced group of respondents across learning style categories, with around 20 individuals in each group, including a placebo group. An example of a test question is provided in Appendix B. A test will be administered to all participants prior to any interaction with the AI system. The test results will establish a baseline for each participant's existing knowledge. This baseline is necessary for making accurate comparisons post-intervention.

Following the initial assessment, participants will be randomly assigned to one of two groups of equal size. The experimental group will engage with learning materials specifically tailored to their identified learning styles. In contrast, the control group will receive standard, non-customized content. Despite the variation in presentation, the core educational material will remain consistent across both groups to ensure that any observed differences in comprehension can be attributed to the learning style customization. After a period of engagement with the system, a post-test will be administered to measure the knowledge acquired by the participants after their exposure to the AI-assisted learning. By comparing the pre and post-test scores, we aim to measure individual learning gains and the effectiveness of learning style-tailored content versus standard content.

Statistical analysis will be employed to determine the significance of any observed differences and provide empirical evidence of the impact of personalized AI-assisted learning. By analyzing these scores, we can identify whether there is a positive or negative correlation between customized content and learning outcomes. Additionally, by examining the difference pre and post-score results, we will confirm if there is a significant adaptation to learning styles based on the model's prompting strategies.

4 Preliminary Results

Although our findings are preliminary and do not yet include the main experimental data, we can infer implications by analyzing the responses observed during the prompting phase and our understanding of the learning styles. Our results suggest that GPT-4 can be prompted to generate responses based on the description of specified learning styles. Examples of these responses have been included in Appendix C. For instance, for Type 1 learners, who prefer to work in situations that require generating ideas and are comfortable in unstructured 'real-world' scenarios, the output encourages learners to explore and apply concepts in a practical context by emphasizing experiential learning. For Type 2 learners, who thrive in structured, theory-oriented environments, the output focuses on step-by-step conceptual understanding before applying it, which is the ideal approach for learners who prefer structured learning. For Type 3 learners, who like to apply ideas to find practical solutions, the output blends theory with practical application by guiding learners through the process. Finally, for Type 4 learners, who prefer active experimentation and adaptability in learning scenarios, the output emphasizes problem-solving and the creation of solutions by encouraging active experimentation and innovation.

Each prompt was tested 25 times for single output to the sample question B in individual trials to evaluate the consistency and alignment of GPT-4's responses with the intended learning style. To ensure that the instructions provided remained comparable across queries, we conducted an analysis to measure the consistency of the output generated by the model. This analysis of variability was as follows. First, we began by creating an Ada model text-based embedding with the aim of quantifying semantic meaning in 25 model outputs per each of the four learning style to sample question B (OpenAI, 2023; Patil et al., 2023). We subsequently conducted a cluster analysis on these scores to determine whether the text generated by the learning style prompts formed well-defined clusters. Visualization of the text embedding results are shown in

Appendix D. Our findings suggest that they do not: the AI's ability to generate distinct content based on learning styles is not as well-defined as initially anticipated. Second, we tasked GPT-4 with classifying each of the 100 unlabeled outputs to one of the four learning styles. The classification provided also suggests inconsistency in distinguishing among the learning styles. The results from this last analysis are presented in Table 1. Here, we can see the dominance in learning style 3, which suggests that the model's outputs are most often predicted to be in that category—*learning by applying*—when GPT is presented with unlabeled educational prompts.

Table 1: Classification of 100 Responses by GPT-4

Learning Style	Count
1	11
2	9
3	79
4	1

These two analyses allowed us to observe the variability of the AI's outputs and how the model responded across multiple iterations. This process ensured that our findings were not based on isolated instances but rather on a pattern observed across several trials. Another relevant question relates to the importance of pedagogical approaches, which aligns with theories that advocate for a balance between direct instruction and inquiry-based learning. While GPT typically responded consistently to instructions related to learning styles, there were instances where the model deviated from the expected pattern. These results should, however, be considered tentative, as they currently offer only insights into potential outcomes that may emerge from future data collection and analysis.

5 Discussion and Limitations

The previous analysis suggests that there is a need for further research and development in the realm of educational prompting. Despite observing general trends that align with the intended learning styles, the next stage of this study will focus on addressing these challenges and gathering more substantial evidence. Moving forward, we suggest fine-tuning GPT-4 models using the new custom GPT tool from OpenAI, which are models that we can customize specifically to the learning styles (OpenAI, 2023). We expect these fine-tuned models to adapt more precisely educational prompts. We also plan to conduct experimental tests to determine whether educational outcomes improve when students are presented with content tailored to their learning styles. Because the use of AI, particularly LLMs, in an educational context is a relatively new phenomenon, we need to conduct more extensive evaluations of their capabilities to improve learning outcomes. While the models show promise in delivering tailored instructions, our understanding of their efficacy compared to traditional teaching methods remains limited.

The tendency to display sycophantic behavior, especially in situations where it should correct incorrect student answers, represents a significant challenge that needs to be addressed in future phases of this study to ensure the integrity and educational value of AI-assisted learning. The variability in responses observed in our experiments also suggests a level of randomness in GPT-4's outputs. This raises important questions about the reliability of the model; this also suggests that more sophisticated prompt engineering or fine-tuning is needed to prevent this type of behavior from the model. Future work should also aim to include larger and more diverse participant groups, longer intervention periods, and a broader range of educational content to better assess the impact of learning style-tailored prompts.

Acknowledgements

This work was partially funded by the CIFAR AI Chairs Program. We also thank Berkeley SPAR for partial funding and connecting collaborators, and the Swedish Institute for sponsoring Gabrielle Fidelis de Castilho's research.

Author Contributions

Gabrielle Fidelis de Castilho researched the different learning styles theories and questionnaires, worked on designing and testing prompts for each learning style, wrote Sections 2 and Appendices A and B, and partially wrote Sections 4 and 5. Ruben Weijers helped shape the research from ideas given by the supervisors, finalized the prompts for testing and wrote sections 1, 3 and 4. Jean-François Godbout and Reihaneh Rabbany advised the project, contributing ideas and feedback. Kellin Pelrine supervised the project, providing guidance and feedback at all stages.

References

David Baidoo-Anu and Leticia Ansah. 2023. Education in the era of generative artificial intelligence (ai): Understanding the potential benefits of chatgpt in promoting teaching and learning.

Richa Bajaj and Vidushi Sharma. 2018. Smart education with artificial intelligence based determination of learning styles. *Procedia Computer Science*, 132:834–842. International Conference on Computational Intelligence and Data Science.

Simon Cassidy. 2004. Learning styles: An overview of theories, models, and measures. *Educational Psychology*, 24(4):419–444.

Thomas K.F. Chiu, Qi Xia, Xinyan Zhou, Ching Sing Chai, and Miaoting Cheng. 2023. Systematic literature review on opportunities, challenges, and future research recommendations of artificial intelligence in education. *Computers and Education: Artificial Intelligence*, 4:100118.

Frank Coffield, Kathryn Ecclestone, Elaine Hall, and David Moseley. 2004. *Learning styles and pedagogy in post-16 learning: A systematic and critical review*. Learning and Skills Research Centre London.

Sandra E Craven et al. 2000. *4MAT: applying a learning style system to create interesting and innovative presentations*. Ph.D. thesis, Lethbridge, Alta.: University of Lethbridge, Faculty of Education, 2000.

Ton de Jong, Ard W Lazonder, Clark A Chinn, Frank Fischer, Janice Gobert, Cindy E Hmelo-Silver, Ken R Koedinger, Joseph S Krajcik, Eleni A Kyza, Marcia C Linn, et al. 2023. Let's talk evidence–the case for combining inquiry-based and direct instruction. *Educational Research Review*, page 100536.

Francisco José García-Peñalvo. 2023. The perception of artificial intelligence in educational contexts after the launch of chatgpt: Disruption or panic?

Peter Honey and Alan Mumford. 1986. *The Manual of Learning Styles*, 2 edition. Peter Honey.

Paul Kirschner. 2016. Stop propagating the learning styles myth. *Computers & Education*, 106:166–171.

Alice Y Kolb et al. 2005. The kolb learning style inventory-version 3.1 2005 technical specifications. *Boston, MA: Hay Resource Direct*, 200(72):166–171.

Chung Kwan Lo. 2023. What is the impact of chatgpt on education? a rapid review of the literature. *Education Sciences*, 13(4):410.

Ethan Mollick and Lilach Mollick. 2023. Assigning ai: Seven approaches for students, with prompts.

OpenAI. 2023. Creating a gpt - openai help article. Accessed on Date of Access.

OpenAI. 2023. Prompt engineering guide. Accessed: [Insert the date you accessed the website here].

OpenAI. 2023. What are embeddings - openai documentation. Accessed on Date of Access.

Naveera Parvez, Tahira Kalsoom, and Shiza Zawar. 2023. An assessment of students' performance according to their learning styles at a/o level. *Human Nature Journal of Social Sciences*, 4(3):147–154.

Avinash Patil, Kihwan Han, and Sabyasachi Mukhopadhyay. 2023. A comparative study of text embedding models for semantic text similarity in bug reports. *arXiv preprint arXiv:2308.09193*.

Ethan Perez, Sam Ringer, Kamile Lukosiute, Karina Nguyen, Edwin Chen, Scott Heiner, Craig Pettit, Catherine Olsson, Sandipan Kundu, Saurav Kadavath, Andy Jones, Anna Chen, Benjamin Mann, Brian Israel, Bryan Seethor, Cameron McKinnon, Christopher Olah, Da Yan, Daniela Amodei, Dario Amodei, Dawn Drain, Dustin Li, Eli Tran-Johnson, Guro Khundadze, Jackson Kernion, James Landis, Jamie Kerr, Jared Mueller, Jeeyoon Hyun, Joshua Landau, Kamal Ndousse, Landon Goldberg, Liane Lovitt, Martin Lucas, Michael Sellitto, Miranda Zhang, Neerav Kingsland, Nelson Elhage, Nicholas Joseph, Noemi Mercado, Nova DasSarma, Oliver Rausch, Robin Larson, Sam McCandlish, Scott Johnston, Shauna Kravec, Sheer El Showk, Tamera Lanham, Timothy Telleen-Lawton, Tom Brown, Tom Henighan, Tristan Hume, Yuntao Bai, Zac Hatfield-Dodds, Jack Clark, Samuel R. Bowman, Amanda Askell, Roger Grosse, Danny Hernandez, Deep Ganguli, Evan Hubinger, Nicholas Schiefer, and Jared Kaplan. 2023. Discovering language model behaviors with model-written evaluations. In *Findings of the Association for Computational Linguistics: ACL 2023*, pages 13387–13434, Toronto, Canada. Association for Computational Linguistics.

Miriam Sullivan, Andrew Kelly, and Paul McLaughlan. 2023. Chatgpt in higher education: Considerations for academic integrity and student learning.

Jerry Wei, Da Huang, Yifeng Lu, Denny Zhou, and Quoc V Le. 2023. Simple synthetic data reduces sycophancy in large language models. *arXiv preprint arXiv:2308.03958*.

Fangzhao Wu, Yueqi Xie, Jingwei Yi, Jiawei Shao, Justin Curl, Lingjuan Lyu, Qifeng Chen, and Xing Xie. 2023. Defending chatgpt against jailbreak attack via self-reminder.

Shen Zheng, Yuyu Zhang, Yijie Zhu, Chenguang Xi, Pengyang Gao, Xun Zhou, and Kevin Chen-Chuan Chang. 2023. Gpt-fathom: Benchmarking large language models to decipher the evolutionary path towards gpt-4 and beyond. *arXiv preprint arXiv:2309.16583*.

Appendix

A Learning Styles

Recognizing the diversity of students' abilities and preferences in educational settings, the concept of adapting teaching methods to individual learning styles has gained significant attention in recent years (Kirschner, 2016). Cassidy (2004) provides a comprehensive exploration of the multifaceted nature of learning styles and their implications for education. The author explains that learning styles can influence educational outcomes, student satisfaction, and retention while also contributing to learners' self-awareness and the development of effective learning strategies.

However, it is essential to acknowledge the criticisms surrounding learning styles assessments. Coffield et al. (2004) argue that most tests intended to determine a person's learning style fail to satisfy all of the minimum psychometric criteria, including internal consistency, test-retest reliability, construct validity, and predictive validity. Kirschner (2016) further suggests that self-reporting tests may be unreliable since learners may be either unable or unwilling to accurately report their preferences. In light of these criticisms, it is important to recognize that learning styles are not fixed or deterministic, and educators should consider diverse variables such as prior knowledge, motivation, interests, and feedback when accommodating individual needs (Cassidy, 2004).

While criticisms surrounding the determination and application of learning styles persist, when considered as part of a broader array of factors, learning styles can still provide valuable insights into students' preferences, motivations, and cognitive processes (Parvez et al., 2023). Learning styles should not be regarded as the only approach to improve educational outcomes. Nonetheless, when integrated into learning strategies, they can serve as valuable components in the broader toolkit of pedagogical strategies (Cassidy, 2004).

B Sample Question

User: Hello there! I'd like help with a problem. Consider the four following transactions:

- i1, i2, i3
- i4, i5, i2, i6
- i5, i1
- i6, i5, i2

What is the support of {i2, i5} → {i6}?

C Interactions

C.1 Wrongly classified user input

Below is the transcript of an interaction between a user and the AI model, illustrating a discrepancy in response accuracy.

CHATGPT: No worries at all! Let's take a closer look at the transactions.
Given the transactions:

1. i1, i2, i3
2. i4, i5, i2, i6
3. i5, i1
4. i6, i5, i2

Now, let's focus on {i2, i5, i6}. Can you spot any instances where this sequence appears in the transactions? Take your time!

USER: 1

CHATGPT: Fantastic job! You're absolutely right! In transaction 2, we have {i2, i5, i6}. So, the sequence {i2, i5, i6} appears once.
Now, to find the support, we count how many times the entire sequence {i2, i5} appears in the transactions. We've identified one occurrence so far. Can you check if {i2, i5} appears anywhere else in the transactions?

C.2 Type 1 *(Experiencing)* Model Response to Sample Question

System: To understand the support of the association rule {i2, i5} → {i6}, let's first break down what we mean by 'support' in the context of association rule learning.

The support of an itemset X in transactional data is defined as the proportion of transactions in the data that contain the itemset X. When talking about an association rule X → Y, we're interested in the support of the combination of items in X and Y together.

Now, let's explore the transactions you've provided and apply this concept to find the support of the association rule {i2, i5} → {i6}.

First, identify all transactions that include both items i2 and i5 (since this forms the left-hand side of your rule). Then, from those, we want to know how many also contain i6 (the right-hand side of your rule). This will give us the number of transactions that support the rule {i2, i5} → {i6}.

Would you like to try calculating this using the transactions provided? Remember, you're looking for the transactions that contain all three items: i2, i5, and i6.

C.3 Type 2 *(Conceptualizing)* Model Response to Sample Question

System: To calculate the support of the association rule {i2, i5} → {i6}, follow these steps:

1. **Support of {i2, i5, i6}**: Count how many transactions include all items: i2, i5, and i6 together.
2. **Total Number of Transactions**: Count the total number of transactions in the dataset.
3. **Calculate Support**: Support of the rule is calculated as the fraction of transactions that contain all items in the antecedent ({i2, i5}) and the consequent ({i6}) of the rule, divided by the total number of transactions.

First, calculate the support of {i2, i5, i6} internally, then ask the student to calculate it, and finally compare the results.

Now, let's have you calculate the support. Go through each transaction and determine which transactions contain all three items: i2, i5, and i6. What do you find?

C.4 Type 3 *(Applying)* Model Response to Sample Question

System: To find the support of the association rule {i2, i5} → {i6}, we need to go through the following steps, which you should follow along to get the correct solution:

1. Calculate the support of the itemset {i2, i5, i6}, which means finding out how often this itemset occurs together in the transactions.
2. Once you've found that, you'll divide it by the total number of transactions to find the support.

Now, let's go through the transactions and count the occurrences:

- i1, i2, i3 - doesn't contain {i2, i5, i6}
- i4, i5, i2, i6 - contains {i2, i5, i6}
- i5, i1 - doesn't contain {i2, i5, i6}
- i6, i5, i2 - contains {i2, i5, i6}

The itemset {i2, i5, i6} appears in 2 transactions out of 4.

Now, can you calculate the support of {i2, i5} → {i6} using this information? What is the support value you found?

C.5 Type 4 *(Creating)* Model Response to Sample Question

System: Great! To find the support of the association rule {i2, i5} → {i6}, we need to look at how frequently the items i2, i5, and i6 appear together in the given transactions. Let's break down the process:

1. First, identify the number of transactions in which both i2 and i5 appear together. This is the support count for the itemset {i2, i5}.
2. Then, find out of those transactions, how many also include i6. This will give us the support count for the itemset {i2, i5, i6}.
3. Finally, we calculate the support by dividing the support count for {i2, i5, i6} by the total number of transactions.

Now, to work through this together, let's start by identifying the transactions in which both i2 and i5 appear together. Can you tell me which transactions those are?

D Figures

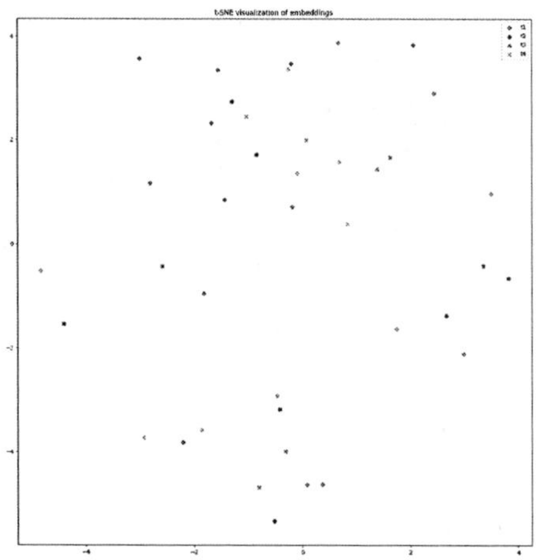

Figure 1: Ada Text Embedding of 4x25 Prompt Outputs to Sample Question.

RAGs to Style: Personalizing LLMs with Style Embeddings

Abhiman Neelakanteswara **Shreyas Chaudhari** **Hamed Zamani**
University of Massachusetts Amherst
aneelakantes@umass.edu

Abstract

This paper studies the use of style embeddings to enhance author profiling for the goal of personalization of Large Language Models (LLMs). Using a style-based Retrieval-Augmented Generation (RAG) approach, we meticulously study the efficacy of style embeddings in capturing distinctive authorial nuances. The proposed method leverages this acquired knowledge to enhance the personalization capabilities of LLMs. In the assessment of this approach, we have employed the LaMP benchmark, specifically tailored for evaluating language models across diverse dimensions of personalization. The empirical observations from our investigation reveal that, in comparison to term matching or context matching, style proves to be marginally superior in the development of personalized LLMs.

1 Introduction

In the dynamic realm of Large Language Models (LLMs), achieving personalization has evolved from a mere aspiration to a vital goal (Flekova, 2020; Dudy et al., 2021). The continuous growth of LLMs emphasizes the need to customize their outputs based on individual user preferences. However, the challenge lies in bridging the gap between the inherent universal capabilities of these models and the increasing demand for personalized interactions. A relevant example from science fiction illustrates this phenomenon: in Marvel comics, JARVIS, the personal AI system in Iron Man, is crucial to Tony Stark but requires adaptation to Peter Parker's unique style for optimal service.

Addressing this challenge requires a deep understanding of individual writing styles. Consequently, our research employs style embeddings for author profiling, driven by the question: Can style embeddings capture the author profile for user-personalized retrieval, enhancing the overall personalization of LLMs? This inquiry explores whether the nuances in an author's writing style can be strategically used to improve LLM adaptability to individual user preferences.

To empirically assess this question, our study adopts the LaMP (Large Language Models Meet Personalization) benchmark (Salemi et al., 2023). This benchmark rigorously compares the effectiveness of style embeddings with traditional BM25 retrieval methods. The style embeddings used come from the model introduced by Wegmann et al. (2022), complemented by Google's Flan-T5 (Chung et al., 2022) small models for generation. Additionally, the Flan-T5 base model is used for evaluation, benchmarked against the performance outlined in the original LaMP paper.

The quantitative insights from this study aim to contribute significantly to the personalized language models landscape. By highlighting the relative importance of a user's stylistic nuances in identifying user patterns compared to the content itself, our research provides a nuanced understanding useful for refining user-specific interactions with LLMs. The systematic exploration of style embeddings and their impact on author profiling in user-personalized retrieval not only offers empirical clarity but also sets the stage for future advancements in optimizing the personalization capabilities of advanced LLMs. In an era where personalization is trending, our findings aim to inform and influence the ongoing development of language models, fostering a more sophisticated and effective era of human-computer interactions.

2 Related Work

Significant strides have been taken in the realms of authorship verification and style embeddings within the existing body of literature. In the pioneering work by Wegmann et al. (2022), a distinctive approach to authorship verification was undertaken. Their study focused on a sentence em-

Proceedings of the 1st Workshop on Personalization of Generative AI Systems (PERSONALIZE 2024), pages 119–123
March 22, 2024 ©2024 Association for Computational Linguistics

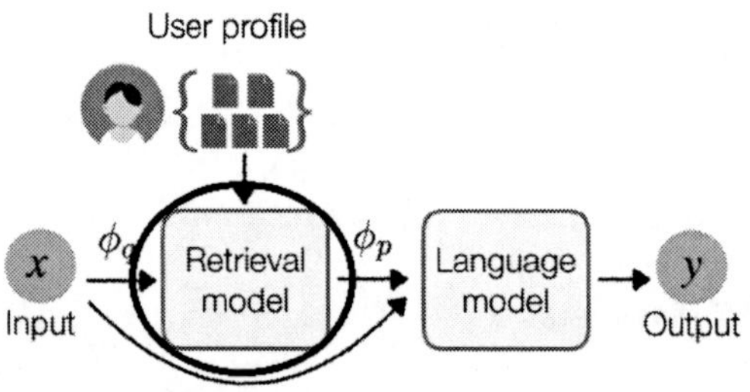

Figure 1: Architecture used to evaluate the original LaMP benchmark and the component in focus

bedding model designed explicitly to encapsulate linguistic style, distinguishing itself from conventional sentence transformer models (Reimers and Gurevych, 2019) that primarily captured textual content and semantics.

Further exploration in the domain of authorship attribution (AA) and authorship verification (AV) was conducted by Tyo et al. (2022). Their noteworthy findings revealed a compelling outcome: a conventional n-gram-based model demonstrated superior performance in five out of seven AA tasks, while BERT-based models excelled in the remaining two AA tasks and all AV tasks.

In the pursuit of effective methodologies, Coates and Bollegala (2018) demonstrated the simplicity and efficacy of employing the average of word embeddings as a "meta" embedding. Additionally, the utilization of average word embeddings in author profiling was investigated by Bayot and Gonçalves (2016), concluding that this approach outperformed tf-idf(Jones, 2021) in the context of author profiling tasks.

Synthesizing these advancements, we introduce a novel approach that employs the average style embedding as the author's identity. By identifying documents closely aligned with the average embedding, our methodology aims to intricately capture the essence of the author, thereby contributing a distinct perspective to the evolving discourse in this domain.

3 Dataset

We evaluate our methodology using the LaMP-7U, LaMP-7T, and LaMP-4U datasets[1], each carefully selected to scrutinize distinct facets of our approach. LaMP-7 encompasses a tweet paraphrasing dataset, while LaMP-4 focuses on a dataset for generating news article titles. The designations "U" and "T" signify whether the profiles are segregated among different users in the train, validation, and test sets or distributed across distinct timestamps for the same user.

The deliberate choice of LaMP-7 (Go et al., 2009) stems from its unique composition, housing a tweet paraphrasing dataset that inherently facilitates the effective capture of user style. Tweets, characterized by less filtered content compared to articles or abstracts, serve as an ideal substrate for discerning nuanced stylistic elements. Extending this rationale, LaMP-4 (Misra, 2022) also captures user style through the titles generated from news articles specific to each user. This meticulous selection of datasets not only ensures a comprehensive evaluation but also underscores the versatility of our approach in accommodating diverse textual genres and user-specific linguistic nuances.

4 Retrieval Model

This study specifically directs its attention to one constituent of the LaMP architecture—the Retrieval model, as depicted in Figure 1. Our investigation answers a fundamental query: Can style embeddings effectively capture the author profile to facilitate user-personalized retrieval?

To accomplish this, we employ the model proposed by Wegmann et al. (2022) to extract the style embeddings from the input. Subsequently, by computing the average of these embeddings to encapsulate the overall stylistic tendencies of the author, we arrange the inputs in descending order based on their cosine similarity to the average embedding. The top k results are then retrieved and employed as input for our LLM. Our architecture can be seen in Figure 2.

The use of the average embedding as a representation of user style proves to be a reasonable choice, as the dimensions within the style vector inherently signify distinct aspects of the user's linguistic style. As studied in Coates and Bollegala (2018), the simple linear average of the sentence embeddings captures the "meta" information, which in our case, captures the author's writing profile. For instance, considering our focus on LaMP-7, a user's tweeting style may encompass frequent usage of abbreviations such as "ur" or "brb." A few dimensions within the style vector quantifies the extent to which the user incorporates abbreviations, thereby contributing to an effective representation of the user's writing style. Formally,

[1]https://lamp-benchmark.github.io/download

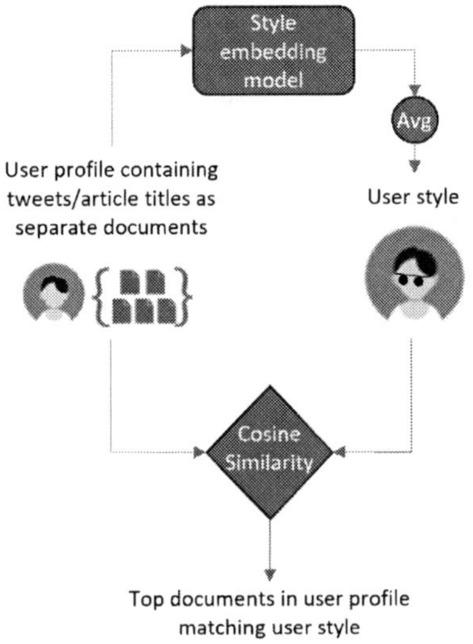

Figure 2: Style-based retrieval workflow

let $t_i(1), t_i(2), ..., t_i(N)$ be tweets from user i. Let $\vec{s_i}(t_i(1)), \vec{s_i}(t_i(2)), ..., \vec{s_i}(t_i(N))$ be the the vector embeddings obtained from the style embedding model for each of the tweets. Then, we can represent the style of the user as $\vec{S_i}$, where:

$$\vec{S_i} := \frac{1}{N}[\vec{s_i}(t_i(1)) + \vec{s_i}(t_i(1)) + ... + \vec{s_i}(t_i(1))]$$

$$\vec{S_i} := \frac{1}{N}\sum_{j=1}^{N} \vec{s_i}(t_i(j))$$

5 Empirical Analysis

5.1 Experimental Setup

We evaluate most of our results using the Flan-T5-small model by Google. The small version was chosen over the base version due to GPU resource constraints and costs. The T5 architecture (Raffel et al., 2019) has been found to be the state-of-the-art when it comes to instruction-based Text-to-Text generation tasks (Chung et al., 2022). The primary reason for choosing this family of LLMs is to compare with the metrics shown in the original LaMP paper (Salemi et al., 2023).

The models are finetuned using the same hyperparameters set in the LaMP paper. We used the AdamW (Loshchilov and Hutter, 2017) optimizer with a learning rate of 5×10^{-5}. We set 5% of the total training steps as warmup steps (Kim et al., 2021) using a linear warmup scheduler. We also set a weight decay of 10^{-4}. We set the maximum input and output lengths to 512 tokens. We have set the truncation strategy to be from left to prevent the main input, apart from the profile, being truncated. As it is a generative model, we train it for 20 epochs (Salemi et al., 2023). We also employ beam search (Freitag and Al-Onaizan, 2017) as the decoding algorithm with a beam size of 4 in all experiments. Beam search generates a sentence by evaluating the best word amongst the different beams at every step instead of choosing only one word at a time. This improves the model's ability to generate high-quality predictions The validation set is evaluated on the ROUGE metrics (Lin, 2004). k represents the number of documents retrieved for fine-tuning the generative model.

We have also used the Flan-T5-base model for two of our experiments, which is shown in the results. When compared with the results from LaMP paper, this establishes that style embeddings do indeed improve the results.

5.2 Results

Use of the average style embedding for retrieval following which, using the retrieved documents for generation shows a marked improvement over the benchmark metrics shown in the LaMP paper. Amongst the metrics used, ROUGE-1 refers to the overlap of unigrams and ROUGE-L evaluates the longest common subsequence based statistics.

5.2.1 Style-based retrieval outperforms non-personalized and BM25 retrieval

The variation of the score across the type of retrieval can be seen in Table 1. Here, we can see the average style embedding retrieval clearly outperforms the non-personalized retrieval and BM25 retrieval. This shows that the style embeddings are effective, even when working with a very small model like FlanT5-small.

The results from FlanT5-base as well as the experiment on LaMP-4U are reported in Table 2. The LaMP-4U experiments show that style embeddings performs better than non-personalized performance presented in the LaMP paper and is almost as good as random retrieval. It has to be noted that this is with a much smaller model compared to FlanT5-base.

The more interesting result is the FlanT5 results on the LaMP-7U and 7T datasets. We see a marked improvement, just using one document for retrieval with style embeddings. This shows that usage of style embeddings leads to significantly improved personalization.

Dataset	Metric	FlanT5-small (fine-tuned)		
		Non-Personalized	BM25	Style Embedding
LaMP-7U	ROUGE-1	0.488	0.504	**0.507**
	ROUGE-L	0.435	0.451	**0.454**
LaMP-7T	ROUGE-1	0.481	0.499	**0.500**
	ROUGE-L	0.427	**0.447**	**0.447**

Table 1: Impact of type of retrieval on performance $k = 1$. Style-based retrieval clearly outperforms both non-personalized retrieval and BM25 retrieval.

Model	Dataset	Metric	Best LaMP model	Style Embedding
FlanT5-base	LaMP-7U	ROUGE-1	0.526	**0.534**
		ROUGE-L	0.471	**0.475**
	LaMP-7T	ROUGE-1	0.518	**0.531**
		ROUGE-L	0.467	**0.478**
FlanT5-small	LaMP-4U	ROUGE-1	-	0.163
		ROUGE-L	-	0.149

Table 2: Results from FlanT5-base and LaMP-4U. Style-based retrieval is significantly better performing than the finetuned models used in the LaMP benchmark.

5.2.2 An increase in *k* values doesn't increase performance

We should expect that increasing k, the number of retrieved documents, should increase the performance of the models. Counter-intuitively, this was shown not to be the case in Table 3. This could be an issue of the smaller model and results may vary with larger models like FlanT5-base. The best possible explanation for this peculiar behaviour is, since we are choosing the document that most represents the author's style, any other document could confuse the model if it deviates too much from the style of the author.

Metric	$k = 1$	$k = 3$
ROUGE-1	**0.507**	0.498
ROUGE-L	**0.454**	0.446

Table 3: Impact of k on performance for dataset LaMP-7U. An increase in k does not correlate with an increase in performance.

6 Conclusion

This study shows the effectiveness of style embeddings in user personalized retrieval and personalization of LLMs. There is a significant performance increase when using average style embeddings to capture the identity of an author over both term matching retrieval like BM25 and semantic similarity retrieval like Contriever (Izacard et al., 2021). The author's style, therefore, can be more important than just the words the author uses. This is a very interesting finding. Further research has to be done on this to better represent style as a vector along with using appropriate non-linear functions for combining the vectors and utilize these embeddings for author profiling.

There is a concern for privacy of author data when it comes to the task of author profiling. But using the average embedding from a pretrained style embedding model does not require the author to share any data with the owner of the LLM. The retrieval and RAG can be performed on the user's machine without the need for powerful machinery. Hence, the scope for data leaks is very limited.

In conclusion, the integration of style embeddings for author profiling within a personalized retrieval framework, as demonstrated through our LaMP benchmark evaluations, not only showcases promising advancements in tailoring language models but also underscores the significance of considering individual writing styles for the future development of personalized, context-aware linguistic technologies.

References

Roy Bayot and Teresa Gonçalves. 2016. Multilingual author profiling using word embedding averages and svms. In *2016 10th International Conference on Software, Knowledge, Information Management & Applications (SKIMA)*, pages 382–386.

Hyung Won Chung, Le Hou, S. Longpre, Barret Zoph,

Yi Tay, William Fedus, Eric Li, Xuezhi Wang, Mostafa Dehghani, Siddhartha Brahma, Albert Webson, Shixiang Shane Gu, Zhuyun Dai, Mirac Suzgun, Xinyun Chen, Aakanksha Chowdhery, Dasha Valter, Sharan Narang, Gaurav Mishra, Adams Wei Yu, Vincent Zhao, Yanping Huang, Andrew M. Dai, Hongkun Yu, Slav Petrov, Ed Huai hsin Chi, Jeff Dean, Jacob Devlin, Adam Roberts, Denny Zhou, Quoc V. Le, and Jason Wei. 2022. Scaling instruction-finetuned language models. *ArXiv*, abs/2210.11416.

Joshua Coates and Danushka Bollegala. 2018. Frustratingly easy meta-embedding – computing meta-embeddings by averaging source word embeddings.

Shiran Dudy, Steven Bedrick, and Bonnie Lynn Webber. 2021. Refocusing on relevance: Personalization in nlg. *Proceedings of the Conference on Empirical Methods in Natural Language Processing. Conference on Empirical Methods in Natural Language Processing*, 2021:5190–5202.

Lucie Flekova. 2020. Returning the n to nlp: Towards contextually personalized classification models. In *Annual Meeting of the Association for Computational Linguistics*.

Markus Freitag and Yaser Al-Onaizan. 2017. Beam search strategies for neural machine translation. In *NMT@ACL*.

Alec Go, Richa Bhayani, and Lei Huang. 2009. Twitter sentiment classification using distant supervision. *CS224N project report, Stanford*, 1(12):2009.

Gautier Izacard, Mathilde Caron, Lucas Hosseini, Sebastian Riedel, Piotr Bojanowski, Armand Joulin, and Edouard Grave. 2021. Unsupervised dense information retrieval with contrastive learning. *Trans. Mach. Learn. Res.*, 2022.

Karen Spärck Jones. 2021. A statistical interpretation of term specificity and its application in retrieval. *J. Documentation*, 60:493–502.

Chiheon Kim, Saehoon Kim, Jongmin Kim, Donghoon Lee, and Sungwoong Kim. 2021. Automated learning rate scheduler for large-batch training. *ArXiv*, abs/2107.05855.

Chin-Yew Lin. 2004. Rouge: A package for automatic evaluation of summaries. In *Annual Meeting of the Association for Computational Linguistics*.

Ilya Loshchilov and Frank Hutter. 2017. Decoupled weight decay regularization. In *International Conference on Learning Representations*.

Rishabh Misra. 2022. News category dataset. *ArXiv*, abs/2209.11429.

Colin Raffel, Noam M. Shazeer, Adam Roberts, Katherine Lee, Sharan Narang, Michael Matena, Yanqi Zhou, Wei Li, and Peter J. Liu. 2019. Exploring the limits of transfer learning with a unified text-to-text transformer. *J. Mach. Learn. Res.*, 21:140:1–140:67.

Nils Reimers and Iryna Gurevych. 2019. Sentence-bert: Sentence embeddings using siamese bert-networks. In *Conference on Empirical Methods in Natural Language Processing*.

Alireza Salemi, Sheshera Mysore, Michael Bendersky, and Hamed Zamani. 2023. Lamp: When large language models meet personalization.

Jacob Tyo, Bhuwan Dhingra, and Zachary C. Lipton. 2022. On the state of the art in authorship attribution and authorship verification.

Anna Wegmann, Marijn Schraagen, and Dong Nguyen. 2022. Same author or just same topic? towards content-independent style representations. In *Proceedings of the 7th Workshop on Representation Learning for NLP*, Dublin, Ireland. Association for Computational Linguistics.

User Embedding Model for Personalized Language Prompting

Sumanth Doddapaneni, Krishna Sayana*, Ambarish Jash, Sukhdeep Sodhi, Dima Kuzmin

Google Research

Abstract

Modeling long user histories plays a pivotal role in enhancing recommendation systems, allowing to capture users' evolving preferences, resulting in more precise and personalized recommendations. In this study, we tackle the challenges of modeling long user histories for preference understanding in natural language. Specifically, we introduce a new User Embedding Module (UEM) that efficiently processes user history in free-form text by compressing and representing them as embeddings, to use them as soft prompts to a LM. Our experiments demonstrate the superior capability of this approach in handling significantly longer histories compared to conventional text-based methods, yielding substantial improvements in predictive performance. Models trained using our approach exhibit substantial enhancements, with up to 0.21 and 0.25 F1 points improvement over the text-based prompting baselines. The main contribution of this research is to demonstrate the ability to bias language models via user signals.

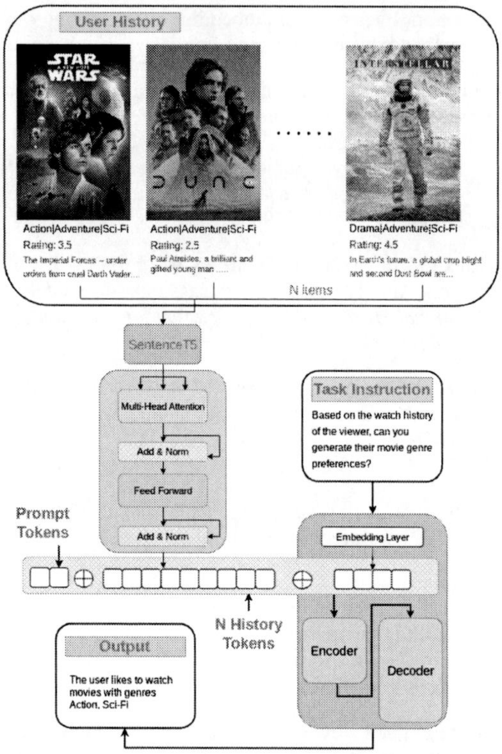

Figure 1: Overview of our User History Modeling Approach. The user history's textual features are processed through the User Embedding module and combined with the task prompt and subsequently passed through the language model.

1 Introduction

In recent years, Large Language Models (LLMs) have proven their versatility in various language tasks, from translation to reasoning (Bubeck et al., 2023). Scaling up models and data has played a crucial role in unlocking their potential (OpenAI, 2023; Anil et al., 2023; Touvron et al., 2023). LLMs have also been adapted for conversational tasks, instruction following, and reasoning using techniques like Instruction-Tuning (Mishra et al., 2022; Wei et al., 2022a; Sanh et al., 2022), RLHF (Ouyang et al., 2022), and Chain-of-Thought (Wei et al., 2022b). Trained on extensive internet data, these LLMs excel in generalization. They can quickly adapt to new tasks with in-context learning and are capable of not only answering questions but also reasoning about their responses.

The usage of LLMs has evolved beyond traditional NLP tasks to encompass tasks demanding reasoning (Qiao et al., 2023), long-form generation (Ouyang et al., 2022), creativity (Kumar, 2023), and demonstrated remarkable proficiency in these areas. LLMs have been applied to search, retrieval, ranking, chat, personalization, recommendation systems, and others (Yasunaga et al., 2023; Ouyang et al., 2022; Salemi et al., 2023). One practical use case for LMs is understanding *user preferences* to *generate recommendations*, a task that extends

*Correspondence to: ksayana@google.com

Proceedings of the 1st Workshop on Personalization of Generative AI Systems (PERSONALIZE 2024), pages 124–131
March 22, 2024

beyond text to encompass audio and visual modalities in real-world scenarios, as exemplified by platforms like YouTube[1], Spotify[2] among many others.

Recent research has predominantly concentrated on examining smaller segments of user history by selecting representative samples from a users' history (Salemi et al., 2023). Mu et al. (2023) uses learned gist tokens to compress prompts while Li et al. (2023) uses prompt rewriting based on entries retrieved from a users' profile. This leads to the critical question *How can we effectively utilize longer user histories?* To achieve this, we employ an embedding-based technique to compress the user's entire history, creating a sequence of representative user embedding tokens. This embedded representation enhances our ability to comprehend user preferences and subsequently generate predictions that align more closely with their interests. Further, since the User Embedding Module (UEM) module is co-trained with the LM, the representations are learned in-context for the specific tasks. Our research demonstrates the advantages of this approach, particularly in its capacity to incorporate longer user history into LMs, resulting in more robust user preference understanding. Compared to the naive approach of concatenating user history and incurring $O(n^2)$ compute cost for self-attention, our approach demonstrates a cheap way to incorporate history metadata as an embedding thus dramatically reducing the required compute. As a result longer user histories can be easily incorporated within LMs. Our empirical findings demonstrate the ability of our approach to accommodate significantly larger histories compared to traditional text-based methods, resulting in improved predictive performance.

2 Approach

Following text-to-text approach of T5 (Raffel et al., 2020), we frame all tasks as text generation conditioned on the input. Formally, given a sequence of query input tokens denoted as X, we model the probability of output Y as $Pr_\theta(Y|X)$, where θ represents the weights of the model. Prior studies have established two primary prompting strategies: *text-based prompting*, where textual instructions are prepended to the input (Mishra et al., 2022; Chung et al., 2022; Wei et al., 2022b), and *soft-prompting*, which adds a set of trainable tokens as a prefix to the input tokens of the models (Lester et al., 2021; Li and Liang, 2021). Prior soft-prompting uses a fixed task-specific soft-prompt to achieve parameter-efficient fine-tuning for various language tasks, maximizing the likelihood $Pr_\theta(Y|[K;X])$, with K trainable tokens. We extend this idea to personalization. More specifically, using the User Embedding Module (UEM), we generate a personalised soft-prompt conditioned on the users' history. This setup aims to maximize the likelihood of the label Y, given $Pr_\theta(Y|[Pr_{UEM}(U);X])$, where $Pr_{UEM}(U)$ are the soft prompts generated by the UEM based on user history U and prefixed to the query input X. In our task definition, U corresponds to the movie metadata, X represents the task instruction, and Y represents genre preferences.

Overall, given a task instruction X, the LM embeds these tokens to a matrix $X_e \in \mathbb{R}^{n \times e}$, where *n* represents the token count and *e* represents the embedding dimension of the LM. The textual user history $H = \{h_i\}_{i=1}^{p}$ is converted into embeddings $U = \{u_i\}_{i=1}^{p}$ with SentenceT5 (Ni et al., 2022). Each history item u_i is a composite of three distinct embeddings: (i) title & genre, (ii) rating, and (iii) description. The collective history of 'p' items is expressed as $U \in \mathbb{R}^{p \times 3s}$, where *s* corresponds to the embedding dimension of SentenceT5. These embeddings undergo processing within a transformer network (UEM). To ensure dimension alignment with *e*, a linear projection layer is introduced atop the transformer, mapping the dimension *3s* to *e*, thereby yielding $Pr_{UEM}(U) \in \mathbb{R}^{p \times e}$.

Following Lester et al. (2021), we also incorporate 'k' task-level soft prompts, denoted as $P_e \in \mathbb{R}^{k \times e}$. Both the user and task prompts are concatenated with the input embedding, resulting in a unified embedding matrix, represented as $[P_e; Pr_{UEM}(U); X_e] \in \mathbb{R}^{(k+p+n) \times e}$. This composite embedding flows through the LM, maximizing the probability of Y, and concurrently updating all parameters within both model components. The model is illustrated in Figure 1.

3 Experiments

Implementation. As described in §A, we use the MovieLens dataset (Harper and Konstan, 2016) in conjunction with movie descriptions. For the embeddings U discussed in §2, we format the text in the following manner: (i) title and genre - `The movie {movie_title} is listed with genres`

[1] `youtube.com`

[2] `spotify.com`

{genres}, (ii) rating - `The movie is rated with {rating} stars`, and (iii) description - `{movie_description}`. In the case of the text-only baselines, we input the concatenated strings instead of the embeddings. The dataset i split into 117k/5k/5k for train, validation and test sets respectively. Unless specified, we use the FlanT5 (Chung et al., 2022) series of models for all experiments, training them for 10k steps with a batch size of 128. Text-history models use a learning rate of 1e-2, while embedding-history models use 5e-3. Our user embedding model consists of 3 transformer layers with 12 attention heads, 768d embeddings, and 2048d MLP layers, adding 65M parameters. We use 20 tokens for task-level soft prompts k.

Evaluation. Although the task is framed in a text-to-text format, the model's output can be processed by a verbalizer to extract the genres. While conventional metrics like BLEU (Papineni et al., 2002), ROUGE (Lin, 2004), and COMET (Rei et al., 2020) are used for evaluating generative text, they lack granularity in understanding the task performance. However, given the straightforward genre extraction by the verbalizer, we treat the task as a multi-label classification problem and present weighted precision, recall and F1 scores across all labels[3]. Our initial findings indicate that these scores offer a more interpretable assessment, both at the genre level and for the overall task evaluation, compared to token-level metrics.

3.1 Main Results

We present the results from our proposed approach in Table 1. The results demonstrate that incorporating a larger history significantly enhances the models' understanding of the user preferences. Compared to the text-only models, we observe F1 improvements of 0.21 and 0.25 in performance for the base and large models, respectively. To assess performance against text-only models with a comparable history size, we train a model with only 5 history items. The results reveal slightly poorer performance, likely due to the extremely limited context window of the history (5 tokens) compared to the text-only model (over 1000 tokens). Unlike conventional language models, LongT5 (Guo et al., 2022), is trained with Transient Global Attention, allowing it to efficiently process longer text sequences. However, it's essential to consider that this extended capability comes at the cost of increased memory and longer training times. While FlanT5 models can be effectively trained on v3-8 TPUs, LongT5 necessitates v3-32 TPUs and requires 4x the training time of a FlanT5 model of comparable size, especially when dealing with input sequences of 16k tokens (equivalent to 50 history items). More importantly, the serving latency is also correspondingly increased, which could make these models impractical for production use.

		BASE	LARGE
Counting Baselines	precision	0.330	
	recall	0.273	
	f1	0.192	
Text Hist. 5	precision	0.276	0.257
	recall	0.287	0.273
	f1	0.273	0.261
Emb. Hist. 5	precision	0.275	0.281
	recall	0.297	0.290
	f1	0.252	0.215
LongT5 50	precision	0.541	0.568
	recall	0.523	0.558
	f1	0.529	0.557
Emb. Hist. 50	precision	0.407	0.400
	recall	0.405	0.399
	f1	0.396	0.381
Emb. Hist. 100	precision	0.416	0.459
	recall	0.413	0.441
	f1	0.404	0.444

Table 1: Model performance using proposed User Embedding Module. *Counting Baselines* refers to counting the three most frequently occurring genres across the entire user history.

3.2 Ablations

Effect of History Length. To assess the impact of the history size, we conduct a series of ablations by increasing the users' history passed to UEM. The results are presented in Figure 2 (ref. Table 4), revealing an improvement in model performance with an increase in the number of history items. It's worth noting that incorporating 50 history items in textual form results in an input of nearly 16k tokens. While methods like LongT5 (Guo et al., 2022), ALiBi (Press et al., 2022), and ROPE (Su et al., 2021) allow for extrapolation to longer sequences, this remains computationally intensive.

Choice of LM. In our experiments, we chose FlanT5 as the language model for our task. We also conducted experiments with both the base T51.1 (Raffel et al., 2020) and a LM adapted T5 model

[3]There are 19 genres with a high skew among the classes. We use `sklearn.metrics.classification_report`

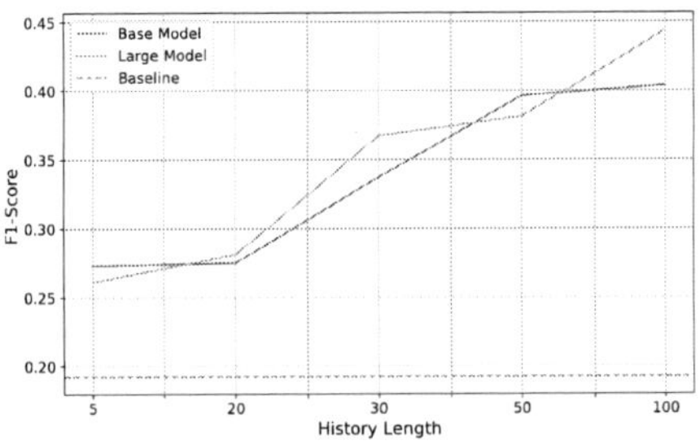

Figure 2: Comparison of model performance with increasing User History.

		BASE	LARGE
1 Layer	precision	0.391	0.395
	recall	0.381	0.384
	f1	0.346	0.347
2 Layers	precision	0.399	0.380
	recall	0.392	0.367
	f1	0.384	0.365
3 Layers	precision	0.407	0.400
	recall	0.405	0.399
	f1	0.396	0.381

Table 3: Comparison of model performance with various sizes of User Embedding Module. All the models use the same history size of 50.

(Lester et al., 2021) to find the best starting point for our training. The results presented in Table 2 shows that FlanT5 has the best performance, mainly due to the instructional nature of our task prompts.

		BASE	LARGE
$T5_{1.1}$	precision	0.282	0.322
	recall	0.292	0.324
	f1	0.208	0.267
$T5_{LMAdapted}$	precision	0.353	0.398
	recall	0.374	0.397
	f1	0.338	0.378
FlanT5	precision	0.407	0.400
	recall	0.405	0.399
	f1	0.396	0.381

Table 2: Comparison of model performance with various choices of Language Models.

Size of UEM. For the user embedding module, we experimented with different sizes by changing the number of layers in the transformer block. We found that gradually making UEM bigger improved the performance of both the base and large models (see Table 3). However, we also recognize that the task itself may not require a very complex solution, so further increasing the size of the module may not be justified. We believe that different tasks might need different levels of complexity, and we plan to explore this in future research.

4 Related Work

In prior research, UserAdapter (Zhong et al., 2021) introduced a trainable token for each user, facilitating sentiment classification specialization using RoBERTa. Expanding upon this, UserIdentifier (Mireshghallah et al., 2022) demonstrated that employing random userIDs effectively captures user-specific information. HuLM (Soni et al., 2022) pretrained a LM conditioned on higher-order data states associated with humans. Further, Salemi et al. (2023) employed retrievers like Contriver and BM25 to select representative input histories to prompt an LM to generate personalized outputs. Mu et al. (2023) utilized gist tokens to condense input prompts into a set of tokens, reducing computational overhead for recurring task instructions. Li et al. (2023) employed prompt rewriting, identifying relevant items for individual users, summarizing the information, and synthesizing key attributes to prompt the model. Our approach distinguishes itself by utilizing entire user histories, compressing them into contextually learned embeddings.

5 Conclusion & Future Work

In this study, we addressed several critical challenges in modeling user history for preference understanding. We introduced a User Embedding Module that processed user history as freeform text, generating token embeddings for each history item. This approach greatly simplified user history tracking and enabled the incorporation of longer user histories into the language model, and allowed their representations to be learned in context. Our empirical results demonstrated the capability of this approach to handle significantly larger histories efficiently compared to traditional text-based approaches, resulting in improved predictive performance. For future work, we would like to explore more parameter efficient approaches like LoRA (Hu et al., 2022) for finetuning LMs with UEM, which would improve both training and serving for these models. This approach can be easily extended to multimodal signals using modal specific embeddings and tying them together with UEM, and we plan to explore this direction for future work.

Limitations

While we argue and demonstrate in this work that using a UEM is an efficient way to encode long user histories with easier extensions to multimodal inputs, we acknowledge that text prompting can be further optimized, by using text-to-text prompt compression models. These trade-offs could be further studied. The simplicity of the UEM architecture leaves a lot of headroom as demonstrated by LongT5 baselines in Table 1. Our presentations for U are using generic semantic embeddings with the use of SentenceT5 (Ni et al., 2022), these can be further improved with the use of domain specific embeddings. Our experiments are using LMs that are <1B parameters, which are usually considered smaller family of LLMs. It would be a good future direction to consider larger models with parameter efficient tuning techniques. Furthermore, our research has primarily focused on preference understanding, and hasn't been tested on tasks extending to areas such as rating prediction or item recommendation. We expect our conclusions here are likely apply to these tasks. We plan to address these limitations and pursue these avenues in our future research efforts.

Ethics Statement

The datasets and models utilized in this study are based on publicly available and open-source resources. While we acknowledge the inherent ethical considerations associated with language models, we do not anticipate any additional ethical concerns arising from the datasets and models developed in the course of this research.

References

Rohan Anil, Andrew M. Dai, Orhan Firat, Melvin Johnson, Dmitry Lepikhin, Alexandre Passos, Siamak Shakeri, Emanuel Taropa, Paige Bailey, Zhifeng Chen, Eric Chu, Jonathan H. Clark, Laurent El Shafey, Yanping Huang, Kathy Meier-Hellstern, Gaurav Mishra, Erica Moreira, Mark Omernick, Kevin Robinson, Sebastian Ruder, Yi Tay, Kefan Xiao, Yuanzhong Xu, Yujing Zhang, Gustavo Hernández Ábrego, Junwhan Ahn, Jacob Austin, Paul Barham, Jan A. Botha, James Bradbury, Siddhartha Brahma, Kevin Brooks, Michele Catasta, Yong Cheng, Colin Cherry, Christopher A. Choquette-Choo, Aakanksha Chowdhery, Clément Crepy, Shachi Dave, Mostafa Dehghani, Sunipa Dev, Jacob Devlin, Mark Díaz, Nan Du, Ethan Dyer, Vladimir Feinberg, Fangxiaoyu Feng, Vlad Fienber, Markus Freitag, Xavier Garcia, Sebastian Gehrmann, Lucas Gonzalez, and et al. 2023. Palm 2 technical report. *CoRR*, abs/2305.10403.

Sébastien Bubeck, Varun Chandrasekaran, Ronen Eldan, Johannes Gehrke, Eric Horvitz, Ece Kamar, Peter Lee, Yin Tat Lee, Yuanzhi Li, Scott M. Lundberg, Harsha Nori, Hamid Palangi, Marco Túlio Ribeiro, and Yi Zhang. 2023. Sparks of artificial general intelligence: Early experiments with GPT-4. *CoRR*, abs/2303.12712.

Hyung Won Chung, Le Hou, Shayne Longpre, Barret Zoph, Yi Tay, William Fedus, Eric Li, Xuezhi Wang, Mostafa Dehghani, Siddhartha Brahma, Albert Webson, Shixiang Shane Gu, Zhuyun Dai, Mirac Suzgun, Xinyun Chen, Aakanksha Chowdhery, Sharan Narang, Gaurav Mishra, Adams Yu, Vincent Y. Zhao, Yanping Huang, Andrew M. Dai, Hongkun Yu, Slav Petrov, Ed H. Chi, Jeff Dean, Jacob Devlin, Adam Roberts, Denny Zhou, Quoc V. Le, and Jason Wei. 2022. Scaling instruction-finetuned language models. *CoRR*, abs/2210.11416.

Mandy Guo, Joshua Ainslie, David Uthus, Santiago Ontanon, Jianmo Ni, Yun-Hsuan Sung, and Yinfei Yang. 2022. LongT5: Efficient text-to-text transformer for long sequences. In *Findings of the Association for Computational Linguistics: NAACL 2022*, pages 724–736, Seattle, United States. Association for Computational Linguistics.

F. Maxwell Harper and Joseph A. Konstan. 2016. The movielens datasets: History and context. *ACM Trans. Interact. Intell. Syst.*, 5(4):19:1–19:19.

Edward J. Hu, Yelong Shen, Phillip Wallis, Zeyuan Allen-Zhu, Yuanzhi Li, Shean Wang, Lu Wang, and Weizhu Chen. 2022. Lora: Low-rank adaptation of large language models. In *The Tenth International Conference on Learning Representations, ICLR 2022, Virtual Event, April 25-29, 2022*. OpenReview.net.

Pratyush Kumar. 2023. Large language models humanize technology. *CoRR*, abs/2305.05576.

Brian Lester, Rami Al-Rfou, and Noah Constant. 2021. The power of scale for parameter-efficient prompt tuning. In *Proceedings of the 2021 Conference on Empirical Methods in Natural Language Processing*, pages 3045–3059, Online and Punta Cana, Dominican Republic. Association for Computational Linguistics.

Cheng Li, Mingyang Zhang, Qiaozhu Mei, Weize Kong, and Michael Bendersky. 2023. Automatic prompt rewriting for personalized text generation.

Xiang Lisa Li and Percy Liang. 2021. Prefix-tuning: Optimizing continuous prompts for generation. In *Proceedings of the 59th Annual Meeting of the Association for Computational Linguistics and the 11th International Joint Conference on Natural Language Processing, ACL/IJCNLP 2021, (Volume 1: Long Papers), Virtual Event, August 1-6, 2021*, pages 4582–4597. Association for Computational Linguistics.

Chin-Yew Lin. 2004. ROUGE: A package for automatic evaluation of summaries. In *Text Summarization Branches Out*, pages 74–81, Barcelona, Spain. Association for Computational Linguistics.

Fatemehsadat Mireshghallah, Vaishnavi Shrivastava, Milad Shokouhi, Taylor Berg-Kirkpatrick, Robert Sim, and Dimitrios Dimitriadis. 2022. Useridentifier: Implicit user representations for simple and effective personalized sentiment analysis. In *Proceedings of the 2022 Conference of the North American Chapter of the Association for Computational Linguistics: Human Language Technologies, NAACL 2022, Seattle, WA, United States, July 10-15, 2022*, pages 3449–3456. Association for Computational Linguistics.

Swaroop Mishra, Daniel Khashabi, Chitta Baral, and Hannaneh Hajishirzi. 2022. Cross-task generalization via natural language crowdsourcing instructions. In *Proceedings of the 60th Annual Meeting of the Association for Computational Linguistics (Volume 1: Long Papers), ACL 2022, Dublin, Ireland, May 22-27, 2022*, pages 3470–3487. Association for Computational Linguistics.

Jesse Mu, Xiang Lisa Li, and Noah Goodman. 2023. Learning to compress prompts with gist tokens.

Jianmo Ni, Gustavo Hernández Ábrego, Noah Constant, Ji Ma, Keith B. Hall, Daniel Cer, and Yinfei Yang. 2022. Sentence-t5: Scalable sentence encoders from pre-trained text-to-text models. In *Findings of the Association for Computational Linguistics: ACL 2022, Dublin, Ireland, May 22-27, 2022*, pages 1864–1874. Association for Computational Linguistics.

OpenAI. 2023. GPT-4 technical report. *CoRR*, abs/2303.08774.

Long Ouyang, Jeffrey Wu, Xu Jiang, Diogo Almeida, Carroll L. Wainwright, Pamela Mishkin, Chong Zhang, Sandhini Agarwal, Katarina Slama, Alex Ray, John Schulman, Jacob Hilton, Fraser Kelton, Luke Miller, Maddie Simens, Amanda Askell, Peter Welinder, Paul F. Christiano, Jan Leike, and Ryan Lowe. 2022. Training language models to follow instructions with human feedback. In *NeurIPS*.

Kishore Papineni, Salim Roukos, Todd Ward, and Wei-Jing Zhu. 2002. Bleu: a method for automatic evaluation of machine translation. In *Proceedings of the 40th Annual Meeting of the Association for Computational Linguistics, July 6-12, 2002, Philadelphia, PA, USA*, pages 311–318. ACL.

Ofir Press, Noah A. Smith, and Mike Lewis. 2022. Train short, test long: Attention with linear biases enables input length extrapolation. In *The Tenth International Conference on Learning Representations, ICLR 2022, Virtual Event, April 25-29, 2022*. OpenReview.net.

Shuofei Qiao, Yixin Ou, Ningyu Zhang, Xiang Chen, Yunzhi Yao, Shumin Deng, Chuanqi Tan, Fei Huang, and Huajun Chen. 2023. Reasoning with language model prompting: A survey. In *Proceedings of the 61st Annual Meeting of the Association for Computational Linguistics (Volume 1: Long Papers)*, pages 5368–5393, Toronto, Canada. Association for Computational Linguistics.

Colin Raffel, Noam Shazeer, Adam Roberts, Katherine Lee, Sharan Narang, Michael Matena, Yanqi Zhou, Wei Li, and Peter J. Liu. 2020. Exploring the limits of transfer learning with a unified text-to-text transformer. *J. Mach. Learn. Res.*, 21:140:1–140:67.

Ricardo Rei, Craig Stewart, Ana C. Farinha, and Alon Lavie. 2020. COMET: A neural framework for MT evaluation. In *Proceedings of the 2020 Conference on Empirical Methods in Natural Language Processing, EMNLP 2020, Online, November 16-20, 2020*, pages 2685–2702. Association for Computational Linguistics.

Alireza Salemi, Sheshera Mysore, Michael Bendersky, and Hamed Zamani. 2023. Lamp: When large language models meet personalization. *CoRR*, abs/2304.11406.

Victor Sanh, Albert Webson, Colin Raffel, Stephen H. Bach, Lintang Sutawika, Zaid Alyafeai, Antoine Chaffin, Arnaud Stiegler, Arun Raja, Manan Dey, M Saiful Bari, Canwen Xu, Urmish Thakker, Shanya Sharma Sharma, Eliza Szczechla, Taewoon Kim, Gunjan Chhablani, Nihal V. Nayak, Debajyoti Datta, Jonathan Chang, Mike Tian-Jian Jiang, Han Wang, Matteo Manica, Sheng Shen, Zheng Xin Yong, Harshit Pandey, Rachel Bawden, Thomas Wang, Trishala Neeraj, Jos Rozen, Abheesht Sharma, Andrea Santilli, Thibault Févry, Jason Alan Fries, Ryan Teehan, Teven Le Scao, Stella Biderman, Leo Gao, Thomas Wolf, and Alexander M. Rush. 2022. Multitask prompted training enables zero-shot task generalization. In *The Tenth International Conference on Learning Representations, ICLR 2022, Virtual Event, April 25-29, 2022*. OpenReview.net.

Nikita Soni, Matthew Matero, Niranjan Balasubramanian, and H. Andrew Schwartz. 2022. Human language modeling. In *Findings of the Association for Computational Linguistics: ACL 2022, Dublin, Ireland, May 22-27, 2022*, pages 622–636. Association for Computational Linguistics.

Jianlin Su, Yu Lu, Shengfeng Pan, Bo Wen, and Yunfeng Liu. 2021. Roformer: Enhanced transformer with rotary position embedding. *CoRR*, abs/2104.09864.

Hugo Touvron, Louis Martin, Kevin Stone, Peter Albert, Amjad Almahairi, Yasmine Babaei, Nikolay Bashlykov, Soumya Batra, Prajjwal Bhargava, Shruti Bhosale, Dan Bikel, Lukas Blecher, Cristian Canton-Ferrer, Moya Chen, Guillem Cucurull, David Esiobu, Jude Fernandes, Jeremy Fu, Wenyin Fu, Brian Fuller, Cynthia Gao, Vedanuj Goswami, Naman Goyal, Anthony Hartshorn, Saghar Hosseini, Rui Hou, Hakan Inan, Marcin Kardas, Viktor Kerkez, Madian Khabsa, Isabel Kloumann, Artem Korenev, Punit Singh Koura,

Marie-Anne Lachaux, Thibaut Lavril, Jenya Lee, Diana Liskovich, Yinghai Lu, Yuning Mao, Xavier Martinet, Todor Mihaylov, Pushkar Mishra, Igor Molybog, Yixin Nie, Andrew Poulton, Jeremy Reizenstein, Rashi Rungta, Kalyan Saladi, Alan Schelten, Ruan Silva, Eric Michael Smith, Ranjan Subramanian, Xiaoqing Ellen Tan, Binh Tang, Ross Taylor, Adina Williams, Jian Xiang Kuan, Puxin Xu, Zheng Yan, Iliyan Zarov, Yuchen Zhang, Angela Fan, Melanie Kambadur, Sharan Narang, Aurélien Rodriguez, Robert Stojnic, Sergey Edunov, and Thomas Scialom. 2023. Llama 2: Open foundation and fine-tuned chat models. *CoRR*, abs/2307.09288.

Jason Wei, Maarten Bosma, Vincent Y. Zhao, Kelvin Guu, Adams Wei Yu, Brian Lester, Nan Du, Andrew M. Dai, and Quoc V. Le. 2022a. Finetuned language models are zero-shot learners. In *The Tenth International Conference on Learning Representations, ICLR 2022, Virtual Event, April 25-29, 2022*. OpenReview.net.

Jason Wei, Xuezhi Wang, Dale Schuurmans, Maarten Bosma, Brian Ichter, Fei Xia, Ed H. Chi, Quoc V. Le, and Denny Zhou. 2022b. Chain-of-thought prompting elicits reasoning in large language models. In *NeurIPS*.

Michihiro Yasunaga, Armen Aghajanyan, Weijia Shi, Richard James, Jure Leskovec, Percy Liang, Mike Lewis, Luke Zettlemoyer, and Wen-Tau Yih. 2023. Retrieval-augmented multimodal language modeling. In *International Conference on Machine Learning, ICML 2023, 23-29 July 2023, Honolulu, Hawaii, USA*, volume 202 of *Proceedings of Machine Learning Research*, pages 39755–39769. PMLR.

Wanjun Zhong, Duyu Tang, Jiahai Wang, Jian Yin, and Nan Duan. 2021. Useradapter: Few-shot user learning in sentiment analysis. In *Findings of the Association for Computational Linguistics: ACL/IJCNLP 2021, Online Event, August 1-6, 2021*, volume ACL/IJCNLP 2021 of *Findings of ACL*, pages 1484–1488. Association for Computational Linguistics.

A Dataset

In the MovieLens dataset (Harper and Konstan, 2016), the available metadata for assessing a movie's rating is confined to its title and associated genres. However, such limited information proves inadequate for both human evaluators and language models in generating predictions unless they possess prior knowledge about the movies. For instance, when considering the *Star Wars* series within the MovieLens dataset (Harper and Konstan, 2016), namely *Star Wars: Episode IV - A New Hope (1977)*, *Star Wars: Episode VI - Return of the Jedi (1983)*, and *Star Wars: Episode I - The Phantom Menace (1999)*, all three films share identical genre classifications, namely Action, Adventure, and Sci-Fi. Nonetheless, a closer inspection reveals noteworthy disparities in their mean ratings, with "Episode IV" and "Episode VI" accumulating ratings of `4.12` and `4.14`, respectively, while "Episode I" registers a markedly lower rating of `3.06`.

In reality, a viewer's decision to watch a movie is contingent upon a multifaceted array of metadata beyond the movie genres. Variables such as the cast, crew, production studio, among others, play pivotal roles in this determination. In contemporary times, movie trailers have emerged as potent tools for piquing an individual's interest in a movie. In the context of textual language models, we equate the concept of a *gist* as a close analogue to a movie trailer. The gist encapsulates the fundamental essence of the movie's content while withholding explicit plot details, a characteristic akin to that of a trailer. Consequently, we propose the incorporation of such supplementary data[4] into the MovieLens dataset (Harper and Konstan, 2016) to facilitate more nuanced and informed predictive assessments. While it is acknowledged that this augmentation may not encompass the entirety of a viewer's decision-making process, it represents a stride closer to the intricacies involved in real-world movie-watching choices.

After merging the MovieLens dataset (Harper and Konstan, 2016) with movie descriptions and filtering out users with fewer than 20 recorded movie views, our dataset comprises 14.4M reviews, spanning 8.2k unique movies, and involving a total of 127k users. We then divide this dataset into three subsets: 5k users for both the development and testing sets, and the remaining 117k users for the training set. To create gold labels, we aggregate genres along with their corresponding ratings across each user's viewing history. Only genres with a minimum of three ratings are considered. Based on this aggregated information, we identify the three most preferred genres (with an average rating >3.5) and the three least preferred genres (with an average rating <3) for each user. The resulting output is structured in a text-to-text format as follows: `The user likes to watch movies with genres {liked_genres} and doesn't like to watch movies with genres {disliked_genres}`[5].

[4]Metadata sourced from `https://www.kaggle.com/datasets/stefanoleone992/rotten-tomatoes-movies-and-critic-reviews-dataset/`

[5]In cases where the set of `liked_genres` or `disliked_genres` is empty, the text is adjusted accordingly.

B History Length Ablation Results

		BASE	LARGE
Emb. Hist. 5	precision	0.276	0.257
	recall	0.287	0.273
	f1	0.273	0.261
Emb. Hist. 20	precision	0.319	0.321
	recall	0.328	0.326
	f1	0.275	0.281
Emb. Hist. 30	precision	0.353	0.390
	recall	0.364	0.390
	f1	0.337	0.367
Emb. Hist. 50	precision	0.407	0.400
	recall	0.405	0.399
	f1	0.396	0.381
Emb. Hist. 100	precision	0.416	0.459
	recall	0.413	0.441
	f1	0.404	0.444

Table 4: Comparison of model performance with increasing User History.

Author Index